♀ WOMEN IN NATIONAL LEGISLATURES

♀ WOMEN IN NATIONAL LEGISLATURES

A Comparative Study of Six Countries

Walter S. G. Kohn

PRAEGER

PRAEGER SPECIAL STUDIES • PRAEGER SCIENTIFIC

Library of Congress Cataloging in Publication Data

Kohn, Walter S G
    Women in national legislatures.

    Bibliography: p.
    1. Women legislators. 2. Comparative government.
I. Title.
JF540.5.K55   328'.33   80-11601
ISBN 0-03-047591-0 (Holt, Rinehart & Winston)

Published in 1980 by Praeger Publishers
CBS Educational and Professional Publishing
A Division of CBS, Inc.
521 Fifth Avenue, New York, New York 10017 U.S.A.

0123456789   145 987654321

Printed in the United States of America

Elizabeth Vallance
1981.

To Rita and Tom, who in so many different ways
helped to make this book a reality.

Whatever women do they must do twice as well as men
to be thought half as good. Luckily, this is not difficult.

───────────

Charlotte Whitton (1896-1975), former mayor of Ottawa, in
Nancy McPhee's The Book of Insults.

ACKNOWLEDGMENTS

I want to express my gratitude to the many people whose help
and assistance was essential in the completion of this book. Various
politicians, party leaders, legislators, and government employees
in the United States, Canada, Britain, the German Federal Republic,
Austria, and Switzerland have contributed in many different ways;
only their large number prevents me from thanking them individually.
Illinois State University has provided me with released time and a
travel grant. The chairman of the Political Science Department,
Professor Hibbert R. Roberts, has been most encouraging and help-
ful. The personnel at Praeger Publishers has made working with
them a joy. My own immediate family had to exercise a lot of
patience, especially my youngest son, Tom, who has waited in so
many outer offices while his father was inside. Last but foremost,
this book demonstrates the importance of partnership among spouses;
many female legislators have pointed out that their success was due
to an understanding husband. I want to say a heartfelt thank you to
a most cooperative wife.

Walter S. G. Kohn

CONTENTS

LIST OF TABLES

♀ WOMEN IN NATIONAL LEGISLATURES

1
INTRODUCTION

"Where are the women?" exclaims Lysistrata in the opening scene of Aristophanes' play when hardly anyone shows up for a meeting she has called for political action by women. This cry of 2,400 years ago has been echoing and reechoing through the ages. Even now, when political equality among the sexes has been formally achieved in most countries, and men and women have the right to vote for, and become members of, the legislatures without constitutional discrimination, one look at the predominantly male parliamentary bodies will inevitably lead to a repetition of the ancient question, "Where are the women?"

Political equality among the sexes is a twentieth-century phenomenon. Before World War I, there were a few isolated cases where women had been given the right to vote; New Zealand had done so in 1893, Finland in 1906, and Norway in 1913.[1] In the United States, Kentucky let women vote in school elections in 1838, and Kansas, in 1861. Similar steps were taken by 15 other states before the turn of the century. Full political participation for women was achieved in Wyoming in 1869 and in Colorado, Utah, and Idaho within the next few decades. After a few more western states had also passed woman suffrage legislation, the concept of sexual equality eventually crossed the Mississippi in 1913, when Illinois allowed women to vote for president. Four years later, New York State amended its constitution in a referendum to give women full political rights. Congress was now ready to write female suffrage into the federal Constitution, and the Nineteenth Amendment was duly ratified and became part of the law of the land in August 1920.[2]

The war also brought the franchise to women in Denmark and the Netherlands and, at its end, to Britain and the new republics of Germany and Austria. In Canada, woman suffrage was very much a local affair, as it had been in the United States. The western provinces took the lead; Manitoba, Saskatchewan, and Alberta preceded the all-dominion franchise for women by two years,* with Quebec the last to enfranchise, in 1940. Even so, Quebec led the French-speaking world because it was 1944 when France and 1948 when Belgium enfranchised women. Switzerland, despite pride in its democratic tradition and practices, waited until 1971 before its female population was able to participate in the determination of the country's political destiny. It was left to some of the smallest countries in Europe to hold out the longest. San Marino failed to let the women vote before 1960, and Liechtenstein's male electorate has thus far steadfastly refused in several plebiscites to extend the franchise to its wives and daughters, despite urgent pleas by a variety of government leaders, parliamentarians, politicians, newspaper editors, and members of the reigning royal family.

Nevertheless, great strides have indeed been made in most nations, especially as a result of wartime upheavals. Just as returning soldiers could not be kept "down on the farm after they had seen Paree," so women were not willing to remain confined to their traditional realms of Kinder, Küche, Kirche after so many had played an active part in the war effort. They realized that there was more to life than looking after the children, working in the kitchen, and going to church. Politics, after all, determines, as Harold Lasswell says, "who gets what, when, and how" and is consequently a matter of vital concern to women as well as men.

Women soon learned to exercise their newly acquired right to participate in voting. Although the voter turnout of women as compared with men naturally varies from election to election and from country to country, by and large women have come to regard voting as an exercise in citizenship that they do not hesitate to perform. Maurice Duverger points this out in his UNESCO study.

> So far as elections are concerned, the proportion of
> women taking part in the political life is large, and
> does not differ materially from that of men, as regards
> either number or composition. It is true that there

---

*In Canadian national elections, relatives of members of the armed forces were enfranchised on September 20, 1917, and all other women on May 24, 1918 (Catherine L. Cleverdon, The Woman Suffrage Movement in Canada [Toronto: University of Toronto Press, 1974], p. 2).

are generally slightly more non-voters among women
than among men, and that the woman's vote is generally
slightly more conservative and more subject to religious influences. But these differences are small and
apply only to a tiny fraction of the female electorate.[3]

Thus, having discovered the political weapon that the ballot represents, women are utilizing it in roughly the same way and manner
as their male counterparts.

However, the active political role that women are playing is
very one-sided. The franchise for women was usually either accompanied or quickly followed by the right to be elected to public
office. It is in this connection that the picture is far from bright.
As members of elected political bodies, women have remained
conspicuous by their absence.

In the present volume, an attempt will be made to give an
account of the female members of the national legislatures in several countries, specifically, the United States, Britain, Canada,
Germany,* Austria,† and Switzerland. All these claim to be
democracies in the Western sense; they have parliamentary bodies
whose membership in at least one house is determined through
direct, popular elections. Eliminated from consideration in this
study are nonelective chambers that coexist with elected ones,
namely, the British House of Lords, the Canadian Senate, and the
Bundesrat (the federal council in both Austria and the Federal
Republic of Germany).‡

Although the selected countries have a common commitment
to elected legislatures based on the principle of representative
democracy, they are also sufficiently different in their particular
democratic procedures and practices to provide interesting con-
trasts (see Table 1.1). Three of the countries are part of the
English-speaking world and its Anglo-Saxon tradition (with due
apologies to Canada's French-speaking Quebec) and are located

----

*Included are the Reichstag, the parliament of the Weimar
Republic from 1919 to 1933, and the present Bundestag of the
Federal Republic.

†The Nationalrat of the two Austrian republics will be considered.

‡It should be noted that in Switzerland the Bundesrat is the
seven-member executive body. Naturally, this does not concern us
here, though we might mention in passing that as of the summer of
1979 no woman has attained membership in that body.

TABLE 1.1

Comparative Data

	United States		British House of Commons	Canadian House of Commons	German		Austrian Nationalrat		Swiss	
	Senate	House of Representatives			Reichstag	Bundestag	1st Rep.	2nd Rep.	Nationalrat	Ständerat
Year of first woman member	1922	1917	1919[a]	1921	1919[b]	1949	1919[c]	1945	1971	1971
Total membership of legislature since women became eligible	96–100	435–37	615–707	235–82	423–558	421–521[d]	165–75	165–83	200	44–46
Frequency of elections	6 yrs.	2 yrs.	varying (max. 5 yrs.)	varying (max. 5 yrs.)	varying (max. 4 yrs.)	4 yrs.[e]	varying (max. 4 yrs.)	varying (max. 4 yrs.)	4 yrs.	4 yrs.
Total number of women elected (by summer of 1979)	14[f]	89	107	33	111	138	13	44	21	2
Maximum number of women serving at one time	2	19	29	12	41	52	12	18	16	1
Number of women serving in 1979	1	16	19	12	n.a.[g]	40	n.a.	18	16	1

[a] One was elected in 1918 but never claimed her seat.
[b] The 1919 body was called German National Assembly.
[c] The 1919 body was called Constituent National Assembly.
[d] Includes representatives from Berlin.
[e] On one occasion, there was a three-year interval.
[f] Includes the appointed members.
[g] Not applicable.
Source: Compiled by the author.

4

either in North America or separated from the European continent proper by the English Channel. The other three countries are central European and part of the German-speaking area (despite the fact that several of the Swiss cantons are inhabited by people whose mother tongue is French, Italian, or Romansh).

The numerical size of these bodies varies considerably from the British House of Commons with its 635 members, to the U.S. Senate with 100, and the Swiss Ständerat with 46. The terms of office fluctuate between two and six years. Some legislatures are elected for fixed periods, while others may be dissolved under specific conditions; consequently, several have lasted only a few months. Such facts have obviously played their part in the frequency of personnel turnover and therefore also in the determination of the number of female members.

Of crucial importance, moreover, is the electoral system itself. There are primarily two methods by which legislators are chosen, although there are many different variations of these models. Under the principle of single-member constituency, a country is divided into a specific number of election districts, each sending one member to the parliament. This is the practice in the Anglo-Saxon countries of the United States, Britain, and Canada. In Austria, and with modifications in Germany and Switzerland, some form of proportional representation prevails, whereby several seats are allocated to a certain larger area, such as a state or province, and each party obtains a number of deputies approximately in proportion to the percentage of votes received in the election. Since the choice of the prospective representatives is up to the party leadership, the nomination process is quite different from that of the English-speaking countries, where individuals are vying with each other for specific seats in the legislature. However, there is no uniform method. Different rules apply in the nations that use proportional representation, but there are variations in the Anglo-Saxon countries also. Thus, in Britain and Canada the local party organizations decide on the candidates, whereas in the United States, through a unique primary system (which in itself may vary from state to state), the voters go to the polls and select the party candidates some time before actually voting for the next officeholder in a general election.

In the following pages, the winning of the franchise and the women who served in the national legislatures will be discussed in detail on a country-by-country basis. For the moment, suffice it to say that although women are playing an increasingly important part in the legislative process of these countries, their total number of participants is still pitifully small, especially when one considers that women make up at least 50 percent of any country's adult population!

NOTES

1. Susanna Woodtli, <u>Gleichberechtigung</u> (Frauenfeld: Verlag Huber, 1975), pp. 247–48.

2. Aileen S. Kraditor, <u>The Ideas of the Woman Suffrage Movement, 1890–1920</u> (Garden City, N.Y.: Doubleday, Anchor Books, 1971), pp. 3–4.

3. Maurice Duverger, <u>The Political Role of Women</u> (Paris: UNESCO, 1955), p. 122.

2
THE UNITED STATES SENATE

WOMEN MEMBERS OF THE U.S. SENATE

The Senate of the United States prides itself on being a great democratic body. It represents all states of the Union on an equal basis. Whether the population is large or small, each state has two senators, who, through the right of unlimited debate or filibuster (still very difficult to curb), can express themselves more fully on matters pertinent or otherwise than almost any legislators elsewhere. Until the Seventeenth Amendment became effective in 1912, senators were chosen by the state legislatures. Today, however, they are elected directly by the people, and therefore the U.S. Senate is included in this study.

But there is one peculiarity that distinguishes the selection of members of the U.S. Senate from that of all other parliamentary bodies here under discussion. The U.S. Constitution provides that, in cases of vacancies in the Senate, "the legislature of any State may empower the executive thereof to make temporary appointments until the people fill the vacancies by election as the legislature may direct."[1] Accordingly, each state has its own provisions for the filling of senatorial vacancies, but in most cases the governor is entitled to appoint a temporary replacement to fill a vacancy until the people are able to elect someone in the next general election. This appointive power of governors has played a major part in getting women into the U.S. Senate. However, it must be said that frequently very little was done to keep them there.

A U.S. senator serves a six-year term beginning on January 3. Before the Twentieth Amendment became operative in 1935, a new congress took over on March 4, despite the fact that in most states the election was held on the Tuesday following the first

7

Monday in November.* In other countries, a newly elected legislator usually assumes office immediately after the election or as
soon as possible thereafter. Not so in the United States, where
even now there is a "lame duck" period of two months. Although
Congress now normally does not meet between the day of the election and the time the new members take their seats, special sessions do occur at which the old members appear, even if they have
retired or have been defeated in the meantime. If there is a vacancy
(that is, if for any reason a former member of Congress is no
longer able to serve), a replacement will be named, and this replacement is sometimes chosen merely for the period between
November and January (or, before 1935, between November and
March). This gives particularly short terms to some people,
especially to women who might be selected more as tokens than as
serious attempts to have the female half of the population represented.

Indeed, the history of women in the U.S. Senate is filled with
examples of tokenism. That there have been only 14 women senators in over half a century is dismal enough. However, the picture
looks much worse when one considers that two women held their
seats for short periods during which the Senate never assembled
and that a third was able to attend two meetings only because the
president called Congress into special session after the legislature
had already adjourned. Altogether ten ladies held the office of
U.S. senator for less than 12 months, and only four were elected
to at least one full six-year term, as Table 2.1 indicates. This
gives U.S. women senators an average service of three years and
eight months (thanks to Margaret Chase Smith's four terms). In
view of the huge discrepancies, however, this figure is not very
meaningful.

The honor of being the first woman to sit in the U.S. Senate
belongs to Rebecca Latimer Felton (1835-1930), a Democrat from
Georgia. She had led a busy life as the wife of a Southern politician
who, in the late nineteenth century, had served in the U.S. House
of Representatives and in the Georgia legislature. Rebecca Felton
was known as an outspoken writer and lecturer. In late September
1922, the incumbent senator, Thomas E. Watson, died suddenly.
The governor of Georgia, Thomas W. Hardwick, now had the chance
to make an appointment to the Senate that might pacify the newly

---

*The Twentieth Amendment became part of the Constitution
on February 6, 1933. Therefore, the first new Congress that could
assemble in January instead of March was the Seventy-Fourth,
elected in November 1934.

enfranchised women voters who had not forgotten his opposition to giving them the vote. He apparently first offered the seat to Senator Watson's widow, who turned it down because of ill health. His second choice was Felton.[2]

TABLE 2.1

Length of Service of Women Senators

Length of Service	Senator(s)
Four six-year terms	Margaret Chase Smith
Three six-year terms	none
Two six-year terms plus a fifteen-month vacancy	Hattie W. Caraway
One six-year term plus a vacancy of almost two months	Maurine B. Neuberger
One six-year term*	Nancy L. Kassebaum
Eleven- to twelve-month vacancy	Rose M. Long
Ten- to eleven-month vacancy	none
Nine- to ten-month vacancy	none
Eight- to nine-month vacancy	Muriel B. Humphrey
Seven- to eight-month vacancy	none
Six- to seven-month vacancy	Eva Bowring
Five- to six-month vacancy	none
Four- to five-month vacancy	Dixie B. Graves, Maryon P. Allen
Three- to four-month vacancy	Elaine S. Edwards
Two- to three-month vacancy	Vera C. Bushfield
One- to two-month vacancy	Rebecca L. Felton, Gladys Pyle, Hazel H. Abel

*Elected in November 1978.
Source: Compiled by the author.

The cynicism of the entire affair was evident because the October 17 Democratic primary was sure to result in the nomination of a man (the governor himself was a candidate). Besides, the Senate was in recess, and therefore Felton would have the honor but no power or authority. However, President Harding called Congress into special session for November 20, and there now began an extraordinary game of tokenism. Although Walter George had been duly nominated in October and elected on the Tuesday following the first Monday in November, he was persuaded to let Felton take the oath of office on November 21 and make a speech on the floor the next day. This done, Senator George was sworn in as her successor.* Felton could now go back to Georgia. She had made history. Due to the appointive powers of the governor of Georgia, she had been the junior senator from the Peach State for less than two months at the age of 87 and had actually occupied a seat in the U.S. Senate and spoken there. It was a nice gesture to the newly enfranchised women of the country, but could anyone really take this seriously?

It was not until 11 years later that another woman was to appear as a member of the Senate. Again she was a Democrat, again she was from the South, and again she was appointed by the governor of her state. When Arkansas, in 1931, mourned the death of Senator Thaddeus Horatius Caraway, Governor Harvey Parnell saw fit to appoint the late senator's widow, Hattie W. Caraway (1878-1950) to her husband's seat. She was 53 years old at that time.

State law provided that a special election had to be called to fill the vacancy until the next general election. The election was scheduled for January 12, 1932. Hattie Caraway ran and won.† She thus became the first elected woman senator. She reached the Senate because she was the widow of the former incumbent. It was expected that she would be satisfied with the distinction of having sat in the Senate and that she would dutifully retire at the end of the year. There were several prominent Arkansas politicians, including Governor Parnell himself, who sought the Democratic nomination for a full six-year term, and Caraway was not supposed to be

---

*Senator George's long career in the Senate ended only with his retirement shortly before his death in 1957.

†Hope Chamberlin states that the Democratic party leaders could not agree on which man to run in the primary and thus selected Caraway, who won "without making a single appearance as a candidate before the Arkansas electorate" (Hope Chamberlin, A Minority of Members [New York: Praeger, 1973], p. 87). However, Diane D. Kincaid reports that Caraway "immediately had to defend her position against two opponents in a special election" (Diane D. Kincaid, "Over His Dead Body: A New Perspective and Some Feminist Footnotes on Widows in the U.S. Congress" [Paper prepared for the 1976 Annual Meeting of the American Political Science Association, Chicago, September 2-5, 1976], p. 9).

among them. However, at the last moment the female senator decided to compete for it. She had built a record as a legislator,
voting the way she felt her husband would have voted. She aligned
herself closely to Senator Huey Long from Louisiana, and that
flamboyant politician came to her aid and campaigned intensively
for her during the week preceding the primary in August. Caraway
not only won over her six opponents, but she received almost as
many votes as the rest of them together.[3] Her victory in the general election in November was a foregone conclusion. Six years
later, in 1938, with a strong New Deal record, she beat back a
challenge from Congressman John McClellan. When McClellan was
elected to the Senate in 1942, Caraway became the senior senator,
another first for a woman. During her time in the Senate, she was
also the first woman head of a senate committee, the first woman
to conduct a senate hearing, and the first woman to preside over the
Senate.[4] Her legislative career ended through defeat in the Democratic primary in 1944.*

This 13-year record for a woman in the Senate remained un-
challenged until it was broken by Margaret Chase Smith in the early
1960s. During the time Caraway was in the legislature, she was
joined by three other women, though not all at once. It was perhaps
poetic justice that the first woman to pair up with her was the widow
of Huey Long, the controversial senator from Louisiana who had
helped the lady from Arkansas in the 1932 primary. After Huey
Long was assassinated, Governor O. K. Allen was apparently the
choice of the Democratic organization, but he died before he could
take up that position. This turn of events threatened to throw the
party into an uproar, so the new governor, James A. Noe, on
January 31, 1936, appointed Rose McConnell Long (1892-1970) to
fill the vacancy. She was the machine's choice in the special election and consequently was elected without opposition on April 21,
1936, for the rest of the term ending on January 3, 1937. Like
Caraway, she thus held an appointive as well as an elective position
as U.S. senator, but, unlike the senator from Arkansas, the 43-
year-old widow from Louisiana was not a candidate for the full
term, which was won by Allen Ellender. While she apparently left
no particularly distinctive legislative marks, her name is in the
record book as belonging to a family that, in addition to filling

---

*She was opposed by several men in the primary, including
the eventual victor, U.S. Congressman and former University of
Arkansas President William Fulbright.

various state offices, has supplied the U.S. Senate with a husband, a wife, and a son.*

The naming of the next woman to the Senate was again a matter of expediency. This time the vacancy occurred in Alabama and was caused in the summer of 1937 when Franklin D. Roosevelt at long last had a chance to make an appointment to the Supreme Court. He chose a U.S. senator, Hugo Black. This presented the governor of Alabama, Bibb Graves, with a hot political issue—which he solved by appointing not someone's widow but his own wife. The appointment came in for much criticism at the time, and, in retrospect, one may wonder whether it set a precedent for the 1960s, when another Alabama governor, George Wallace, found that he could not immediately succeed himself in the governor's mansion and so decided to have his wife elected to that position.

In any event, Dixie Bibb Graves (1882-1965) was appointed by her husband on August 18, 1937, and took her seat two days later, just before the session ended. But another session began in mid-November, and this enabled her to make several speeches on the Senate floor, advocating such things as strong U.S. preparedness and the rights of the "sovereign" U.S. states.

The arrangement was that she would not run in the special election in January 1948. Although it seems that many people would have liked her to continue in office, she returned home after it was clear that Lister Hill was the choice for her seat. Governor Graves died in 1942, but his widow remained active until her own death at the age of 83.

So far, all women senators had been Democrats, and all had come from the deep South. This was changed in 1938. Senator Peter Norbeck from South Dakota had died in office, and in the November election the voters were asked to name someone for the unexpired term, that is, until January 3, 1939. The choice was Gladys Pyle (1890-), who, in a contest with a Democrat, retained the seat for the Republicans on November 8, 1938, but was not a candidate for the full term. Both her parents had been very active in South Dakota politics, and she herself had served in the state legislature, been secretary of state, and competed for the governorship. Her candidacy, therefore, was not based on the fact that she was someone's wife or widow but on her own merits. If married women were scarce in high political offices, unmarried ones were

---

*Her son, Russell B. Long, came to the Senate at the end of 1948 and has been a member ever since, serving together with Senator Ellender for many years.

even scarcer, and Pyle's appearance in Washington was quite unheard-of. To this day, she remains the only U.S. female senator who had never married. However, she did not have a chance to be sworn in. Although she did travel to the nation's capital to claim her office, the Senate was not in session during the two months the 48-year-old lady from South Dakota occupied the position of the state's junior senator.

The scene was repeated a decade later, again involving a Republican lady from South Dakota. Senator Harlan Bushfield had died in office, and on October 6, 1948, Governor George Mickelson appointed the 59-year-old widow of the deceased, Vera Bushfield (1889-), to the U.S. Senate. The object apparently was continuity, with the understanding that the interim senator would resign immediately after the November election in order to give the newly elected person the benefit of a few more days' seniority. This is precisely what happened. When the Senate assembled on December 21, South Dakota's senior senator, J. Chandler Gurney, presented Bushfield's letter of resignation, enabling Karl Mundt to assume the office without delay. Thus, Bushfield never took her seat; as a matter of fact, she did not even bother to put in an appearance in Washington during the time she officially was a member of the Senate.

All this may have helped the morale of U.S. women, but it was hardly of much practical value. However, the situation changed in 1949. That year marked the beginning of the Senate career of the lady with the longest record in that body. Margaret Chase Smith (1897-) was 42 years old when she won a special election in June 1940 to succeed her late husband as Republican member of the House of Representatives from the state of Maine. She won four successive general elections and thus established herself as a politician in her own right, a reputation that, incidentally, preceded her husband's death. In 1948, the incumbent senator from her state, Wallace White, did not seek reelection. Representative Margaret Smith entered the Republican primary against the vigorous opposition of several men, including the incumbent governor and a former governor. She overcame this opposition and received more than half the total vote cast. After that, winning the general election was easy.

For 24 years Smith sat in the U.S. Senate, most of the time as the only woman, usually as an independent spirit. She spoke out against the tactics of Senator Joseph McCarthy when this was quite dangerous and few dared to do so, helped defeat President Eisenhower's nomination of Lewis Strauss to be secretary of commerce, and opposed President Nixon's appointment of Harold Carswell to the Supreme Court. When Senator Barry Goldwater seemed assured of the Republican presidential nomination in 1964, it was Smith who campaigned against him as a rival candidate, and, having entered several primaries, she became the first woman actively to compete for the presidency on a major party ticket, even if her case was doomed from the start. She took her work in the Senate quite seriously and answered almost 3,000 consecutive roll calls, which set an all-time record for attendance. Although many men felt that military matters were not suitable topics for women, she sought and eventually obtained a seat on the Armed Services Committee, ultimately becoming its highest-ranking minority member.

In 1972, shortly before her seventy-fifth birthday, Smith ran for a fifth term. She had become a living institution in Washington and with a Nixon landslide never in doubt and Maine safely in the Republican camp, her reelection seemed assured. Yet the improbable happened, and the voters decided to retire the woman senator from Maine, thereby making the Senate once again an all-male bastion.

Until Smith's election, only South Dakota had provided the Senate with Republican women members. In 1954, Nebraska was also to do so. When Senator Dwight Griswold died, the governor, on April 16, appointed Eva Bowring (1892-), a 62-year-old widow who had been very much involved in politics, as indicated by eight years of service as vice-chairperson of the Nebraska Republican Central Committee. When she was sent to Washington, Eisenhower was in the White House, and the Senate was controlled by the Republicans only because Wayne Morse of Oregon, who had deserted his party during the previous presidential campaign, voted with the Republicans for organizational purposes. Bowring was expected to add strength to the Eisenhower forces, and she did. However, her time on Capitol Hill was limited. State law required that the appointee should serve only until the next regular election, that is, the Tuesday following the first Monday in November.

But on that day, Nebraska elected another woman to the Senate, again for a short time, because the law also stipulated that no one elected for the unexpired two months between early November and early January could be a candidate for election to a full six-year term.[5] Despite this rule, which made the race almost meaningless, there was much interest in the contest. The Republican nomination was won by a 66-year-old widow, Hazel Abel (1888-1966), who became Nebraska's second interim senator. As in 1938, when the voters in Arkansas and in South Dakota elected females to the Senate, so in 1954 the electorate in widely different parts of the country chose two women; Margaret Chase Smith was reelected in Maine, and Hazel Abel was elected to fill a vacancy for

a few weeks by the people of Nebraska. But while Pyle never had
the opportunity to appear on the floor and vote, Abel did. The Senate
was back in session after the November election to decide whether
to censure a fellow senator, Wisconsin's Joseph McCarthy. The
junior senator from Nebraska followed the debate closely, and when
the roll was eventually called, she voted for censuring her Republican colleague. Although her term ended on January 3, she decided
to resign on December 31 so that the winner of the six-year term,
Carl Curtis, would have the opportunity to gain some seniority.

Margaret Chase Smith was once again the only woman in the
Senate, and she was to hold this distinction until November 1960,
when she was joined by a woman from the opposite party and opposite part of the country. Maurine Neuberger (1907-), Democrat
from Oregon and the first woman senator to be born in the twentieth
century, was no newcomer to the legislative scene. While her husband Richard was a member of one branch of the Oregon legislature, she sat in the other. Moreover, when in 1954 he was elected
the first Democratic senator from his state in quite a while, his
wife became closely associated with his activities in Washington.
Although suffering from cancer, Dick Neuberger had decided to file
for renomination in the spring of 1960 but died just before the filing
deadline. Never one to shun publicity, Maurine Neuberger knew
that she was a controversial figure, especially as a Democrat in
what was still basically a Republican state. As a woman who had
just lost her husband, she faced quite a dilemma. However, she
eventually determined to run in the primary and won, defeating
several men. She went on to beat her Republican opponent, former
Governor Elmo Smith, in November, even though Richard Nixon
carried the state in his unsuccessful attempt for the presidency.
Later on, she was asked what she considered the hardest thing
about being a woman senator and replied, "Being elected."[6]

Maurine Neuberger was 53 years old when she entered the
Senate. The Democrats controlled the White House during her
term of office, just as they controlled the Congress. The junior
senator from Oregon voted with her party when she thought it wise
and opposed her party's administration when she deemed it necessary. She supported truth-in-lending and spoke at length against
a proposed corporation that would make use of space satellites for
communication systems.

In 1964, the senator married a Boston psychiatrist, Philip
Solomon, and moved to New England, an action that was not too
kindly perceived by many of her constituents in the West. When
her term neared its end, she announced that she would not seek reelection. She retired into private life in Massachusetts, and after
her marriage ended in divorce, took up residence again in Portland,
Oregon.

As the political career of Margaret Chase Smith drew to a close in 1972, another woman made a brief appearance as member of the Senate. She was Elaine S. Edwards (1929-), Democrat from Louisiana. It will be recalled that Rose Long was succeeded by Allen Ellender in 1937. He held the seat until his death on July 27, 1972, at the age of 81. Preceded by a woman, he also was followed by one. On August 1, Governor Edwin Edwards copied Governor Graves of Alabama by appointing his own wife to the vacancy. At the time, she was, like Rose Long, 43 years old. Allen Ellender, who was running for renomination and facing a serious challenge from State Senator J. Bennett Johnson, died. There were others who now coveted the appointment, and the choice of Elaine Edwards was, from her husband's point of view, a good solution. He called it "a meaningful gesture"[7] in spite—or because ?—of the assurance that she was not a candidate for the full term. From Washington, Senator Edwards kept in close touch with Baton Rouge by telephone, and there was even the unfriendly remark that "the Senator doesn't go to the bathroom without calling the governor."[8] Bennett Johnson won the senatorial primary in August and was duly elected in November. On November 13, Edwards resigned, allowing the newly elected senator to be appointed ahead of time in order to acquire seniority, and thereby ending her brief career as a legislator.

This action, followed by the replacement of Margaret Chase Smith in early January 1973, again deprived the Senate of any female members. No new woman senator was in sight. The three women who braved the odds in 1974 and the one who did so in 1976 were not much more than political sacrificial lambs. However, the situation changed in 1978, first through tragedy and later through the will of the people. In January 1978, Minnesota's senior senator, former Vice-President and presidential candidate Hubert Humphrey, lost his battle against cancer. Shortly after his death, his 65-year-old widow Muriel (1912-) was appointed to his seat. She had been intimately associated with her husband's many campaigns and numerous projects, and she certainly was no stranger to either Washington or the political scene. Her appointment was therefore regarded by many as natural. She was given her husband's office and his seat on the Foreign Relations Committee. Her maiden speech was in support of the Panama Canal Treaty, then a hotly disputed item. After a mere ten weeks in office, a reporter could write that during that time

> she has proposed a nationwide advocacy system to assist
> seriously disabled psychiatric patients, urged the ex-
> pansion of a supplemental food program for women,
> infants and children, proposed a plan to train economically

disadvantaged students for biomedical careers and
advocated universal testing to prevent mental retarda-
tion. She has also seen the passage of the Humphrey-
Hawkins full employment bill, which had been a project
of her husband's.[9]

Whether or not to run for the remaining four years of her husband's
term posed a difficult question for her, but she finally decided to
retire from politics at the end of the year.

Much more unexpected was the vacancy that occurred in
Alabama. On June 1, 1978, Senator James B. Allen died suddenly
of a heart attack. Governor George Wallace appointed Allen's
widow Maryon (1925-) to the seat left vacant. Accustomed to public
life, the new senator had been a newspaper reporter and met her
husband, then the lieutenant governor, when interviewing him for
the press. Allen ran for the unexpired two years of her husband's
term and entered the primary accordingly. However, she met with
defeat and has since not been a candidate.

However, in November 1978, the very time that Senators
Humphrey and Allen terminated their service in Washington, another woman was elected to the Senate, Nancy Landon Kassebaum
(1932-), Republican from Kansas. At age 46, she thus became only
the fourth woman to be elected to a full six-year term. Kassebaum,
unlike many of her predecessors, did not enter the Senate on her
husband's coattails (she is separated from him), although being the
daughter of Alf Landon—former governor, the 1936 Republican
presidential candidate, and grand old man of Kansas politics—certainly did not hurt. Her only previous political office had been that
of school board member, and one year as aide to outgoing Senator
James Pearson had been her only other political experience. She
has promised to run for no more than one additional term, saying
that after 12 years it is possible to ". . . lose touch with your
constituents and . . . lose perspective."[10]

DISCUSSION

It is unfortunate that this brief sketch of 14 women exhausts
the list of the female senators. In terms of age, they cover a wide
span; only four were under 50 when they reached the Senate, six in
their fifties, three over 60, and one 87. This means that on the
average a female senator was about 56 when first entering the
Senate. Seven, or 50 percent of the total, served by appointment
only, and two more were originally appointed and then successfully
ran for election. Of the remaining five, two were elected to two

months' vacancies, and only Senators Smith, Neuberger, and Kassebaum won full six-year terms without previous appointments.

Quite clearly, appointment was the key in most instances. It is unlikely that any of the ladies involved except Kassebaum would have entered the Senate had it not been for the death of an incumbent. Only Smith and Kassebaum stepped into vacancies caused by decisions of U.S. senators not to seek reelection; 12 others filled seats left empty by the death of the incumbents. Technically, Abel falls into a different category, because the person she replaced was Bowring, who, it will be recalled, was appointed to the late Senator Griswold's position. When this appointment expired, Abel was elected to fill the remaining two months of the unexpired term. Six of the women senators succeeded their own husbands, one through election and the other five through appointment.

The "widow syndrome" will be discussed again in some of the following chapters. In the case of the U.S. Senate, ten of the 14 women were widows, including the six who inherited their husbands' seats. Excluding Kassebaum, only two of the female senators still had spouses when they came to the Senate, and both of them were the wives of the governors who appointed them. Pyle was the only one who never married. It is, of course, an indication of the chauvinistic character of our society that it is even necessary to mention the marital status of women senators. Whether or not he is married is hardly a piece of vital information about a male legislator. In a woman, however, it seems to indicate a certain degree of reliability and success, though no one appears to be interested in finding out whether the marriage was bliss, hell, or in-between!

Politically, the female senators consisted of eight Democrats and six Republicans. For whatever reasons, they were grouped together in terms of entrance to the Senate. The first four to reach the Senate, those entering between 1922 and 1938, were all Democrats; the second group, who arrived between 1938 and 1954, all Republicans; the next four, who came in 1960, in 1972, and in 1978, again Democrats; and the last one, elected in 1978, a Republican. Geographically, the South accounted for six female senators (two from Alabama, two from Louisiana, and one each from Arkansas and Georgia), the Middle West was represented by another six (two from Nebraska, two from South Dakota, and one each from Minnesota and Kansas), and the Pacific Northwest (Oregon) and New England (Maine) each elected one. It should be noted that none of the states with large populations are among these. Using the rank order established by the 1970 census, Georgia, the most populated state of those sending women to the Senate, ranks fourteenth, Minnesota nineteenth, Louisiana twentieth, and Alabama twenty-first.

None of the other states with female senators rank in the top half of the list. Perhaps it would be wrong to draw any conclusions from this. Nevertheless, the fact remains that, as we shall see, California, New York, and Illinois together account for more than 25 percent of the congresswomen in the House of Representatives. In the Senate, the big states so far have never been represented by women.

We have mentioned repeatedly that only four women were successful in winning election to full six-year terms in the Senate. Does this mean that there is a strong antifeminist feeling as far as women legislators are concerned? Not necessarily. Women do get elected to the House of Representatives on a continuing basis. However, in contests for the U.S. Senate, very few women compete. Table 2.2 shows that during the last ten general elections, with one-third of the 100 Senate seats at stake every time, only between one and three women competed on each occasion on the Republican or Democratic lists. For example, in November 1976, 33 senatorial contests took place. Not a single woman was elected. Actually, only one ran on a major party ticket, Connecticut's Democratic Secretary of State Gloria Schaffer, who, despite demonstrated popularity at the polls, could not overcome incumbent Senator Lowell Weicker's strong appeal as an anti-Nixon Republican. Two other women, from Hawaii and New York respectively, gave up almost certain reelection to the House of Representatives in their unsuccessful attempts to obtain the Democratic nomination for the Senate. Patsy Mink's loss to her fellow congressman, Spark Matsunaga, and Bella Abzug's, by one percentage point, to Patrick Moynihan, cannot be attributed to antifeminism, for in both cases there were good political reasons for people's supporting the male candidates. Had the two women succeeded in the primaries, they might well have won the general election, for both previously Republican seats were captured by the Democrats that year. Thus, the country came close to having two women senators instead of none.

There were several other occasions when women decided to give up their seats in the House of Representatives in order to try their luck as candidates for the Senate. The very first congresswoman, Republican Jeannette Rankin, had won an at-large seat in Montana in November 1916. When the state legislature created two congressional districts, she opted to run for the Senate in 1918. She narrowly lost the Republican nomination but stayed in the race as candidate of the National party, coming in third in the general election, which was won by Democrat Thomas Walsh. Other notable women representatives who lost senatorial races include Ruth Hanna McCormick, Republican from Illinois, who, after two terms in the House, successfully challenged an incumbent senator

TABLE 2.2

Women as Senatorial Candidates of Major Parties, 1960–78

Year	Number of Women Candidates	Name(s) of Candidates	State	Party	Result
1960	3	Lucia Cormier	Maine	Democratic	lost
		Margaret C. Smith	Maine	Republican	won
		Maurine Neuberger	Oregon	Democratic	won
1962	1	Gracie Pfost	Idaho	Democratic	lost
1964	2	Elly Peterson	Michigan	Republican	lost
		Genevieve Blatt	Pennsylvania	Democratic	lost
1966	2	Margaret C. Smith	Maine	Republican	won
		Ruth Briggs	Rhode Island	Republican	lost
1968	1	Katherine Peden	Kentucky	Democratic	lost
1970	1	Leonore Romney	Michigan	Republican	lost
1972	2	Margaret C. Smith	Maine	Republican	lost
		Louise Leonard	West Virginia	Republican	lost
1974	3	Barbara Mikulski	Maryland	Democratic	lost
		Betty Roberts	Oregon	Democratic	lost
		Gwenyfred Bush	South Carolina	Republican	lost
1976	1	Gloria Schaffer	Connecticut	Democratic	lost
1978	2	Nancy Kassebaum	Kansas	Republican	won
		Jane Eskind	Tennessee	Democratic	lost

Source: Compiled by the author.

TABLE 2.3

Women Members of the U.S. Senate

Senator	Dates	Party	State	Means of Entry	Entry Date	Reasons for Departure	Departure Date
Rebecca Felton	1835–1930	Democratic	Georgia	appt.[a]	October 3, 1922	res.	November 22, 1922
Hattie Caraway	1878–1950	Democratic	Arkansas	appt.[a]	November 13, 1931	def.	January 1945
Rose Long	1892–1970	Democratic	Louisiana	appt.[b]	January 31, 1936	ret.	January 1937
Dixie Graves	1882–1965	Democratic	Alabama	appt.[b]	August 18, 1937	res.	January 10, 1938
Gladys Pyle	1890–	Republican	South Dakota	elec.	November 8, 1938	ret.	January 1939
Vera Bushfield	1889–	Republican	South Dakota	appt.[a]	October 6, 1948	res.	December 1948
Margaret C. Smith	1897–	Republican	Maine	elec.	September 1948	def.	January 1973
Eva Bowring	1892–	Republican	Nebraska	appt.	April 16, 1954	ret.	November 7, 1954
Hazel Abel	1888–1966	Republican	Nebraska	elec.	November 2, 1954	res.	December 31, 1954
Maurine Neuberger	1907–	Democratic	Oregon	elec.[a]	November 8, 1960	ret.	January 1967
Elaine Edwards	1929–	Democratic	Louisiana	appt.[a]	August 1, 1972	res.	November 13, 1972
Muriel Humphrey	1912–	Democratic	Minnesota	appt.[a]	January 25, 1978	ret.	November 1978
Maryon Allen	1925–	Democratic	Alabama	appt.[a]	June 8, 1978	def.	November 1978
Nancy Kassebaum	1932–	Republican	Kansas	elec.	November 1978	n.a.[c]	n.a.

[a]To husband's seat.

[b]By husband.

[c]Not applicable.

Note: Abbreviations used under Means of Entry and Reason for Departure are the following: appt., appointed; elec., elected; res., resigned; def., defeated; and ret., retired.

Source: Compiled by the author.

TABLE 2.4

The U.S. Senate and Female Members

Congress	Years	Senators
66th	1919-21	none
67th	1921-23	Felton
68th	1923-25	none
69th	1925-27	none
70th	1927-29	none
71st	1929-31	none
72nd	1931-33	Caraway
73rd	1931-35	Caraway
74th	1935-37	Caraway, Long
75th	1937-39	Caraway, Graves, Pyle
76th	1939-41	Caraway
77th	1941-43	Caraway
78th	1943-45	Caraway
79th	1945-47	none
80th	1947-49	Bushfield
81st	1949-51	Smith
82nd	1951-53	Smith
83rd	1953-55	Smith, Bowring, Abel
84th	1955-57	Smith
85th	1957-59	Smith
86th	1959-61	Smith, Neuberger
87th	1961-63	Smith, Neuberger
88th	1963-65	Smith, Neuberger
89th	1965-67	Smith, Neuberger
90th	1967-69	Smith
91st	1969-71	Smith
92nd	1971-73	Smith, Edwards
93rd	1973-75	none
94th	1975-77	none
95th	1977-79	Humphrey, Allen
96th	1979-81	Kassebaum

Source: Compiled by the author.

in the primary only to be defeated in the general election; Helen
Gahagan Douglas, Democrat from California, a three-term congresswoman whose failure in the senatorial contest in 1950 took on
nationwide significance since it made famous the personality and
tactics of her Republican opponent, Congressman Richard M.
Nixon; and Idaho's Democratic Congresswoman Gracie Pfost, who,
in 1962 after spending ten years in the House, only barely missed
winning the Senate seat to which former Governor Len Jordan had
recently been appointed.

When one looks at the handful of women who run each year for
the Senate on a major party ticket, one may be forgiven the assump-
tion of a certain death wish on the part of these candidates. Did
anyone, male or female, really have a chance against Republican
Lowell Weicker from Connecticut in 1976, against Republican
Charles Mathias from Maryland in 1974, or against Democrat
Jennings Randolph from West Virginia in 1972? Did the three
brave women who took on these men really think they could win any
more than did Elly Peterson and Leonore Romney, who ran against
Philip Hart in Michigan in 1964 and 1970, respectively, or than
did Pennsylvania's proven vote-getter, Genevieve Blatt, who could
not defeat Hugh Scott in 1964? Luck is certainly a factor in politics. At the same time, a particular contest in a particular year
may prove unwinnable. More women will be elected to the U.S.
Senate when more enter primaries, when more are willing to run,
and when more get the nod in races where they have at least a
fighting chance of winning. (For a concise listing of the women
members of the U.S. Senate, see Tables 2.3 and 2.4.)

NOTES

1. U.S., Constitution, Amend. 17.

2. Hope Chamberlin, A Minority of Members (New York:
Praeger, 1973). Many of the anecdotal details in this and the next
chapter are taken from this work. It contains articles on all female
members of both houses of Congress between 1917 and 1972.

3. Ibid., p. 87.

4. U.S., Congress, Women in Congress: 1917-1976, 94th
Cong., 2nd sess., 1976, Rept. 1732, p. 20. This contains details
of all women who have served in both houses of Congress up to
1976.

5. Chamberlin, op. cit., p. 244.

6. Peggy Lamson, Few Are Chosen: American Women in
Political Life Today (Boston: Houghton Mifflin, 1968), p. xii.

7. Chamberlin, op. cit., p. 346.
8. Ibid., p. 347.
9. New York Times, April 8, 1978.
10. New York Times, November 29, 1978.

3
THE UNITED STATES
HOUSE OF REPRESENTATIVES

WOMEN MEMBERS OF THE U.S. HOUSE
OF REPRESENTATIVES

As we have seen in the previous chapter, there had been
only 14 women in the U.S. Senate up to the summer of 1979. None
were on the roster when the nation celebrated its two hundredth
birthday in 1976, although the situation changed only two years
later, when, upon the death of two male members, their widows
were appointed to their seats. However, the House of Representatives presents quite a different story. By 1979, a total of 89 women
had held membership in the House. * The first, Jeannette Rankin,
served one term from 1917 to 1919, giving the United States the distinction of having had female representation in the national legislature before any of the other countries here under discussion. Her
departure, however, left Congress again without women. Then
four females served for very short periods until Florence Kahn,
after winning a special election in February 1925, provided continuity by remaining in Congress for a dozen years. Since that time,
the House has never been without its women members, even though
there have not yet been more than 19 in any one session. Since this
"high" constitutes only 4.37 percent of the total membership of 435,
the situation is obviously far from satisfactory to anyone interested
in proper representation of the population.

---

*Not included in all the figures cited is Mary Elizabeth
Farrington, who from August 1954 to January 1957 was a nonvoting
delegate from the territory of Hawaii.

When Jeannette Rankin was elected in November 1916, only very few countries allowed their women to vote, as we have seen. The United States was still struggling with the problem; the Nineteenth Amendment did not become effective until August 1920. But while this amendment extended the right to vote and to hold office to women throughout the United States, the female population had been accorded voting rights piecemeal before that date. The West especially pioneered in that respect. By the time the Nineteenth Amendment was incorporated into the U.S. Constitution, nearly 18 million women were already entitled to vote, and the amendment enfranchised another 9.5 million.[1]

As indicated by Table 3.1, the western state of Montana gave women the right to vote in 1914. Among those working for the suffrage movement was Jeannette Rankin (1880-1973). She had traveled across the United States, studied in New York, visited New Zealand, and in the summer of 1916 announced that she would run for a seat in the House of Representatives. She came from a Republican family and entered the primary of that party, although she remarked many years later, "I never was a Republican, I ran on the Republican ticket."[2] She outpolled the other seven contenders and in her campaign against the Democrats emphasized woman suffrage, Prohibition, and "preparedness for peace." Just as Woodrow Wilson went to bed on that election night believing he had lost, so did Jeannette Rankin, and it was several days before it became clear that she had indeed won, the only Republican to do so that year in Montana.

Her career in Washington is overshadowed by two votes, cast a generation apart, against war. Shortly after she arrived in Congress in 1917, the legislature was called upon to declare war on Germany. The president's recommendation was voted for by 374 members of the House, while 50 voted against it, among them Jeannette Rankin. She followed her conscience, even though public sentiment ran against her. This action and her general outspokenness made her vulnerable when it came time to seek reelection. Before 1918, the two congressional members from Montana had run at large; now the state was divided into two districts, and Rankin's home area was so gerrymandered as to make it predominantly Democratic. Although not wanting to avoid battle, she thought she could not win as candidate for the House under these circumstances and therefore decided to try for the Senate. She entered the Republican primary but came in second in a field of four. She then fought it out in November on a third-party ticket, but once again was unsuccessful. When her term ended in March 1919, both houses of Congress were without female representation.

TABLE 3.1

Woman Suffrage in the United States before
the Nineteenth Amendment

Year	State(s)	Extent of Suffrage
1838	Kentucky	School elections
1861	Kansas	School elections
1875	Mississippi, Minnesota	School elections
1887	Kansas	Municipal elections
1890	Wyoming*	Full suffrage
1893	Colorado	Full suffrage
1896	Utah, Idaho	Full suffrage
1910	Washington	Full suffrage
1911	California	Full suffrage
1912	Oregon, Kansas, Arizona	Full suffrage
1913	Illinois	Presidential elections
1914	Montana, Nevada	Full suffrage
1917	New York, Michigan, Oklahoma, South Dakota	Full suffrage

*The territory of Wyoming enfranchised women in 1869.
Sources: Martin Gruberg, Women in American Politics
(Oshkosh, Wis.: Academia, 1968); and Aileen S. Kraditor, The
Ideas of the Woman Suffrage Movement, 1890-1920 (Garden City,
N.Y.: Doubleday, Anchor Books, 1971).

But Washington had not seen the last of Jeannette Rankin.
When in the 1930s the peace of the world was threatened again,
Rankin felt that the United States was drifting toward war and that
this trend ought to be stopped. In 1940 she again ran for Congress.
She defeated three men in the Republican primary and then won over
her Democratic opponent, an incumbent New Dealer, although she
apparently received little help from the Republican organization.

By the time she returned to Congress, she was of course no
longer the only woman in the House but joined six others. She again
showed her independence, especially when on December 8, 1941,
the day after the Japanese attack on Pearl Harbor, hers was the
only vote cast against the declaration of war. However courageous
this might have been, the action made her not only unpopular but
destroyed her effectiveness in Congress and, together with financial
and family reasons, persuaded her to retire from Congress at the
end of her term.

The congressional career of Jeannette Rankin was in several ways unorthodox. While she succeeded in breaking the sex barrier, her activities in Washington were obviously not particularly successful, as illustrated by her antiwar votes as well as by the shortness of her stays in Congress. She was, incidentally, one of only two congresswomen to serve two scattered terms.

The Sixty-Seventh Congress

Rankin's departure in March 1919 left Congress without women for two years, until the arrival of Alice Mary Robertson (1854-1931), who in her campaign in 1920 declared, "The men have thrust the vote on us and now I am going to see whether they mean it."[3] Although she opposed woman suffrage as "bartering the birthright for a mess of pottage,"[4] she now decided to make use of it. She was 66 years old and had taught and worked with Indians all her life. Like Jeannette Rankin, she was outspoken, articulate, and knew what she wanted, and she, too, was unmarried. A Republican from Oklahoma, she defeated the Democratic incumbent but did not stay in Washington very long. She also took a number of unpopular stands; notably, she opposed a measure giving bonuses to war veterans. The man she defeated two years earlier was eager for a rematch, which he won, whereupon Robertson went home, denouncing politics "as too unclean for women."[5]

However, by that time she was no longer the only woman in the House. Two others had joined her during her term, and here we meet for the first time a phenomenon that was so frequent in the Senate, namely that of a woman entering to fill a vacancy. However, in contrast to the Senate, appointments are not possible in the House. Every member has to be elected. Special elections are held in the district to fill the vacancy, although the way these elections are held, indeed, whether they are held at all, or whether the vacancy is allowed to exist until the next general election, are matters of state law as interpreted by the governor. In any event, beginning in 1922, it seems to have occurred to the political leaders in the various states and congressional districts that there was sentiment for filling a vacancy with a close relative of the deceased and that this sentiment ought to be utilized politically. The close relative was usually the wife. Interestingly enough, however, in the very first instance it was the daughter. Winnifred Mason Huck (1882-1936), daughter of the Illinois Republican pacifist Congressman William E. Mason, campaigned for and won the four months of her father's unexpired term upon his death. She was the first wife and mother to go to Congress, reportedly with the full support and agreement of her civil-engineer husband and their four children.[6] But she was unsuccessful in two attempts to return to the House and had to devote her energies to investigative reporting instead.

Mae Ella Nolan (1886-1973) became the first widow to take her late husband's position in the House. She was persuaded to run for the unexpired term and the full two years for which her husband had just been elected. A Republican from California, she served from January 1923 to March 1925, at which time she retired, explaining that "politics is entirely too masculine to have any attraction for feminine responsibilities."[7] But she had made history by becoming the chairperson of the Committee on Expenditures in the Post Office Department and thus Congress' first female committee head.[8]

The Sixty-Eighth Congress

Shortly before Nolan's term was up, she was joined by the second woman in the Sixty-Eighth Congress. Another widow, Florence P. Kahn (1868-1948), followed her husband as Republican member from California. She was the first woman of Jewish faith to enter the House. Unlike those of the other women, however, hers was not a short career. Time after time she ran for reelection and won, and it was not until November 1936 that she was defeated by a New Dealer. By that time the presence of six women in the House at one time had become a fait accompli. Kahn provided continuity. She insisted on adequate committee appointments and eventually received those of Education, Military Affairs, and Appropriations. The latter two at least were not those originally regarded as suitable for women. She had first been assigned to Indian Affairs, which she rejected since "the only Indians in my district are in front of cigar stores,"[9] a remark echoed more than four decades later by Shirley Chisholm, who refused to serve on the Agriculture Committee, saying that the only agricultural connection of her district was the proverbial tree that grows in Brooklyn. Refusing a committee assignment had been unthinkable, especially for a woman, but Florence Kahn was determined to "obliterate sex in politics."[10]

The Sixty-Ninth Congress

The three women who sat in the House in 1925 all were to be around for quite some time. In addition to Kahn, there was Mary T. Norton (1875-1959), the first Democratic woman in the House and the first from an eastern state. It may be that New Jersey's political boss, Frank Hague, believed that she would bring respectability to his political organization.[11] In any event, she made a name for herself as an advocate of social reform and a friend of the underdog, until ill health finally forced her retirement at the age of 75 after she had been in the House for a quarter of a century.

A total of 35 years of service was accumulated by another 1925 newcomer, Edith Nourse Rogers (1881-1960). A Republican from Massachusetts, she won a special election for the seat previously held by her late husband. She entered the House at the age of 44, won election after election every two years, and was headed for another victory at the polls when she died. She had been a member of Congress longer than any other woman, and her record has thus far not been surpassed.

The Seventieth Congress

Joining the Kahn-Norton-Rogers trio in 1927 was Katherine G. Langly (1888-1948). She was another wife succeeding her husband—but under somewhat unusual circumstances. Congressman John Wesley Langley, Republican from Kentucky, had run afoul of the law because he dealt in whiskey during the Prohibition era. When, after conviction, he was forced to go to jail, his wife competed for his seat and won, first in a special election in 1927 and then in the regular one the following year. When her husband was released from prison, he wanted his congressional job back, but his wife was unwilling to give it up. Eventually, she prevailed and became a candidate for reelection, but the family disagreement had caused enough of an uproar to defeat her in the election. When her husband was in Congress, Langley had been his secretary. When she held the seat, she appointed her married daughter to the job. This led Hope Chamberlin to maintain that Katherine Langley's major claim to fame was her ability to show "how the House of Representatives can be used to keep a family on the public payroll."[12]

Arriving early in 1929 was Pearl Peden Oldfield (1876-1962), Democrat from Alabama. Her husband had died the previous November, and she had agreed to fill his unexpired term. She never felt adequate for the job without her husband's guidance and, at the end of her term, expressed happiness about retiring "to the sphere in which I believe women belong—the home."[13]

The Seventy-First Congress

Oldfield's attitude was certainly not typical of women representatives, and one of the best examples of an opposite position was Ruth Hanna McCormick (1880-1944), Republican from Illinois. She came from a prominent political family; her father was Ohio's "king-maker," Senator Mark Hanna. She had also married into a financially and politically important Illinois family. President Theodore Roosevelt attended her wedding, and her husband eventually sat in the U.S. Senate. However, shortly before his death, he was defeated for renomination in the Republican primary, and the victor, Charles S. Deneen, now became the widow's target. As a prelude, she contested an at-large seat in the House of Representatives in 1928, overwhelmed her primary opponents, and then led the state ticket in November. In 1930, she was ready to do battle with Deneen. Although it meant giving up her seat in the House, she challenged him in the primary and beat him. However, in November, the Democrats took the seat, and McCormick thus failed in her attempt to become the first elected female senator. She did remain active in politics, ran a farm and a newspaper, and married a politician from New Mexico, Albert Gallatin Simms, who had been a colleague of hers while in Congress.

Another woman from a prominent political family came to Washington at the same time, even though party, background, and region could not have been more different. Ruth Bryan Owen, Democrat from Florida (1885-1954), was the daughter of three-time presidential contender William Jennings Bryan and as such had been involved in politics at an early age. She married young, was divorced soon afterward, then married a British officer in the Royal Engineers, accompanying him to many parts of the world. Owen tried for Congress in 1926, losing the primary by a few hundred votes. By 1928, her husband had died. She ran again and this time succeeded, a particularly difficult task since Florida had rejected ratification of the Woman Suffrage Amendment and was therefore not too well disposed to women in politics.* She was reelected in 1930 but failed in the primary in 1932, because the tide was turning against Prohibition and the family was identified with the antiliquor forces. However, Owen did vote for repeal of Prohibition after her defeat,

---

*Chamberlin reports that, in a gesture of good will, the Florida legislature in 1969 voted to grant women the right to vote!

because this clearly seemed to be the will of the people. Her daughter attempted to continue the family tradition by twice running for
Congress from California, albeit unsuccessfully.[14]

Also entering the House in 1929 was Ruth Baker Pratt (1877-
1965). A Republican, she was born into a well-to-do family, was
highly educated, and married a wealthy man. She fought Tammany
Hall as an alderwoman and reached Congress from New York's Silk
Stocking district, which later sent to Washington such notables as
John Lindsay and Ed Koch and, in 1978, rejected Bella Abzug.
Pratt's views on women in politics are worth recalling.

> A man enters public life and not the slightest attention
> is paid to the fact that he is a man. A woman runs for
> office and there is more interest in the fact that she is
> a woman than in her qualifications for the job she seeks.
> She is completely shackled by her sex. At every turn
> she is confronted with the fact that the activities of the
> world have been cut from a he pattern.
>
> She is a woman candidate, not merely a candidate,
> as a man is. If elected, she becomes the woman this or
> that, not simply the title. Where the masculinity of her
> confreres is taken for granted, her femininity always
> causes mild surprise and is good for an old-fashioned
> debate on whether women generally are not miscast
> when assuming roles which have heretofore been re-
> served for the other sex.[15]

Pratt tried to help all her constituents, even those whose poor
standards of living had been completely unfamiliar to her. In 1930,
she won reelection, but in 1932, was unable to withstand the Roosevelt
tidal wave and was defeated.

The next woman to enter the House was a Democrat from
Arkansas, chosen to fill the unexpired term of her late husband.
Effiegene Wingo (1883-1962) had taken care of the needs of her husband's congressional district during his lifetime while he recuper-
ated from a car accident. So natural was it for her to succeed him
that she was endorsed not only by her own party but by the Republican organization as well. She entered Congress in December 1930,
served the remainder of her husband's unexpired term plus the two
years after that, and then retired for reasons of health.

The Seventy-Second Congress

The only newcomer to the Seventy-Second Congress among
women was Willa B. Eslick (1878-1961). She was in the gallery

when her husband, a Democrat from Tennessee, made a speech on the floor, during which he suffered a heart attack and died. In August 1932, the people back home chose her to succeed him. She took her seat in December and served only until the new session began the following March.

The Seventy-Third Congress

When Franklin Roosevelt assumed the presidency, some of the old Republican districts elected Democrats, two of whom were women. Virginia E. Jenckes (1882-1975) was elected from Indiana on an anti-Prohibition platform. She won the Democratic primary against a former congressman and in the general election defeated the eight-term Republican incumbent. The 50-year-old widow came to Washington with high hopes but was frustrated because she was put on committees that were of little interest to the people in her district. She did manage to win reelection repeatedly but failed in 1938, when she got caught in a squabble within her own party.

Only one term was granted to Kathryn O'Loughlin McCarthy (1894-1952), a 38-year-old Democratic lawyer who had been actively fighting for the underdog. She defeated eight men in the primary and went on to win election in traditionally Republican Kansas. She must have been quite persuasive, for during the campaign she met a candidate for state senator, converted him from hostility to support for the cause of women in public office, and married him a month before taking her seat in Congress. McCarthy had a rough time in the House. She rejected her assignment to the Insular Affairs Committee and eventually received Education rather than the coveted Agriculture. Because it was felt that she and the New Deal were not doing enough for the farmers of Kansas, she was defeated for reelection.

Even shorter was the congressional career of Marian Clarke (1880-1953). She was elected in late December 1933 to serve out the second half of her deceased husband's term as Republican from upstate New York. Though well-qualified, she did not seek reelection the following November.

In late 1933, there was also a vacancy for the one congressional seat in Arizona when President Roosevelt appointed Congressman Lewis W. Douglas to be director of the budget. Chosen at a special election and reelected the following year was politically active, twice-widowed Isabella Greenway (1886-1953). She had gone to school with Eleanor Roosevelt, had been a bridesmaid at her wedding, and was on intimate terms with the occupants of the White House. Although in sympathy with the New Deal, Greenway did oppose the president on several occasions when she thought him to be wrong or his policy not in the interests of Arizona. She eventually even opposed Roosevelt for reelection in 1940 by joining the "Democrats for Willkie." Four years earlier, she had decided not to seek reelection, supposedly for family reasons.

The Seventy-Fourth Congress

Another friend of the Roosevelts was Caroline O'Day (1875-1943), whose work in New York with social welfare and labor had brought her close to Eleanor Roosevelt and Frances Perkins. Elected as a Democrat for an at-large seat, her campaign made history because it was the first time that a first lady campaigned on behalf of a candidate. O'Day generally backed New Deal legislation, with some exceptions. Although born in Georgia, she firmly supported minority protection. She was also strongly pacifist and opposed various defense measures right up to Pearl Harbor. Ill during the 1940 campaign, she won in spite of her absence from the hustings. In all of her contests for election and reelection, she had female opposition. In 1942, when she decided to retire, she was succeeded by a Republican woman, Winifred Stanley. O'Day died the day after she left public office.

The Seventy-Fifth Congress

Also associated with the Roosevelts was Nan Wood Honeyman (1881-1970), who, in 1936, surprisingly captured a Republican-held congressional seat for the Democrats in Oregon. She failed to repeat her victory two years later and tried again in 1940, again without success. Married and active in politics, she was the only female among the 95 newcomers to Congress in 1937. Chamberlin sums her up as "shamelessly opportunistic yet politically naive. Because she broke promises and failed to communicate with constituents, she wrote her own congressional obituary."[16]

A rather unique case, reminiscent of some of the appointed women senators, was Elizabeth Gasque (1896-), Democrat from South Carolina. Her husband had been in Congress for over a decade when he died. She was duly elected to succeed him, but, since Congress was not in session between September 1938 and January 1939, she did not have the opportunity to be sworn in. Gasque had decided to run only for the unexpired term, so that her congressional career was actually over before it had begun.

The Seventy-Sixth Congress

The only woman who was a newcomer at the beginning of the Seventy-Sixth Congress in 1939 was Jessie Sumner (1898-). A lawyer and unsuccessful candidate for nomination for state's attorney, she had been elected to a county judgeship formerly held by an uncle. A Republican from Illinois, she has been called "the only woman ever to serve from the extreme right in American politics"[17] because of her strong anti-Roosevelt, anti-New Deal, anti-United Nations, and pro-"peace and neutrality" attitudes. In that, she was perhaps typical of what, during her eight years in Congress, could be described as midwestern isolationism. Very articulate and a good debater, she voluntarily retired at the end of 1946. Sumner never married. "A woman who has neither husband nor children is in an enviable position to do anything she pleases," she is quoted as saying. "Lots of women could succeed in politics if they did not prefer the so-called A-1 career, marriage."[18]

Also opposed to war, but eventually becoming convinced that the United States had to be prepared for one, was the next woman to enter Congress in 1939, Clara McMillan (1894-). She filled a vacancy of 14 months left in the term of her late husband, a Democrat from South Carolina. She did not seek reelection, apparently in order not to have to compete with her eventual successor, Mendel Rivers.

If McMillan is a good example of a widow who takes her late husband's place, finishes his term, and then quietly fades away, the next two are not. Margaret Chase Smith, Republican from Maine, has been discussed in a previous chapter, since she left her major mark in the U.S. Senate, in which she served for 24 years with distinction. After the death of her congressman-husband in 1940, she successfully competed for his seat and presumably could have been reelected as often as she wished. She sat in the House for over eight years, then gave up her safe position in order to face the uncertainty of a bitterly contested primary for the Senate in 1948. There were several other women who took a similar course; Smith, however, was the first and thus far the only one to succeed in going from one congressional house to the other.

Shortly before Smith, another congressional widow entered the House, Frances Bolton (1885-1977), Republican from Ohio. Well-to-do, she was a descendant of a signer of the Declaration of Independence, the granddaughter of a congressman and senator (even if a Democrat!), and the mother of a congressman, with whom she served for a while as the only mother-son combination in the House. Bolton was a member of the Foreign Relations Committee and in time became its ranking Republican. After entering Congress at the age of 54, she decided to remain, which she did for a total of 29 years, becoming the woman with the second-longest service record, surpassed only by Edith Rogers. But whereas Rogers died while a member of the House, Bolton, at age 83, fell victim to a liberal Democrat, Charles Vanik, when in 1968 redistricting threw them into competition for the same seat.

The next few women were all widows serving for brief periods after their husbands' deaths had terminated congressional careers. None of them sought reelection. Florence R. Gibbs (1890-1964) was a Democratic representative from Georgia for three months in late 1940.

The Seventy-Seventh Congress

In May 1941, Katharine Byron (1903-1976) was elected as Democrat from Maryland. Hers was a hard-fought battle that saw prominent Democrats like Eleanor Roosevelt and Estes Kefauver speaking on her behalf. Her husband had been killed in a plane crash. Years later, her son was to represent the same congressional district, and when he suddenly died in 1978, his widow followed him in Congress, too.

Veronica Boland (1899-) was a Democrat from Pennsylvania who served for two months in late 1942. By the time the Seventy-Seventh Congress had passed into history, a record-breaking nine women were on its roster, including Jeannette Rankin, who was completing the second of her two, widely dispersed two-year terms.

The Seventy-Eighth Congress

We have previously mentioned Congresswoman O'Day from New York, who retired in January 1943. At that time, her place was taken by another woman, Republican Winifred Stanley (1909-). She was a lawyer and assistant district attorney, who, by prevailing over seven opponents (including two other women), at age 33 became the youngest female to sit in the House. Seniority and an antifeminist attitude prevented her from getting the Judiciary Committee assignment that she coveted. Reapportionment meant the disappearance of her at-large seat two years later, and this ended her congressional career.

If the last few women mentioned did not leave much of a mark, this can hardly be said of Clare Boothe Luce (1903-), Republican from Connecticut. She was born poor but married into money; her second husband, Henry Luce, was the publisher of Time and Life magazines. At one time close to Franklin Roosevelt, she became one of his harshest critics, a position that, in 1942, made her contest the Connecticut congressional seat once held by her stepfather. She won it and defended it against a Roosevelt-backed woman two years later. Author and actress, she was famous when she got into the House, attracted attention through her hard work and verbal skills while there, and remained in the public view in diplomatic and political capacities after voluntarily giving up her two-term seat.

As Luce's first term came to an end, another woman made a brief appearance, Willa L. Fulmer (1884-1968), Democrat from South Carolina. Immediately after the death of her congressman-husband, she was elected to the remaining two months of his term. She faced no opposition, but little more than 2 percent of the population voted. In January 1945, her tenure ended without her seeking reelection.

The Seventy-Ninth Congress

When the Seventy-Ninth Congress convened, two extraordinary ladies with the same last name came to Washington. From Illinois arrived Emily Taft Douglas (1899-). Active in public affairs and a Democrat, she was married to the Chicago alderman and economics professor, Paul Douglas—who had run for the Senate in 1942 and lost, enrolled in the Marine Corps at the age of 50 during World War II, and in 1948 was to begin a famous 18-year career in the U.S. Senate. The daughter of a sculptor and herself an actress, Emily Douglas won an at-large seat in 1944, thereby reversing the usual role of a wife following her husband to Congress. Although like so many other liberals she was defeated in 1946 in her bid for reelection, there is no question that by that time women had, in her own words, "come a long way, and in a hurry."[19]

Emily Taft Douglas's defeat had important repercussions for Illinois, since it launched the career of William Stratton. The eventual defeat of the other Congresswoman Douglas helped the rise of another politician, Richard M. Nixon, who beat her in a highly publicized and dirty Senate campaign in 1950. Helen Gahagan Douglas (1900-), an accomplished actress, was drawn into California politics by her strong feelings of social justice and by her abhorrence of Hitler, whose atrocities she experienced first-hand during European engagements. She had worked hard in Democratic campaigns and was therefore well-known when she ran and won her House seat in 1944. She was reelected twice before her ill-fated try for the U.S. Senate.

Another Democrat who moved into the House in 1945 was Chase Going Woodhouse (1890-), Democrat from Connecticut. Her election gave the Nutmeg State two female representatives. Married to a college professor and herself a member of that profession, she had served as secretary of the state of Connecticut. Except for Jeannette Rankin, she is the only woman member of Congress to serve two scattered terms. After two years in the House, she was defeated for reelection, then ran again in 1948 and won, only to lose once more at the end of her second term.

Next in chronological order are two Democrats from the South, who, in 1946, served briefly to fill unexpired terms, though not those of their own husbands. A vacancy, caused by a resignation in Georgia, led to the victory in a special election of Helen Douglas Mankin (1896-1956), an attorney and state legislator who overcame the opposition of 17 men to win the primary, largely with the support of organized labor and blacks. When she attempted to run for a full term, she lost in the primary, not by popular vote (for she did get a majority), but because of Georgia's unit rule that gave rural counties a bigger weight than the more populated ones. Mankin fought this in court but in vain. She then attempted to organize a write-in campaign, but did not get enough support to win. Two years later she failed again. She was killed in a car accident in 1956, several years before Georgia's undemocratic unit rule was declared unconstitutional.

Jane Pratt (1902-), Democrat from North Carolina, had been administrative assistant to several congressmen for more than 20 years when she was called upon to fill the vacancy caused by the death of her boss, William O. Burgin. She won overwhelmingly. Although she certainly had the background, Pratt did not enter the next primary because she could not afford the campaign costs.

The Eightieth Congress

Of greater length was the career of Katharine St. George (1896-), Republican from New York. A first cousin of Franklin Roosevelt, she did not share his political philosophy but was quite conservative in her outlook, as befitted someone who had been born and had married into well-to-do families. St. George proved that women were no exception to the seniority rule in Congress. She did not at first receive the committee assignments she wanted but eventually landed on the powerful Rules Committee, the first woman to do so. She was an early advocate of the Equal Rights Amendment to the Constitution, which at that time did not get anywhere. The Goldwater debacle of 1964 was accompanied by her own defeat by a liberal Democrat after 18 years in Congress. She is quoted as saying: "At the federal level, I feel that politics is not the ideal task for a woman. It interferes with her private and family life, and should certainly not be undertaken until the children are grown. Even then it is questionable whether it is worth giving up so much of intimate and family ties."[20]

Another newcomer in 1946, but lasting only one term, was Georgia Lusk (1893-1971), a Democrat from New Mexico. A widowed educator, she competed against nine men and another woman for one of the two congressional at-large seats and won, coming in second in the primary and first in the election. Her attempt to win renomination was less successful, however. She lost by fewer than 3,000 votes but did not have the money to finance a recount. She had this to say about women in politics: "They could get ahead faster if they didn't get off on tangents, expect too much and get discouraged too easily. They'd be better off, too, if they would go into some other line first and demonstrate that they have ability. That's the way men do it."[21]

The Eighty-First Congress

In 1948, Utah sent its first woman to Congress in the person of Democrat Reva Beck Bosone (1898-), a lawyer, member of the state legislature, and municipal judge. A reformer and humanitarian, she ran for a second term against Ivy Baker Priest, later Eisenhower's treasurer of the United States. Bosone won this all-female contest but was less successful when she tried to keep her job in 1952 or regain it in 1954.

In 1948, Cecil M. Harden (1894-) also arrived in Washington, having captured for the Republicans the Indiana district that had once been represented by Democrat Virginia Jenckes. Although originally winning by fewer than 500 votes, Harden personified Hoosier thinking, so that she was reelected with increasing majorities the next few times, until defeated in 1958. All her life she was involved in politics, working her way up from the precinct to the national committee level.

Equally active in politics, but on the Democratic side, was Edna F. Kelly from Brooklyn, New York (1906-). She was the widow of a city court judge when she first ran for Congress, believing that a woman should not have a political career if her husband was in politics, especially if they had children.[22] She first competed for an unexpired term and then was reelected again and again with clockwork regularity, all the time accumulating seniority that placed her high in rank on the Foreign Affairs Committee. In 1968, redistricting forced Kelly to compete with another Democrat, Congressman Emanuel Celler, who at the age of 80 was practically a political institution, and this terminated her political career after almost two decades in the House.

The Eighty-Second Congress

The Eighty-Second Congress was a milestone in female representation. During its two years, a total of ten women were sitting in the House. Never again were there fewer, and eventually the figure was almost doubled, though thus far the 20-mark has not been reached. To the six holdovers from the previous Congress,* two newcomers were added straight away and two more a few months later. Marguerite Stitt Church (1892-), 58 years old, was chosen in the regular election to follow her recently deceased husband as a Republican from Illinois. Educated at Wellesley and Columbia, she was an internationalist and served for a decade on the Foreign Affairs Committee together with Frances Bolton and Edna Kelly. When she was 70 years old and her district was reapportioned, Church decided that it was time to retire from Congress.

Another midwestern Republican was Ruth Thompson (1887-1970) from Michigan. Legal secretary, attorney, probate judge, and state legislator before her arrival in Washington, she breached the previously all-male bastion of the Judiciary Committee. She was reelected twice but in her third try was defeated for renomination by Robert Griffin (later a U.S. senator), largely because a scandal developed over the costly relocation of an air force base.

The next woman to enter the House in 1951 was Elizabeth Kee (1894-1975), who won a special election for a seat from West Virginia upon the death due to heart attack of her Democratic congressman-husband. Possession of this seat became a family tradition. Kee was reelected six times until she decided to retire in January 1965 so that her son could follow her in the House.

Also elected in July 1951 was Vera D. Buchanan (1902-1955), Democrat from Pennsylvania. She, too, followed her late husband and was twice reelected. She continued with her congressional duties even after she was taken ill and hospitalized in mid-1955, suffering from cancer that caused her death a few months later while still a member of Congress.

----

*There had been seven women in the Eighty-First Congress. Smith switched over to the Senate; the other six were reelected.

The Eighty-Third Congress

In November 1952, as Eisenhower swept the nation, Democrat Gracie Pfost (1906-1965) won a congressional seat in Idaho by 591 votes, having lost the same contest two years earlier by a 783-vote margin.[23] She had held county offices before and made a name for herself as an old-fashioned populist, fighting private interests on behalf of the public.[24] She sat in the House for a decade, then decided to try for the Senate—in which race she was defeated by a mere handful of votes.

Like so many other congresswomen, Leonor K. Sullivan (1903-) was the widow of a U.S. representative, a Democrat from Missouri. In 1951, the party leaders refused to endorse her for the vacant seat because they felt she could not win.[25] She took a job as an administrative assistant to a congressman in order to earn some money, then entered the primary for her husband's old seat the next year, which by that time was occupied by a Republican. She barely got the nomination but won overwhelmingly in November 1952, thus setting the stage for a career in Congress that was to last until her retirement 24 years later. In the meantime, she had become secretary of the House Democratic Caucus and the only woman on the House Democratic Steering Committee, positions of leadership in her party's hierarchy in Congress. She was the only woman representative to vote against the Equal Rights Amendment, explaining that passage would lead to a "break-down in family life." "ERA says you are my equal," she declared. "I think I'm a whole lot better."[26]

It is debatable whether the next woman should be included in this list. Martin Gruberg[27] and the congressional publication Women in Congress[28] do include her; Hope Chamberlin does not. Mary Elizabeth Farrington (1898-) was duly elected to take her late husband's place as delegate to Congress from the territory of Hawaii. She was a Republican who served from August 1954, and was reelected in November but defeated two years later. Although she had the right to speak from the floor, offer legislation, and serve on committees, she was denied the right to vote since Hawaii at that time was not yet a state. For this reason, she is mentioned here without counting her as a full-fledged member of Congress.

The Eighty-Fourth Congress

Four newcomers swelled the number of women to 15 in January 1955, not counting Farrington. Ira Blitch (1912-), Democrat from Georgia, had served in both houses of the Georgia legislature when she upset the incumbent congressman in the primary. She had been instrumental in legislative efforts to give women the right to sit on juries in her state. In the House, she opposed desegregation and the extension of voting rights to blacks. For eight years she represented her district; then arthritis forced her into retirement.

A much longer period of service was chalked up by Edith Green (1910-), Democrat from Oregon, who passed two decades in the House. The child of teachers, she also became a teacher, and education was her speciality. She became a high-ranking and very influential member of the Education and Labor Committee. Strongly independent and not always on the liberal side, Green was quite a force in the House and Oregon politics until her retirement in 1975.

Starting at the same time and eventually compiling an identical record of 20 years in the House was Martha Griffiths (1912-), Democrat from Michigan. But while Green (despite her devotion to the cause of equality) opposed the Equal Rights Amendment, Martha Griffiths was one of its strong advocates. She was also responsible for making discrimination on account of sex, in addition to race, color, and national origin, an offense under the 1964 Civil Rights Act. A lawyer, Griffiths became a member of the state legislature and, after one unsuccessful attempt to enter Congress, succeeded two years later in the 1954 election with her lawyer-husband acting as campaign manager. Despite her husband's close connection to Governor Mennen Williams and the Democratic organization in Michigan, she met with party and labor opposition because of her independence.[29] However, this did not seem to have retarded her effectiveness as a legislator or her popularity as a vote-getter. Like Green, she retired in January 1975.

From Minnesota in 1955 came Coya Knutson (1912-), another Democrat. A teacher and state legislator, she became a member of the House Agriculture Committee. But her career in Washington was short; she was defeated in 1958, the only Democratic representative to be unsuccessful for reelection that year. Whereas Green's husband (from whom she was later divorced, however) moved his electrical heating business from Oregon to Washington, D.C.,[30] and whereas Griffiths' spouse (who had been her fellow student at law school and with whom she was associated in a law practice) had managed her campaign, Knutson's husband was back on the farm and issued the famous "Coya, come home" letter. Although he was apparently an alcoholic and the marriage in bad shape, the publicity was enough to bring about Knutson's defeat. In 1960, she unsuccessfully tried a comeback. The whole episode is a good example of how devastating sympathy for an allegedly lonely husband and a presumably neglected teenage son can be to a woman's political career.

In 1956, the death of a congressman paved the way for another widow, Kathryn E. Granahan (1906-), Democrat from Pennsylvania. She not only succeeded her late husband in Congress but assumed his position as Philadelphia ward leader as well, a position not usually associated with a woman. Her Irish-Catholic background made her fight to have Good Friday declared a national holiday, and her placement on the Post Office Committee put her in the forefront of the battle against obscenity and pornography. She did not seek reelection in 1962 after President Kennedy had named her treasurer of the United States.

The Eighty-Fifth Congress

If so many of the female newcomers to Congress in the early 1950s were Democrats, the late 1950s saw another crop of Republicans. Florence Dwyer (1902-1976), Republican from New Jersey, arrived in 1956, probably on the Eisenhower coattails, although she continued to win on her own record until her retirement in 1973. She started as a lobbyist and served in the state legislature before entering Congress, which she did with the full support of her husband. "You do have to break a barrier," she is quoted as saying. "Some women who try for office say 'Vote for me because I will be the first woman in the office.' That's an insult to women. . . . I never try to stand on the fact that I wear skirts."[31]

The Eighty-Sixth Congress

Catherine May (1914-) was a Republican from the state of Washington. She captured a formerly Democratic seat, utilizing her ability as a professional broadcaster, which had also helped her to gain a seat in the state legislature. The fact that she was able to get on the Agriculture Committee was of importance to her largely agricultural district. Unlike Knutson, however, it was not her eventual estrangement from her husband (she got an amicable divorce during her tenure in Congress and remarried afterward) that defeated her after 12 years, but the bad state of the economy under a Republican administration and her inability to provide a satisfactory answer to the proverbial question, But what have you done for me lately?

When after 38 years of marriage and 16 years in Congress, Congressman Sidney Simpson died nine days before the November election, his widow Edna (1891-) was persuaded to take his place as Republican from Illinois. Quiet and unassuming, she served two years and then retreated back into private life.

Widowed shortly after she decided to run for Congress was Jessica McCullough Weis (1901-1963), Republican from upstate New York. Well-to-do and active in Republican politics, she took on three men to run for the seat vacated by Kenneth Keating when he ran for the Senate. After she won the nomination, she proceeded to win the election and repeated this feat two years later. She was not a candidate in November 1962 and died of cancer the following May.

In the election of November 1960, Julia Butler Hansen (1907-), Democrat from Washington, ran both for an unexpired term of two months and for a full two-year term. She won both and continued to hold the seat until she decided to retire in January 1975. Her background included service on a local city council and more than two decades of membership in the state legislature, where she advanced to a position in the Democratic leadership. All of this prepared her well for service in Congress, where she sat on the coveted Appropriations Committee.

The Eighty-Seventh Congress

Much shorter was the tenure of Catherine Norrell (1901-). A Democrat from Arkansas, Norrell, at the age of 60, competed for her late husband's congressional seat against determined male opposition. Having won the 20-month term, she pursued the interests of her district. Reapportionment, which would have thrown her into a primary battle with another incumbent Democrat, and high campaign costs figured in her decision not to seek reelection.

Also filling in for her deceased husband was Louise Goff Reece (1898-1970). A Republican from Tennessee, she was the daughter and granddaughter of two U.S. senators (the Goffs from West Virginia). She defeated her Democratic opponent overwhelmingly in a special election in May 1961, but arthritis prevented her from running for reelection the following year.

Corinne Boyd Riley (1893-), Democrat from South Carolina, was another congressional widow. With a special election coming up for the unexpired term due to her husband's death, she was persuaded to run, even though another woman, a state representative, claimed a far better qualification than having been married to the late congressman. Without a single campaign appearance, Riley won by a huge margin in the primary and was unopposed in the special election. Once in Congress, she turned down committee assignments until she got what she wanted, Science and Astronautics. The eight months in Congress were a "pleasant interlude" to her,[32] after which she returned to private life.

Somewhat different was the career of Charlotte T. Reid (1913-),who, in a sense, also followed her husband. However, Frank T. Reid, an attorney and son of a former congressman, was not an incumbent but had received the Republican nomination for an Illinois district when he died. The state Republican executive committee replaced him on the ballot with his widow, who went on to victory in November and was reelected four more times. She resigned in October 1971, the only woman representative ever to do so. She gave up her seat in Congress in order to accept President Nixon's nomination to membership on the Federal Communications Commission.

The Eighty-Eighth Congress

We have earlier referred to families of politicians like the Kees in West Virginia. A similar situation existed with the Bakers in Tennessee. When Republican Congressman Howard H. Baker died suddenly in early 1964, it was almost natural for his widow to take his place. She had to defend the seat against a Democrat, but Irene B. Baker (1901-) won at the age of 62. She did not run for reelection, but her son, Howard Baker, Jr., kept the family in politics when he eventually was elected to the U.S. Senate.

The Eighty-Ninth Congress

Hawaii had already sent a female representative to Congress before statehood was achieved. In 1964, as a state, it elected Democrat Patsy T. Mink (1927-) to the House as full-fledged member. A lawyer, she had been involved in politics and had become a member of the territorial legislature. Statehood for Hawaii had been one of her projects; equality for women was another. Her husband, a geologist, managed her campaign and relocated in Washington, D.C., after she was elected. After winning reelection several times, she decided to give up her seat in 1976 in order to contest the Democratic nomination for senator, where she faced a man, Hawaii's other Democratic congressperson. Both were popular, but Patsy Mink lost.

Much more short-lived was the political career of Lera M. Thomas (1900-), Democrat from Texas. She filled the unexpired vacancy created upon the death of her husband, who had been in Congress almost three decades. An attempt was made to have her nominated for the full term, but this required a rather complicated maneuver, since her husband had already filed for the primary. The efforts failed, limiting her to nine months in Congress.

The Ninetieth Congress

Margaret Heckler (1931-), Republican from Massachusetts, arrived in the House in 1966. An attorney and member of the Governor's Council, her major feat was not so much getting elected and reelected in a district that was becoming increasingly Democratic, but winning the Republican nomination in the first place. Her opponent was Joseph Martin, former Speaker of the House of Representatives, at the age of 81 very much an institution and almost a legend in Massachusetts and Republican politics. Less than half her opponent's age, Heckler campaigned and won, thereby beginning a career that still continues.

The Ninety-First Congress

With Bolton and Kelly both denied continuation of their service in Congress, only nine of the previous incumbents were reelected to the Ninety-First Congress. These were joined by Shirley Chisholm (1924-). A Democrat from Brooklyn, New York, she became the first black congresswoman in history. She claimed that she had "suffered worse discrimination as a woman than as a black."[33] Chisholm had served in the state legislature and as a former teacher had championed causes helping children, especially poor ones. This she was to continue in Congress. She was a candidate for the Democratic presidential nomination in 1972 and received 150 votes at the convention. Marital difficulties, including divorce and a second marriage, do not seem to have made any dent in her popularity. Her district will apparently send her back to Washington as long as she wants, even though she occasionally faces determined opposition from Republicans and fellow Democrats alike.

The Ninety-Second Congress

Also well known beyond her district, but more controversial than Shirley Chisholm, is Bella Abzug (1920-), Democrat from New York. Loved or hated, called "an outstanding liberal" by some and "abrasive" by others, she was a practicing attorney married to a stockbroker and the loud champion of such causes as the antiwar movement during the U.S. involvement in Vietnam. She competed for and won a congressional seat in 1970. But reapportionment in 1972 abolished that seat. Abzug decided on a primary fight against a fellow liberal, Congressman William Fitts Ryan, who at the time was dying from cancer. Ryan won overwhelmingly in a contest that caused much bad blood. Two months before the election, Ryan died and the Democratic county commission named Abzug as replacement. More bitterness followed, especially since the Liberal party nominated Priscilla Ryan for her late husband's seat. Abzug was victorious and was able to win again in 1974. Two years later, she gave up the seat and entered the Democratic primary for the U.S. Senate, losing in a runoff against Patrick Moynihan. She next ran for the office of mayor of New York but did not even get into the runoff primary. In early 1978, she tried once more for public office when the congressional seat in the Silk Stocking district (previously held by New York City's newly elected mayor, Ed Koch) was at stake. As the Democratic candidate she was the favorite; yet she lost. Much of the antagonism toward her, as well as the support she received, was personal, and Abzug's recent inability to win public office (and, for that matter, the difficulties she has had with the Carter administration) should not be attributed to a general antipathy toward women in politics, although her strong identification with "women's causes" sometimes leads to such a conclusion.

Voluntarily retiring after only four years in the House was Ella Grasso (1919-), Democrat from Connecticut. She had served in the state legislature and eventually became Democratic floor leader. Then she was elected to the office of secretary of state, from which she went to Congress. Her service there included membership on the Veterans Affairs and Labor and Education Committees. In 1974, she returned to Connecticut to become one of the nation's very few female governors, a position to which she was reelected four years later.

A woman had defeated a former Republican Speaker of the House of Representatives from Massachusetts, so it seemed appropriate that the retiring Democratic Speaker from the same state also should be succeeded by a woman. Louise Day Hicks (1923-), a 48-year-old attorney, made quite a name for herself as the leader of the antibusing efforts by Boston citizens. A widow and the daughter of a judge, her ambitions, however, were not in Washington but in her own hometown. Hicks had been on the school committee, had run unsuccessfully for mayor of Boston, and had served on the city council before obtaining her seat as a Democratic congresswoman in 1971. Once more she ran for mayor of Boston and lost and in 1972 was defeated for reelection to Congress by a Democrat running against her as an Independent.

In the same Congress, Elizabeth B. Andrews (1911-) had an even shorter career. As a Democrat from Alabama, she filled the remaining nine months of her late husband's unexpired term. There was some opposition inside the party organization, but as she put it: "Womanhood per se was never an issue. In Alabama today if a

woman is qualified and capable, she can obtain political support."[34]
She had ruled out reelection from the start and retired accordingly
in 1973.

The Ninety-Third Congress

In January 1973, five more women came to Congress, and
before the year was over, two more had joined to fill the unexpired
terms of their late husbands. From California came Democrat
Yvonne Braithwaite (1932-), who during the campaign married
William Burke and later, while a member of Congress, gave birth
to a baby girl. She had served in the state legislature and had
reached national prominence when, a black, she presided over part
of the 1972 National Democratic Convention as vice-chairperson.
She was repeatedly reelected to her House seat but gave it up in
order to run in 1978 for the post of attorney general of California.
She won the nomination by a narrow margin but lost the contest in
November.

Maryland's new congresswoman was Republican Marjorie
Holt (1920-). A lawyer and former clerk of the circuit court, her
congressional committee appointments have included Armed Services and Budget, committees that are not usually identified with
"women's matters"—a clear indication that no longer are such assignments meted out according to sex. She has been reelected continually.

We have pointed out that occasionally women act as "giant
killers," and Margaret Heckler's victory over Joseph Martin is a
good example. A similar feat was performed by Elizabeth Holtzman
(1941-), Democrat from New York. She unseated Congressman
Emanuel Celler, who had already been in Congress for almost two
decades before Holtzman was born. Celler had successfully overcome redistricting and had, as previously mentioned, defeated
longtime Congresswoman Edna Kelly in the Democratic primary of
1968. Four years later he himself was beaten in the primary by
Holtzman. A Brooklyn attorney, she had worked for New York City
Mayor John Lindsay and was a Democratic state committee member
when she engaged in a tireless, if greatly underfunded, campaign
that won her the nomination and the election as the youngest woman
ever to be sent to Congress. Since that event, reelection time and
again has been easy. She not only replaced Celler in Congress but
on the Judiciary Committee as well.

In the six years she served in the House, Barbara Jordan
(1936-) probably became one of the best-known political figures of
her time. A black Democrat from Texas, she is remembered as

giving a particularly moving address during the 1976 Democratic Convention. Her activities as a member of the Judiciary Committee during the Nixon impeachment proceedings also caused widespread attention. She is an attorney who had tried twice to get into the Texas legislature before succeeding on the third attempt. She entered Congress in 1973 and served three terms before retiring in January 1979 "for personal reasons."

Another member of the "class of 1973" is Patricia S. Schroeder (1940-), a Democrat from Colorado. She is also an attorney, married to an attorney, and the mother of two small children, thus proving that having a young family is not necessarily a hindrance to a congressional career for a woman. Schroeder had been active in citizen groups, such as Planned Parenthood and environmental organizations, and had entered the Democratic primary short on funds and organizational support. After winning the primary, she proceeded to defeat the Republican incumbent and has been successful in her reelection bids ever since. She serves on the Armed Services Committee.

Tragedy brought another woman into the House shortly after the beginning of the Ninety-Third Congress. Corinne (Lindy) Boggs (1916-) was the wife of a prominent Louisiana Democratic congressman, majority leader Hale Boggs, whose plane had disappeared over Alaska the previous October. Hale Boggs had won reelection in November despite his absence, but several months later his seat was declared vacant, and, in the primary that followed, Corinne Boggs won overwhelmingly over four other opponents and has been continually elected and reelected since. In 1976, she presided over the Democratic National Convention.

Another woman following her congressman-husband upon his death was Cardiss Collins (1931-). She is a Democrat from Illinois and became that state's first black congresswoman. Steeped in local politics, she won the primary over an antiorganization opponent and has continued to represent her Chicago district. She is one of the Democratic whips and serves on the International Relations Committee.

The Ninety-Fourth Congress

Martha Keys (1930-) was elected as a Democrat from Kansas in November 1974. She is the sister of one of the chief strategists of the 1972 Democratic campaign, Gary Hart, who later became senator from Colorado. Keys was assigned to the powerful Ways and Means Committee. Divorced, she married Indiana's Democratic Congressman Andy Jacobs while both were in the House.

Theirs was the first wedding of two members of Congress and constituted the first husband-wife combination serving in the House. Both continued to maintain legal residences in their respective districts. Keys was reelected in 1976. In 1978, however, the absentee issue was raised against her and was apparently sufficient to ensure her defeat. Thus, Kansas retired its only congresswoman at the same time that it elected its first woman senator.

Also newly elected in 1974 was Gladys N. Spellman (1918-), Democrat from Maryland, a former county commissioner and later head of that body. She is married, a schoolteacher by profession, and a member of the Committee on Banking, Currency, and Housing.

Virginia Smith (1911-) entered Congress as a Republican from Nebraska. She and her husband are farmers. Although long active in public and civic services, this was her first elective office. She was reelected to the Ninety-Fifth and Ninety-Sixth Congresses and serves on the Education and Labor Committees.

Millicent Fenwick (1910-), Republican from New Jersey, was divorced and in her sixties when she came to Congress. She had been elected to the state legislature, then became director of New Jersey's consumer affairs before making her successful try for a congressional seat, which she has been occupying ever since. After trying for several years, she became a member of the International Relations Committee.

The second congresswoman newly arriving from New Jersey in 1975 was Democrat Helen Stevenson Meyner (1929-). Her father was president of Oberlin College, her husband had served as governor of New Jersey, and her cousin, Adlai Stevenson, had been governor of Illinois and a presidential candidate. She had been involved in newspaper and television work and had first run for Congress in 1972 and lost. She won in 1974, won again in 1976, but was defeated in 1978.

Also active in the media had been Marilyn Lloyd (1929-), Democrat from Tennessee, who entered Congress on her forty-sixth birthday. Her husband had just won the Democratic primary when he was killed in a plane accident. She allowed her name to be put before the voters in his stead and went on to defeat the incumbent. With science and technology as well as the problems of the aging among her interests, she has represented her district since that time.

Thus, the election of 1974 brought six new women into the House, raising the number of women to 18. When Shirley Pettis (1924-) replaced her deceased husband in May 1975, an all-time high was reached that has been neither paralleled nor surpassed since that Congress. Pettis, a Republican from California, was reelected in 1976 but retired two years later. She is the mother of

two children and felt that the size of her district made it difficult
for her to be in touch with the voters while attending to her job in
Washington. [35]

The Ninety-Fifth Congress

By January 1977, when the new Congress assembled, three
of the former women members were no longer present: Leonor
Sullivan had retired, and Patsy Mink and Bella Abzug had attempted,
unsuccessfully as it turned out, to enter the Senate. Two newcomers
appeared. Barbara Mikulski (1936-) was a social worker with
strong political ties in Baltimore. She had failed to take Senator
Mathias's seat away from him in 1974. In 1976, she became a
Democratic congresswoman from Maryland and successfully defended her seat two years later.

From Cleveland came Mary Oakar (1940-), an Ohio Democrat
and former schoolteacher. On her way to Washington, she had to
defeat 11 men in the primary. After that it was easy, since she
met no Republican opposition in the general election. Oakar was
reelected in 1978 and now serves on the Committee on Banking,
Finance, and Urban Affairs.

The Ninety-Sixth Congress

The November 1978 election was not a good one for women in
the United States. True, Kassebaum became the first woman elected
to a six-year term in the Senate without the help of any coattails of
husbands, living or dead. But this did not erase the fact that the
number of women in the Senate was down by one. In the House, the
number of women had stood at 18 but was reduced to 16 as a result
of the election. Three (Barbara Jordan, Shirley Pettis, and Yvonne
Burke) had vacated their seats voluntarily, and two (Martha Keys
and Helen Meyner) had been defeated. In all, 31 women across the
nation had received major-policy endorsement in their attempts to
enter the House as members of the 1979 freshman class; only three
succeeded. All three were from the East.

It will be recalled that Katharine Byron was elected in 1941 to
fill the unexpired term of her deceased husband. Eventually, her
son also became a Democratic congressman from Maryland, and
when, at the age of 49, he died suddenly while jogging, his widow
Beverly (1932-) consented to take his place. No stranger to politics,
she had campaigned with her husband when he first ran for the state
legislature, explaining, "It meant I either stayed at home by myself
or joined him."[36] She was placed on the Armed Services Committee.

A second Democratic newcomer arrived from Queens in New York City, despite attempts to gerrymander the district. Geraldine Ferraro (1935-) is a 43-year-old wife and mother of three children. She had not held political office previously.

Youngest among this group and youngest among the women now in Congress is Olympia Snowe (1947-), a Republican from Maine. Her husband was a member of the state house of representatives when he was killed in a car accident. She ran for her husband's old seat and won it, later competing for and winning a seat in the state senate. When in 1978 Congressman Cohen vacated his place in the U.S. House of Representatives in order to run for the Senate, Snowe followed him to the lower house in Washington.

DISCUSSION

These 89 women sat in the House of Representatives in the 62 years following Rankin's breach of the sex barrier in 1917. (Not included in all these calculations is Farrington, Hawaii's nonvoting delegate from 1954 to 1957.) When first elected, the eldest of the female representatives was 67, the youngest 31. Their average age on first arrival in the House was slightly over 48 years. Their length of service varied from two months (Boland and Fulmer) to 35 years (Rogers). The average length of service for all former female representatives (that is, those who by 1979 were no longer in Congress) is about six years and eight months.

If such statistics compare favorably with those cited earlier for the U.S. Senate, it must be remembered that the House membership is 435 as compared to 100 for the upper chamber. Moreover, two-year terms greatly increase the number of contests and give more people the opportunity to compete. It is also easier to develop a personal following in a congressional district, which is usually a smaller area than an entire state, although several congresswomen from Montana, Illinois, and New York have indeed been elected from the entire state.

There are many one-party districts in the United States. This means, in effect, that once established, a member of Congress is difficult to dislodge, and we have mentioned several instances where a member of Congress was removed from office only when the district was reapportioned. Many congresswomen, like their male colleagues, have enjoyed relative job security once they got into office. Though Neuberger is accurate in saying that the most difficult thing for a woman is to be elected, perhaps Sullivan comes even closer to the truth with her remark that the hardest thing for a woman is to be nominated.[37] Sullivan learned this the hard way, for she was denied

the nomination for her late husband's seat and had to do it on her
own a year later. Of course, even getting into office may not be the
end of the problem as far as the powers-that-be are concerned. To
quote Congresswoman Heckler, "Usually the party hierarchy is the
last to see your potential as a candidate."[38]

The first five women in the House were Republicans; indeed
eight of the first ten belonged to the GOP. In the course of time,
this one-party predominance has shifted. Altogether, there have
been 32 Republican congresswomen compared to 57 Democrats,
about a three-to-five ratio. This reflects the fact that during the
last few decades many more Democrats were elected to Congress
than Republicans. In the Ninety-Sixth Congress, we find five Republican and 11 Democratic women, which is perhaps not too surprising in view of the almost two-to-one advantage that the Democrats hold in the total congressional membership.

Although marital status should be a person's private affair,
it is important to raise the issue here because of the public image.
Ten of the 89 congresswomen never married, including the first
two to enter Congress. Of those ten, two were in their sixties when
they first became members, one was in her midforties, and the remaining seven, the vast majority, were 40 or younger. Considering the average age of 48, which we previously mentioned, it is important to note that the unmarried congresswomen were younger
when they first entered the House; on the average, their age comes
to 42.6 years. This group includes the youngest ever, Elizabeth
Holtzman, who was 31 when first elected. The only other 31-year-
old newcomer was Olympia Snowe, who had been married but lost
her husband and was without children. There is some significance
in this, since raising a family is often an obstacle to entering politics. A woman representative with young children is a rare and
recent phenomenon, only surpassed in rarity by a congresswoman
giving birth to a child while in office.

Of the 89, 32 were married at the time they became congresswomen. In many cases, they had the full support of their spouses.
Some husbands died while their wives were in Congress, and there
were some divorces. One woman was married, got divorced, and
married a fellow congressman from another state. This did not affect her reelection the first time, but she was defeated two years
later. The ages of this group vary between 32 and 63 for an average of almost 46 years. Before they came to Washington, 15 other
female representatives had been married and were either widows
not immediately preceded by their husbands to Congress or as candidates for Congress, or divorcées. These range in age from 31 to
64, and their combined average comes to 50.4 years, somewhat
older than the previous category.

A most interesting group is that of wives immediately following their husbands into Congress. There were 32 cases where a
wife was called upon to take her husband's place. Usually a vacancy
occurred due to the death of the incumbent. Sometimes the wife
met with no opposition whatever. Sometimes the nomination was
hers for the asking, and she met competition only during the election campaign itself. In some cases, however, hostility had to be
overcome either in the primary or in the party organization. Between 1917 and 1976, 351 representatives died in office, and a wife
followed her husband, therefore, only 9 percent of the time.[39] Nevertheless, taking the place of one's husband is one of the most traveled roads into the House by women. By 1979, 36 percent of all
congresswomen had gone this route. The 32 cases include 29 where
a congressman had died, two where the husband died after receiving
the nomination for Congress, and one where the husband had to be
replaced because he was serving a prison sentence. Not included
is Sullivan, who was refused the nomination and therefore did not
immediately replace her late husband. The ages of the women who
succeeded their spouses range from 36 (Nolan)—an age that is
rather young for this group and quite an exception—to 68 (Riley),
which amounts to an average entry age of 51.4 years.

Table 3.2 shows that there were many congresswomen who
had husbands at the time they entered the House (32 not including
Langley), but by far the largest proportion, 63 percent, did not.
As to age groups, 20 percent were 40 or under, 64 percent were 50
or under, and 11 percent were over 61.

Regarding the question of where in the United States these
women came from, it should be noted from Table 3.3 that, while only
10 states have had female senators, a total of 37 have had congresswomen, with New York and Illinois providing the largest number.
There seems to be very little connection between states that had
women senators and those that had congresswomen, as the case of
Kansas in 1978 clearly illustrates. However, several congresswomen gave up their House seats in order to seek a place in the
Senate, with Margaret Chase Smith the only woman so far to succeed in this endeavor.

One rather striking fact that can be seen from Table 3.3 is
that the ten states with the largest populations account for 41, or
almost 50 percent, of all the women who ever sat in the House of
Representatives. The seven states with the smallest number of
people have never been represented by a woman in the House,
though one of them has had two female senators. Whether this is
due to more broad-mindedness and enlightenment among the indus-
trialized states or to more one-party districts in New York and
California is hard to tell.

TABLE 3.2

Ages of Women Entering the House

	Age Group				
	31–40	41–50	51–60	61–70	Total
Total	18	39	22	10	89
Never married					
Democrat	4	1	0	0	5
Republican	3	0	0	2	5
Total	7	1	0	2	10
Wives					
Democrat	4	14	5	1	24
Republican	3	3	2	0	8
Total	7	17	7	1	32
Widowed/Divorced					
Democrat	0	5	3	0	8
Republican	1	2	3	1	7
Total	1	7	6	1	15
Followed husband					
Democrat	1	10	6	3	20
Republican	2	4	3	3	12
Total	3	14	9	6	32

Source: Compiled by the author.

There is another way of looking at the same phenomenon. The larger states, which have more representation in Congress, present a much greater opportunity. Is Arkansas with its four congressional seats at this time really more male chauvinist than New York, which has a delegation of 39, even though Arkansas has had only three congresswomen compared to New York's 11? Leaving aside the fact that the number of congressional seats a state is allotted may vary slightly from decade to decade, we may get some idea of the relationship between population and female representation in the House by looking at Table 3.4. Again, it has to be considered that in the more populated states there is numerically more opportunity, due to the fact that there simply are more congressional seats. With 239 seats available over the years, 41 women elected is after all not so great a number, especially when one remembers that some of them have served many years.

TABLE 3.3

Female Representatives and Senators per State, 1917–79

State	Ranking*	Representatives	Senators	State	Ranking*	Representatives	Senators
Alabama	21	1	2	Montana	43	1	0
Alaska	50	0	0	Nebraska	35	1	2
Arizona	32	1	0	Nevada	46	0	0
Arkansas	33	3	1	New Hampshire	42	0	0
California	1	5	0	New Jersey	9	4	0
Colorado	28	1	0	New Mexico	37	1	0
Connecticut	24	3	0	New York	2	11	0
Delaware	47	0	0	North Carolina	11	1	0
Florida	8	1	0	North Dakota	45	0	0
Georgia	14	3	1	Ohio	6	2	0
Hawaii	40	1	0	Oklahoma	27	1	1
Idaho	41	1	0	Oregon	30	2	0
Illinois	5	8	0	Pennsylvania	4	3	0
Indiana	12	2	0	Rhode Island	39	0	0
Iowa	25	0	0	South Carolina	26	4	0
Kansas	31	2	1	South Dakota	44	0	2
Kentucky	23	1	0	Tennessee	17	4	0
Louisiana	20	1	2	Texas	3	2	0
Maine	38	2	1	Utah	36	1	0
Maryland	18	5	0	Vermont	48	0	0
Massachusetts	10	3	0	Virginia	13	0	0
Michigan	7	2	0	Washington	22	2	0
Minnesota	19	1	1	West Virginia	34	1	0
Mississippi	29	0	0	Wisconsin	16	0	0
Missouri	15	1	0	Wyoming	49	0	0

*The ranking is according to population, based on the 1970 census.

Source: Compiled by the author.

TABLE 3.4

Female Representation in the U.S. House
by Population of States

State Ranking by Population (1970 Census)	Number of Women to Serve (1917-79)	Percent of the Total Congresswomen	Total Number of Seats (mid-1970s)
1 – 10	41	46	239
11 – 20	18	20	93
21 – 30	15	17	59
31 – 40	13	15	30
41 – 50	2	2	14

Source: Compiled by the author.

Looking at length of service, we find that almost half the women, 42 to be precise, have served not longer than five years. One-half of those following their husbands were in the House for two years or less. On the other hand, six served 20 years or more and between them accumulated 133 years of service. Four eventually retired voluntarily, one was defeated after 29 years in Congress, and one died while running for reelection. Of the 13 women who returned to the House in 1979 (there were three newcomers), one had completed 12 years of service, one had completed ten years of service, three had completed six years of service each, two had completed more than five years of service each (winning special elections), four had completed four years of service each, and two had completed two years of service each. Table 3.5 provides details on the 73 women who by 1979 had completed their stay in the House.

Of the 73 congresswomen who have served in the past, two died in office, and 48 voluntarily retired, although Diane Kincaid points out that the decision to withdraw was often surrounded by "considerable circumstantial doubt"—reasons of health (real or otherwise), political motivations, financial problems, and family considerations (such as the inability to replace a nurse for five young children when the nurse went on army duty during the war).[40] Congresswomen were defeated 25 times, either for renomination or re-election. Only Jeannette Rankin had the chance to retire twice from the House. Only Chase Woodhouse had the misfortune to be defeated twice as incumbent member of the House. Woodhouse is the only woman who staged a successful comeback after she lost her seat. Several others tried but in vain. There were a number of women who did not win in their first attempt to get into the House but succeeded in a later try. Such a bouncing back from defeat is much more widespread in Britain. However, it is worth noting that it is not unknown in this country either.

TABLE 3.5

Length of Service of Congresswomen

Length of Service (in years)	Number of Congresswomen	Percent of Total Congresswomen	Congresswomen Succeeding Husbands
0 – 0.5	7	9.6	5
0.5 – 1	8	11.0	7
1 – 2	11	15.1	4
2 – 3	3	4.1	2
3 – 4	13	17.8	3[a]
4 – 5	2	2.7	1
5 – 6	6	8.2	0
6 – 7	1	1.4	1
7 – 8	3	4.1	0
8 – 9	2	2.7	1[b]
9 – 10	2	2.7	0
10 – 12	4	5.5	1
12 – 14	1	1.4	1
14 – 16	2	2.7	0
16 – 18	1	1.4	0
18 – 20	3	4.1	0
20 – 25	2	2.7	0[c]
25 – 30	1	1.4	1
30 – 35	1	1.4	1
Total	73	100.0	28

[a]Including Langley.
[b]Excluding Reid.
[c]Excluding Sullivan.
Source: Compiled by the author.

TABLE 3.6

Women Members of the U.S. House of Representatives

Congresswoman	Dates	Party	State	In Office	Reason for Departure
Jeannette Rankin	1880–1973	Republican	Montana	1917–19	Retired[a]
				1941–43	Retired
Alice Robertson	1854–1931	Republican	Oklahoma	1920–23	Defeated
Winnifred Huck[b]	1882–1936	Republican	Illinois	1922–23	Defeated
Mae Nolan[c]	1886–1973	Republican	California	1923–25	Retired
Florence Kahn[c]	1868–1948	Republican	California	1925–37	Defeated
Mary Norton	1875–1959	Democratic	New Jersey	1925–51	Retired
Edith Rogers[c]	1881–1960	Republican	Massachusetts	1925–60	Died
Katherine Langley[c]	1888–1948	Republican	Kentucky	1927–31	Defeated
Pearl Oldfield[c]	1876–1929	Democratic	Arkansas	1929–31	Retired
Ruth McCormick	1880–1944	Republican	Illinois	1929–31	Retired[a]
Ruth Owen	1885–1954	Democratic	Florida	1929–33	Defeated[d]
Ruth Pratt	1877–1965	Republican	New York	1929–33	Defeated
Effiegene Wingo[c]	1883–1962	Democratic	Arkansas	1930–33	Retired
Willa Eslick[c]	1878–1961	Democratic	Tennessee	1932–33	Retired
Virginia Jenckes	1882–1975	Democratic	Indiana	1933–39	Defeated
Kathryn O'Loughlin McCarthy	1894–1952	Democratic	Kansas	1933–35	Defeated
Marian Clarke	1880–1953	Republican	New York	1934–35	Retired
Isabella Greenway	1886–1953	Democratic	Arizona	1934–37	Retired
Caroline O'Day	1875–1943	Democratic	New York	1935–43	Retired
Nan Honeyman	1881–1970	Democratic	Oregon	1937–39	Defeated
Elizabeth Gasque	1896–	Democratic	South Carolina	1938–39	Retired
Jessie Sumner	1898–	Republican	Illinois	1939–47	Retired

(continued)

Table 3.6, continued

Congresswoman	Dates	Party	State	In Office	Reason for Departure
Clara McMillan[c]	1894–	Democratic	South Carolina	1939–41	Retired
Frances Bolton[c]	1885–1977	Republican	Ohio	1940–69	Defeated
Margaret Chase Smith[c]	1897–	Republican	Maine	1940–49	Retired[a]
Florence Gibbs[c]	1890–1964	Democratic	Georgia	1940–41	Retired
Katharine Byron[c]	1903–1976	Democratic	Maryland	1941–43	Retired
Veronica Boland[c]	1899–	Democratic	Pennsylvania	1942–43	Retired
Winifred Stanley	1909–	Republican	New York	1943–45	Retired
Clare Boothe Luce	1903–	Republican	Connecticut	1943–47	Retired
Willa Fulmer[c]	1884–1968	Democratic	South Carolina	1944–45	Retired
Helen G. Douglas	1900–	Democratic	California	1945–51	Retired[a]
Emily T. Douglas	1899–	Democratic	Illinois	1945–47	Defeated
Chase Woodhouse	1890–	Democratic	Connecticut	1945–47	Defeated
				1949–51	Defeated
Helen Mankin	1896–1956	Democratic	Georgia	1946–47	Defeated[d]
Jane Pratt	1902–	Democratic	North Carolina	1946–47	Retired
Georgia Lusk	1893–1971	Democratic	New Mexico	1947–49	Defeated[d]
Katharine St. George	1896–	Republican	New York	1947–65	Defeated
Reva Bosone	1898–	Democratic	Utah	1949–53	Defeated
Cecil Harden	1894–	Republican	Indiana	1949–59	Defeated
Edna Kelly	1906–	Democratic	New York	1949–69	Defeated[d]
Marguerite Church[c]	1892–	Republican	Illinois	1951–63	Retired
Ruth Thompson	1887–1950	Republican	Michigan	1951–57	Defeated[d]
Elizabeth Kee[c]	1894–1975	Democratic	West Virginia	1951–65	Retired
Vera Buchanan[c]	1902–1955	Democratic	Pennsylvania	1951–55	Died
Gracie Pfost	1906–1965	Democratic	Idaho	1953–63	Retired[a]
Leonor Sullivan[c]	1903–	Democratic	Missouri	1953–77	Retired

Name	Years	Party	State	Service	Status
Iris Blitch	1912–	Democratic	Georgia	1955–63	Retired
Mary Farrington[c]	1898–	Republican	Hawaii[e]	1954–57	Defeated
Edith Green	1910–	Democratic	Oregon	1955–75	Retired
Martha Griffiths	1912–	Democratic	Michigan	1955–75	Retired
Coya Knutson	1912–	Democratic	Minnesota	1955–59	Defeated
Kathryn Granahan[c]	1906–	Democratic	Pennsylvania	1956–63	Retired
Florence Dwyer	1902–1976	Republican	New Jersey	1957–73	Retired
Catherine May	1914–	Republican	Washington	1959–71	Defeated
Edna Simpson	1891–	Republican	Illinois	1959–61	Retired
Jessica Weis	1901–1963	Republican	New York	1959–63	Retired
Julia Hansen	1907–	Democratic	Washington	1960–75	Retired
Catherine Norrell[c]	1901–	Democratic	Arkansas	1961–63	Retired
Louise Reece[c]	1898–1970	Republican	Tennessee	1961–63	Retired
Corinne Riley[c]	1893–	Democratic	South Carolina	1962–63	Retired
Charlotte Reid[f]	1913–	Republican	Illinois	1963–71	Resigned
Irene Baker[c]	1901–	Republican	Tennessee	1964–65	Retired
Patsy Mink	1927–	Democratic	Hawaii	1965–77	Resigned[a]
Lera Thomas[c]	1900–	Democratic	Texas	1966–67	Retired
Margaret Heckler	1931–	Republican	Massachusetts	1967–	n.a.
Shirley Chisholm	1924–	Democratic	New York	1969–	n.a.
Bella Abzug	1920–	Democratic	New York	1971–77	Resigned[a]
Ella Grasso	1919–	Democratic	Connecticut	1971–75	Resigned[g]
Louise Hicks	1923–	Democratic	Massachusetts	1971–73	Defeated
Elizabeth Andrews[c]	1911–	Democratic	Alabama	1972–73	Retired
Yvonne Braithwaite Burke	1932–	Democratic	California	1973–79	Resigned
Marjorie Holt	1920–	Republican	Maryland	1973–	n.a.
Elizabeth Holtzman	1941–	Democratic	New York	1973–	n.a.
Barbara Jordan	1936–	Democratic	Texas	1973–79	Retired

(continued)

Table 3.6, continued

Congresswoman	Dates	Party	State	In Office	Reason for Departure
Patricia Schroeder	1940–	Democratic	Colorado	1973–	n.a.
Corinne Boggs[c]	1916–	Democratic	Louisiana	1973–	n.a.
Cardiss Collins[c]	1931–	Democratic	Illinois	1973–	n.a.
Martha Keys Jacobs	1930–	Democratic	Kansas	1975–79	Defeated
Gladys Spellman	1918–	Democratic	Maryland	1975–	n.a.
Virginia Smith	1911–	Republican	Nebraska	1975–	n.a.
Millicent Fenwick	1910–	Republican	New Jersey	1975–	n.a.
Helen Meyner	1929–	Democratic	New York	1975–79	Defeated
Marilyn Lloyd[f]	1929–	Democratic	Tennessee	1975–	n.a.
Shirley Pettis[c]	1924–	Republican	California	1975–79	Retired
Barbara Mikulski	1936–	Democratic	Maryland	1977–	n.a.
Mary Oakar	1940–	Democratic	Ohio	1977–	n.a.
Beverly Byron[c]	1932–	Democratic	Maryland	1979–	n.a.
Geraldine Ferraro	1935–	Democratic	New York	1979–	n.a.
Olympia Snowe	1947–	Republican	Maine	1979–	n.a.

[a]In order to run for Senate.
[b]Followed father into office.
[c]Followed husband into office.
[d]In primary.
[e]Nonvoting delegate.
[f]Followed husband as party nominee.
[g]In order to run for governor.

Notes: Data were verified wherever possible. In cases of discrepancies, official publications, such as Biographical Directory of the American Congress, were given preference. Abbreviation n.a.: not applicable.

Source: Compiled by the author.

TABLE 3.7

The House of Representatives and Female Members

Congress	Years	Number of Women	Names
65th	1917–19	1	Rankin
66th	1919–21	0	
67th	1921–23	3	Robertson, Huck (November 1922), Nolan (January 1923)
68th	1923–25	2	Nolan, Kahn (February 1925)
69th	1925–27	3	Kahn, Norton, Rogers (June 1925)
70th	1927–29	5	Kahn, Norton, Rogers, Langley, Oldfield (January 1929)
71st	1929–31	9	Kahn, Norton, Rogers, Langley, McCormick, Pratt, Oldfield, Wingo (November 1930)
72nd	1931–33	7	Kahn, Norton, Rogers, Owen, Pratt, Wingo, Eslick (August 1932)
73rd	1933–35	7	Kahn, Norton, Rogers, Jenckes, McCarthy, Greenway (October 1933), Clarke (December 1933)
74th	1935–37	6	Kahn, Norton, Rogers, Jenckes, Greenway, O'Day
75th	1937–39	6	Norton, Rogers, Jenckes, O'Day, Honeyman, Gasque (September 1938)
76th	1939–41	8	Norton, Rogers, O'Day, Sumner, McMillan (November 1939), Bolton (February 1940), Smith (June 1940), Gibbs (October 1940)
77th	1941–43	9	Norton, Rogers, O'Day, Sumner, Bolton, Smith, Rankin, Byron (May 1941), Boland (November 1942)
78th	1943–45	8	Norton, Rogers, Sumner, Bolton, Smith, Luce, Stanley, Fulmer (November 1944)

(continued)

Table 3.7, continued

Congress	Years	Number of Women	Names
79th	1945–47	11	Norton, Rogers, Sumner, Bolton, Smith, Luce, Douglas, Douglas, Woodhouse, Mankin (February 1946), Pratt (May 1946)
80th	1947–49	7	Norton, Rogers, Bolton, Smith, Douglas, Lusk, St. George
81st	1949–51	9	Norton, Rogers, Bolton, Douglas, Woodhouse, St. George, Bosone, Harden, Kelly (November 1949)
82nd	1951–53	10	Rogers, Bolton, St. George, Bosone, Harden, Kelly, Church, Thompson, Kee (July 1951), Buchanan (July 1951)
83rd	1953–55	11	Rogers, Bolton, St. George, Harden, Kelly, Church, Thompson, Kee, Pfost, Sullivan, Buchanan (plus Farrington, July 1954)
84th	1955–57	16	Rogers, Bolton, St. George, Harden, Kelly, Church, Thompson, Kee, Buchanan (died November 1955), Pfost, Sullivan, Blitch, Green, Knutson, Griffiths, Granahan (November 1956) (plus Farrington)
85th	1957–59	15	Rogers, Bolton, St. George, Harden, Kelly, Church, Kee, Pfost, Sullivan, Blitch, Green, Knutson, Griffiths, Granahan, Dwyer
86th	1959–61	17	Rogers (died September 1960), Bolton, St. George, Kelly, Church, Kee, Pfost, Sullivan, Blitch, Green, May, Griffiths, Dwyer, Granahan, Simpson, Weis, Hansen (November 1960)
87th	1961–63	19	Bolton, St. George, Kelly, Church, Kee, May, Pfost, Sullivan, Blitch, Green, Griffiths, Dwyer, Granahan, Weis, Hansen, Norrell (April 1961), Reece (May 1961), Riley (April 1962), Reid (November 1962)
88th	1963–65	12	Bolton, St. George, Kelly, Kee, Sullivan, Green, Griffiths, Dwyer, May, Hansen, Reid, Baker (March 1964)

64

89th	1965–67	11	Bolton, Kelly, Sullivan, Green, Griffiths, Dwyer, May, Hansen, Reid, Mink, Thomas (March 1966)
90th	1967–69	11	Bolton, Kelly, Sullivan, Green, Griffiths, Dwyer, May, Hansen, Reid, Mink, Heckler
91st	1969–71	10	Sullivan, Green, Griffiths, Dwyer, May, Hansen, Reid, Mink, Heckler, Chisholm
92nd	1971–73	13	Sullivan, Green, Griffiths, Dwyer, Hansen, Reid (resigned October 1971), Mink, Heckler, Chisholm, Abzug, Grasso, Hicks, Andrews (April 1972)
93rd	1973–75	16	Sullivan, Green, Griffiths, Hansen, Mink, Heckler, Chisholm, Abzug, Grasso, Burke, Holt, Holtzman, Jordan, Schroeder, Boggs (March 1973), Collins (June 1973)
94th	1975–77	19	Sullivan, Mink, Heckler, Chisholm, Abzug, Burke, Holt, Holtzman, Jordan, Schroeder, Boggs, Collins, Keys, Spellman, V. Smith, Fenwick, Meyner, Lloyd, Pettis (May 1975)
95th	1977–79	18	Heckler, Chisholm, Burke, Holt, Holtzman, Jordan, Schroeder, Boggs, Collins, Keys, Spellman, V. Smith, Fenwick, Meyner, Lloyd, Pettis, Mikulski, Oakar
96th	1979–81	16	Heckler, Chisholm, Holt, Holtzman, Schroeder, Boggs, Collins, Spellman, V. Smith, Fenwick, Lloyd, Mikulski, Oakar, B. Byron, Ferraro, Snowe

Notes: Unless otherwise indicated, dates in parentheses show when congresswoman entered the House. The 66th through 72nd Congresses were in session from March to March of the given years; the remainder extended from January to January.

Source: Compiled by the author.

In conclusion, it is obvious that the number of women in the House is still far too small. Former Congresswoman Hansen comments, "Every essence of a woman's life prevents her involvement in politics." To which Neuberger adds that "women are such late starters in public life," because, while men are making names for themselves in service organizations and in their jobs, women are raising families.* But Grasso feels neither advantaged nor disadvantaged by being a woman.[41] Perhaps the last word belongs to Schroeder, who declared, "Yes, I have a uterus and a brain, and they both work."[42] (For a concise listing of the women members of the U.S. House of Representatives, see Tables 3.6 and 3.7.)

NOTES

1. Martin Gruberg, Women in American Politics (Oshkosh, Wis.: Academia, 1968), p. 6.
2. Hannah Josephson, Jeannette Rankin (Indianapolis: Bobbs-Merrill, 1974), p. 52.
3. Hope Chamberlin, A Minority of Members (New York: Praeger, 1973), p. 39.
4. Ibid.
5. Gruberg, op. cit., p. 152.
6. Chamberlin, op. cit., p. 45.
7. Ibid., p. 47.
8. U.S., Congress, Women in Congress, 1917-1976, 94th Cong., 2d sess., 1976, Rept. 1732, p. 57.
9. Ibid., p. 41.
10. Chamberlin, op. cit., p. 51.
11. Ibid., p. 53.
12. Ibid., p. 65.
13. Ibid., p. 66.
14. Ibid., pp. 73-78.
15. Ibid., p. 79.
16. Ibid., p. 115.
17. Women in Congress, 1917-1976, p. 78.
18. Chamberlin, op. cit., p. 153.
19. Ibid., p. 180
20. Ibid., p. 207.
21. Ibid., p. 203.

---

*The same point was made time and again in private conversation by female members of the Swiss Parliament. See Chapter 8.

22. Gruberg, op. cit., p. 292.

23. Chamberlin, op. cit., p. 229.

24. Women in Congress, 1917-1976, p. 63.

25. Chamberlin, op. cit., p. 237.

26. Women in Congress, 1917-1976, p. 107.

27. Gruberg, op. cit., pp. 164, 292.

28. Women in Congress, 1917-1976, p. 24.

29. Susan and Martin Tolchin, Clout: Womanpower and Politics (New York: Coward, McCann & Geoghegan, 1973), p. 75.

30. Chamberlin, op. cit., p. 257.

31. Ibid., pp. 270-71.

32. Ibid., p. 291.

33. Ibid., p. 324.

34. Ibid., p. 344.

35. Congressional Quarterly 36 (1978): 278.

36. Congressional Quarterly 36 (1978): 3,520.

37. Tolchin and Tolchin, op. cit., p. 71.

38. Congressional Quarterly 28 (1970): 1,746.

39. Diane D. Kincaid, "Over His Dead Body: A New Perspective and Some Feminist Footnotes on Widows in the U.S. Congress" (Paper prepared for the 1976 Annual Meeting of the American Political Science Association, Chicago, September 2-5, 1976), p. 5.

40. Ibid., p. 16.

41. Congressional Quarterly 28 (1970): 1,746.

42. Tolchin and Tolchin, op. cit., p. 87.

4

THE BRITISH HOUSE OF COMMONS

HISTORY

When turning to the British Parliament, we are concerned with one of the oldest governmental institutions in the world, one that dates back to the Middle Ages. At that time, and during the centuries that followed, the concept of equality for women was too ridiculous for words. Among the poorer classes, women were equal to men only in the sense that they both led downtrodden, often animallike existences. Upper-class women, on the other hand, had become objects for admiration and chivalrous inspiration, but certainly not those to become involved in the rough and tumble of the affairs of state. There would obviously have been general agreement with a remark made in the House of Commons as recently as 1918, when it was maintained that Parliament was not "a fit and proper place for any respectable woman to sit in."[1]

Notable exceptions to keeping women out of the political arena occurred when a woman succeeded to the throne in her own right. As queen, she was expected to function politically as well as, if not better than, any man. But these were exceptional, God-ordained events, and the queen herself would not accept the notion of political equality for her own sex. In a letter to William Gladstone, Queen Victoria, in 1870, left no doubts about her own sentiments.

> The Queen feels so strongly upon the dangerous and
> unchristian and unnatural cry and movement of
> "women's rights" . . . that she is most anxious that
> Mrs. Gladstone and others should take some steps to
> check this alarming danger and to make whatever use
> they can of her name.[2]

No wonder progress was slow. It took much agitation and many marches, together with jail terms, hunger strikes, and forcible feedings before the goal was finally achieved. As in the United States, advances in Britain were piecemeal. In 1869, women received the vote in municipal elections. In 1870, they were allowed to sit on school boards. In 1907, they could become members of county and borough councils and even be elected to the office of mayor.[3] But the major goal, the right to participate in parliamentary elections both as voters and candidates, still eluded them.

As in the United States, it was the end of World War I that brought about female enfranchisement, but the methods of accomplishment were different. In the United States, a constitutional amendment was passed, which required two-thirds majorities in both houses of Congress, followed by ratification by three-fourths of the states. In Britain, all that was necessary was a majority vote in the House of Commons and a concurring vote in the House of Lords. On the other hand, no county, borough, or any other unit below the national level could pass enfranchising legislation the way Montana and other states had done.

In February 1918, the House of Commons gave the right to vote to women over 30 years of age. In October, it passed a bill making it possible for women to become members of the House of Commons. The House of Lords quickly agreed, and the measure became law through royal assent. The country was just getting ready for its first post-World War I election, which thus became the first one in which women could vote and also be candidates.[4] In anticipation of this event, several women had earlier announced their candidacies. To the 13 million men entitled to vote, there were now added 9 million women. Ten years later, in 1928, the discrepancy in age was removed through the Equal Franchise Act, enabling 15 million women to vote alongside 13.7 million men on the same legal basis.[5]

THE BRITISH ELECTORAL SYSTEM

Before we begin a brief sketch of all the women who have been members of the House of Commons, a few general remarks are necessary. The members of the House of Commons, like those in the U.S. House of Representatives, are elected in single-member districts where the "first past the post" wins, no matter with how small a plurality. Runoff elections are completely unknown. There are, at present, 635 of these single-member constituencies, but the figure has varied. (There were 707 in 1918, 615 from 1922 to 1935, 640 in 1945, 625 in 1950 and 1951, and 630 from 1955 to 1970.)

No appointments to the House of Commons are possible; each member of Parliament (M.P.) is elected by the voters in one of the districts. In the United States, we are used to fixed congressional terms; a congressman serves for two years, a senator for six. In Britain, the law merely states that an election must be held within five years of the last one* and leaves it up to the discretion of the prime minister to determine the precise date. Since 1918, there have been 18 general elections. If a vacancy occurs due to death, resignation, or elevation to peerage, a by-election is held within a few months. Two dozen women have, over the years, successfully contested such by-elections.

Getting on the ballot is relatively easy. A handful of signatures has to be collected, and £150, about $300, have to be deposited (the money is returned if the candidate receives at least 12.5 percent of the total vote at the election). As a result, many compete. In October 1974, there were 2,252 candidates for 635 positions, almost four for each seat.[6] But in order to get elected, it is almost essential to have the endorsement of a major party. There are exceptions. In the two 1974 general elections, the nationalist movements in Scotland and Wales made headway, but in 1979 they lost ten of their previously held 14 seats. Occasionally, a Bernadette Devlin can win in Northern Ireland, or an Eleanor Rathbone may get a chance to represent the English universities, a possibility that no longer exists because of the abolition of the university seats. But most seats are still held by the two major parties, and, in 1979, 607 of 635 seats (or 95.6 percent) were taken by either Conservative or Labour candidates.

"Adoption" of an individual as candidate of a major party is handled by the local party organization with varying degrees of interference from national headquarters. Residence requirements do not exist; anybody can "stand" for Parliament in any constituency regardless of where he or she lives. Some of the seats are "safe" for a particular party, others are hopeless, still others may be "marginal." Where one competes is therefore of crucial importance. It is most unlikely for an unknown newcomer to be "adopted" by a "safe" constituency. The career of Margaret Thatcher, Britain's first female prime minister, may serve as an example. She first

---

*However, Parliament has the power to prolong its own life and in an emergency does so. Thus, in order to avoid holding an election during World War II at a time when the enemy was at the gate, the 1935 Parliament extended its existence every year, and the election was finally held in 1945, ten years after the last one.

contested the constituency of Dartford in Kent in 1950, after having
met local Conservative party leaders at a national party conference.
She received 36.3 percent of the vote in what was then a Labour
party stronghold. In 1951, she was able to obtain 41 percent in the
same district, while still coming in second. But her performance
apparently impressed the party leaders at Finchley, a relatively
safe Conservative seat, where she was "adopted" a few years later.[7]

Thatcher has been a member of Parliament ever since. Others
have not been as lucky. We find a sizable number of representatives
being defeated in every general election, with some of them bouncing back sooner or later. Whether the second time around they are
in a safer position depends on the circumstances. Women generally seem to be at a disadvantage. "Selection committees appear to
be prejudiced against women because it is easier for a woman to
obtain the nomination for a seat unlikely to be won than for a seat
where the chances are good."[8] The frequency of defeat bears this
out. About 50 percent of the female M.P.'s careers in politics were
terminated through defeat as compared to one-third for the women
in the U.S. House of Representatives. However, a number of
others returned at a later date in Britain and only one in the United
States. Family connections are occasionally notable in Britain,
though the "widow syndrome" is less frequent than in the United
States.

Furthermore, it must be remembered that the British government depends on having a majority in the House of Commons. While
people vote for individual members, they do so in the realization
that a vote for a candidate of a particular party is also a vote for an
administration formed by that party. Alternatively, members may
face defeat, not because of anything they have or have not done, but
because their party is unpopular. This results normally in a much
larger turnover of seats at a British general election than in the
United States. For example, a 43-seat loss of Republican seats in
the House of Representatives in 1974 was termed a "landslide";[9] in
the British general elections of 1970, February 1974, and 1979, the
victorious parties gained 67, 14, and 57 seats, respectively,* a
quite normal occurrence. Such a system may make life less secure
for a British legislator. However, it also provides an opportunity to
become a member of the executive, something not possible under
the U.S. system.

---

*In several respects, the 1974 elections were not typical,
since the two major parties together received less popular support
than usual.

WOMEN MEMBERS OF THE BRITISH
HOUSE OF COMMONS

The Parliament of 1918

In the general election of 1918, 17 women were among the
1,623 candidates for 707 seats. The Labour and Liberal parties
had four women candidates each, and there were several Independents. When a Conservative candidate died suddenly during the
campaign, his widow was persuaded to take his place—"Probably
she was the first woman to discover that there is nothing like be-
reavement, injury or childbirth to commend a candidate to the
British electorate."[10] She missed winning by a handful of votes,
as did several others. The only woman who won was Countess
Constance Markievicz (1884-1927). She was born in Ireland and
had married a Polish count. Because she was involved in the Irish
struggle against British rule, Markievicz was in jail during the
campaign. Released a few months after the election, she joined the
rest of the Irish Sinn Fein M.P.s in refusing to take their seats,
and so the first female member of the British Parliament actually
made herself a "nonperson" as far as parliamentary history is
concerned.

Before this Parliament was dissolved almost four years later,
two women did make their entires. The first was U.S.-born Lady
Nancy Astor (1879-1964). Her husband, a Conservative member
of Parliament who inherited a peerage, had to give up his seat in
the House of Commons in order to get into the House of Lords. In
a by-election in November 1919, his wife successfully competed
for his Plymouth seat. Reelected time after time until her retirement in 1945, she became known for her strong views on a number
of issues, including antialcoholism, and for her biting tongue,
which led her into many sharp encounters. Those with Winston
Churchill are especially famous. Jean Mann quotes Professor
Brogan as describing Lady Astor, together with George Bernard
Shaw, as "a National Monument, a National Nuisance, a National
Joke, a National Irritation, and in old age, part of the landscape"
as well as one who possessed "courage, generosity, energy and
wit."[11]

In 1921, there was a vacancy in Parliament created through
the sudden death of a Liberal in Lincolnshire, and his widow,
Margaret Wintringham,* was chosen to take his place. At age 42,

---

*It has not been possible to find birth dates for about a dozen
female M.P.s, while on another dozen or so, only the age at the

she was a magistrate and involved in various other public affairs
and therefore well-known in the district. Although she did not speak
on her own behalf during the campaign,* she won the election, if
only by under 1,000 votes. Wintringham managed to win reelection
by about the same number of votes in 1923 but in 1924 was one of
many Liberals to lose. Despite several other attempts to return to
Parliament, she was not successful.

The Parliament of 1922

The general election of 1922 saw a doubling of female candidates, 33 in all, including five Conservatives, ten Labourites, and
16 Liberals.[12] Only the two incumbents won. However, in 1923
another woman arrived. Captain Hilton Philipson had been elected
in 1922 as a National Liberal. The following April he was unseated
and prohibited from occupying the seat for seven years because of
"fraudulent practices" by his agent, even though Philipson himself
was unaware of them.[13] His wife, Mabel Hilton Philipson, 36 years
old and mother of three small children, accepted the nomination
for her husband's seat but decided to run as a Conservative. She
was a well-known actress. She won and continued to sit in Parliament until 1929, by which time she announced that since her husband was no longer interested in a political career, "The reason
why I have held the seat has ceased to exist."[14] Although quite
active in such areas as nursing-home legislation, she apparently
saw her parliamentary role primarily as a seat-warming operation.

The Parliament of 1923

The 1923 general election had revolutionary results since it
produced the first Labour government, albeit a minority administration. Eight women were elected. The three incumbents won and
among the five newcomers were the first female Labour members.
The new Conservative member was the duchess of Atholl
(1874-1960), Scotland's first female M.P. Her husband had represented the district several years earlier. The duchess was a

---

time of becoming an M.P. or at the time of death could be ascer-
tained. The figures used in the text reflect this circumstance.
    *See Chapter 9.

public-spirited aristocrat.* Although she won by only a handful of votes, she was reelected several times. She opposed the notion of giving women the vote on the same basis as men, saying that "it would give franchise to tinkers and people who wandered about and lived in caravans." The average homemaker and mother, she maintained, did not want to vote, since mothers with large families had no time for political meetings.[15] She strongly disagreed with her party over its India policy, so that she not only voted against it but even left the party and sat as an Independent in 1934-35. However, in the 1935 general election she again ran as a Conservative; the threat from Mussolini and fascist Italy, she felt, had to be met by Conservative unity. She took serious issue with Chamberlain's appeasement policy at Munich, and, facing expulsion from the party and strong opposition in her constituency, she applied for the Chiltern Hundreds.† In the resulting by-election she fought for her old seat but received only 47 percent of the vote in a two-way contest, running as an Independent against a Conservative in an election marked by bad weather.

On the Liberal side, Lady Vera Terrington in 1923 captured the Wycombe seat. For the first and only time in the twentieth century, this district was taken by the Liberals. The new M.P., who was 35 years old when elected, was defeated at the next general election.

Also winning in 1923 were three women from the Labour party. All three were unmarried. Dorothy Jewson, of middle-class origin, was youngest, at age 39. Her stay in Parliament lasted only until the following year, when she was defeated for reelection.

---

*When appearing in Canada with Agnes Macphail, Canada's first female M.P., Atholl wore a feather boa and "non-descript headgear," causing Macphail to remark, "The Duchess is really wonderful, considering the way she was brought up" (Margaret Stewart and Doris French, Ask No Quarter [Toronto: Longman, Green, 1959], p. 136).

†Strictly speaking, a member of Parliament holds a seat until the next general election and cannot resign. But since one cannot be in Parliament and hold an office of profit under the crown at the same time, the M.P. who wants to resign applies for the position of steward and bailiff of the Chiltern Hundreds. The application is never refused and, upon being granted, makes the appointee ineligible to continue as member of Parliament.

Also born into a middle-class family and a socialist by conviction was Susan Lawrence (1871-1947), the oldest of the women
in that Parliament. An unsuccessful candidate in several previous
elections, she was defeated again in 1924. However, a by-election
in 1926 brought her back, and she stayed in the House for another
five years until her final defeat during the Labour debacle in 1931.
During the first Labour government, she became parliamentary
private secretary (P.P.S.) to the president of the Board of Education, a largely honorary position, which, however, is often regarded as the first rung up the ministerial ladder. From 1929 to
1931, she served as parliamentary secretary to the minister of
health, a junior government post.

Margaret Bondfield (1873-1953) was of working-class origin,
with first-hand knowledge of privation. She was an ardent labor
union member and organizer and had previously attempted to enter
Parliament. She succeeded in 1923, lost her seat in 1924, came
back in a 1924 by-election, and left the House for good following
her defeat in 1931. Having served as parliamentary secretary to
the minister of labor in 1924, she held the office of minister of
labor from 1929 to 1931. This made her the first woman to head a
government department and the first woman to sit in the cabinet.

The Parliament of 1924

The general election of 1924 saw a decisive swing to the right.
Labour lost heavily and so did the women in Parliament. Their
only gain was that the incoming Conservative government felt com-
pelled to follow Labour's example and appoint a woman to office.
(The duchess of Atholl was parliamentary secretary to the president
of the Board of Education from 1924 to 1929.) Of the incumbents,
only the duchess, Lady Astor, and Philipson returned, which meant
defeat for all previous Labour members. Indeed, Labour would
have been without any female representation in Parliament had it
not been for the one newcomer, Ellen Wilkinson (1891-1947). "Red
Ellen" stood at the extreme end of her party, embraced communism
for a short time after the Russian Revolution, and then became
permanently attached to moderate democratic socialism. She
stayed in Parliament for seven years and held the position of parliamentary private secretary to the parliamentary secretary of the
Ministry of Health from 1929 to 1931. Defeated for reelection in
1931, she traveled abroad, wrote, and lectured until she was able
to stage a comeback in 1935. When Churchill formed his coalition
wartime government, she first became parliamentary secretary to
the minister of pensions. Later in 1940 and for the rest of the war,

she was parliamentary secretary to the Ministry of Home Security, a very important assignment in beleaguered wartime Britain. In the postwar Clement Attlee government, she became minister of education and held the position at the time of her death in 1947.

During the five years following the 1924 general election, the four female M.P.s were joined by six more. We have already mentioned the return of Susan Lawrence and Margaret Bondfield in by-elections. In 1927, Countess Gwendolyn Iveagh (1881-1966), who had been involved in Conservative politics, successfully contested her husband's seat when the latter moved to the House of Lords. She remained in Parliament until her retirement in 1935, when the seat passed on to her son-in-law. She was the fourth Conservative woman M.P., all of whom had "inherited" their seats from their husbands.

Two other women substituted for their husbands, but in different ways. Hilda Runciman's spouse was a Liberal member of Parliament who wanted to represent another constituency at the next general election. He had already been "adopted" by St. Ives when an unexpected by-election occurred there in 1928. His wife contested it and won by a handful of votes. In 1929, it was her husband who "stood" in St. Ives while she ran in another district, which she lost by 62 votes.[16]

Similarly, Ruth Dalton, whose husband sat in the House of Commons as a Labour member and who wanted to change seats, won that particular district in a by-election and kept it "warm" for him until the next general election, when she retired from the House. The Runcimans and the Daltons were the first instances of husband and wife together in the House of Commons.

In 1929, again in a by-election, Jennie Lee (1904-) captured a previously Conservative seat in a poor industrial area in Scotland where many people were "embittered by long years without work and desperate in their needs."[17] At 24, she was the youngest woman to enter Parliament at a time when her female contemporaries could not yet vote. She retained her seat later that year at the general election but lost it in 1931. Her political leanings were to the left of the British Labour party, from which she departed for a while. She contested parliamentary seats unsuccessfully under various labels. Lee rejoined the Labour party and, in 1945, returned to Parliament, where she was to stay for 25 years. Meanwhile, she had married Aneurin Bevan, a left-wing Labour leader and member of the House of Commons. After her husband's death and during the early years of the Harold Wilson administration in the 1960s, Lee held junior governmental positions in the Ministry of Works and Buildings and then in the Department of Education and Science. In 1967, she became minister of state in the Department of Education and Science with special responsibility for the arts. She lost her seat in 1970 and accepted a life peerage, a rather interesting development since she had earlier favored the abolition of the House of Lords altogether.

The Parliament of 1929

The general election of 1929, which brought about the second Labour government, also found more women than ever before in the House of Commons: nine Labourites, three Conservatives, one Liberal, and one Independent. Of the seven newcomers, five were from the Labour party, and all of them were gone again in 1931.

Edith Picton-Turbervill (1872-1960) was later to relate details about a woman's life in the House of Commons. She was a former suffragette and, while in Parliament, succeeded in the passage of a bill preventing the death penalty from being imposed on expectant mothers.[18] She was defeated for reelection in 1931.

A physician, Ethel Bentham (1861-1931) entered the House in 1929 but died while an M.P. in January 1931.

Marion Phillips was born in Australia in 1881. She was a trade-union organizer, a journalist, and an economist. She died in 1932, after being unable to return to Parliament in 1931.

Mary Agnes Hamilton (1884-1966) also was victorious in 1929 but lost in 1931. During her brief stay in Parliament, she represented Britain at a League of Nations meeting in Geneva and served as P.P.S. to future Prime Minister Attlee, then chancellor of the Duchy of Lancaster and later postmaster general.

Lady Cynthia Mosley joined her husband on the Labour benches, then left the party with him as he turned more and more to the right, eventually becoming the leader of the British fascists. She did not live to see this turn of events, dying in 1933 at the age of 34.

Also arriving in 1929 was Eleanor Rathbone (1872-1946). Before the Attlee government abolished this practice, university graduates had their special representatives in Parliament, and Rathbone was elected by the combined English universities. She served until her death in 1946, a tireless campaigner "for all lost causes."[19] She sat as an Independent and spoke her mind fearlessly, whether to warn of the impending danger from fascism in Spain, Italy, and Germany, or to ask for support for refugees, or to advocate government-financed allowances for families.

Another newcomer in 1929 was Megan Lloyd George (1902-1966), daughter of the World War I prime minister, together with whom she served in Parliament for a number of years. She represented a Welsh constituency as a Liberal continually until she was defeated in 1951. Unlike her brother, who felt that the true inheritor of the Liberal philosophy was the modern Conservative party, she turned to Labour and entered Parliament as a Labourite for another Welsh district in 1955, representing it until her death in 1966.

A by-election in 1930, for the seat left vacant by her husband when he entered the House of Lords, brought victory to Lady Noel-Buxton. She was the first peeress to represent the Labour party. She served until her defeat in 1931. However, she returned for another constituency 14 years later and sat in Parliament until her retirement in 1950.

Replacing the late Ethel Bentham was another woman from the Labour party, U.S.-born Leah Manning. She won the by-election in February 1931 but was defeated in the general election in October. Like Lady Noel-Buxton, she staged a comeback in 1945 but was unsuccessful in her attempt to stay on in 1950.

The Parliament of 1931

The general election in 1931 sent 15 women to Parliament. Not surprisingly, in view of the decimation of the Labour party, there was not a single Labourite among them. The ten new women were Conservatives, the first time that female members of that party reached the House without their husbands' names or reputations.[20] Six had rather short parliamentary careers. Shortest was that of Mary Pickford. Daughter of a peer, she was 47 years old on arrival but died in March 1934.

Ida Copeland defeated Sir Oswald Mosley among others but was herself defeated for reelection at the next general election.

Marjorie Graves (1884-1961) was victorious over Herbert Morrison in a London constituency; however, she, too, was unsuccessful in 1935.

Sarah Ward, age 35, Norah Runge, age 47, and Helen Shaw, age 51, brought various degrees of expertise to the House but met with defeat after four years of service.

Thelma Cazalet (1899-) fought Manning for Bentham's seat in the 1931 by-election. Cazalet lost in February but won in October. Reelected in 1935, she was from 1938 to 1940 a P.P.S., the fourth woman but only the first Conservative female to hold such a post. In May 1945, after the collapse of the wartime coalition and the formation of the Conservative caretaker government, she became parliamentary secretary to the minister of education. In the general election that followed, the Conservatives lost their majority, and Cazalet her seat. In the summer of 1939, she had married and become Thelma Cazalet-Keir.

Mavis Tate entered Parliament in 1931 at the age of 38 and, before the next general election, decided to compete for another seat elsewhere, a move that turned out to be successful. She fought for equality for women as did Cazalet-Keir and, like her, accumulated 14 years of parliamentary service until defeated in 1945.

Florence Horsbrugh (1889-1969) was rather unexpectedly elected in 1931. Reelected four years later, she became parliamentary secretary to the minister of health in 1939. Though appointed to this post by Neville Chamberlain, she retained it under Churchill until the caretaker government was formed. She then was shifted to the Ministry of Food as parliamentary secretary. Defeated in 1945, Horsbrugh was persuaded to try again in 1950. She lost, but due to an immediate vacancy caused by the unexpected death of the Conservative candidate, she was "adopted" elsewhere and won. She remained in Parliament for the next nine years. After Churchill's return to power in 1951, Horsbrugh was made minister of education, although she had to wait several years before she was also given a seat in the cabinet, eventually becoming the first Conservative woman to attain cabinet rank. She left the government in 1954 and became a private member of Parliament as Dame Florence Horsbrugh. Five years later, she accepted a peerage and departed for the House of Lords.

Irene Ward (1895-), later Dame Irene, was the final new female M.P. to arrive in 1931. She began her political career by defeating Margaret Bondfield and remained in the House until she herself was beaten in 1945. Five years later, she returned and continued to be reelected until she retired in 1974. Her 38 years in the House constitute a record for a woman. Although never attaining ministerial rank, Ward was certainly a colorful person. Brookes calls her "too independent and obstinate," while at the same time possessing "prodigious industry and a shrewd grasp of affairs."[21]

The Parliament of 1935

No women entered the House as a result of by-elections between 1931 and 1935. In 1935, only nine of the incumbents returned, and no new ones were added immediately. Considering that this Parliament was to last a full decade because of wartime circumstances, it is remarkable that in the many by-elections that were held, only six women were elected. It is perhaps less surprising that four of the six followed their husbands, while one joined her husband.

A by-election in 1937 was necessitated when a Conservative M.P. was being elevated to the House of Lords. His wife, Lady

Joan Davidson (1894-), won his seat. Daughter of a one-time member of Parliament, she was no stranger to political life. Davidson was reelected until retiring in 1959. In 1964, she accepted a peerage and joined her husband in the House of Lords. While in the House of Commons, she had been elected to the executive of the "1922 Committee," a very influential organization of Conservative back-benchers—no small achievement for a woman at that time.

The death of her husband brought Labour's Agnes Hardie, the sister-in-law of the famed Keir Hardie, into the House, where she was the only one of her sex to oppose conscription of women in wartime.[22] She declined to run again in 1945.

A 22-year career in the House of Commons, with continuing service in the House of Lords, began when, in April 1938, Edith Summerskill (1901-) captured a Conservative seat in London for the Labour party. She holds a medical degree, is married to a doctor, and is the mother of Shirley Summerskill, who also combines medical training with parliamentary service. Edith Summerskill was a member of the postwar Labour government, serving for five years as parliamentary secretary to the Ministry of Food and for another year as minister of national insurance, thus following Bondfield and Wilkinson as a full-fledged department head. She terminated her career in the House of Commons by accepting a peerage in January 1961.

Another Labour victor who took a seat away from the Conservatives in 1938 was Jennie Adamson (1882-1962). Her husband was already a member of the House of Commons. During the war, she served as P.P.S. to the minister of pensions and in 1945 joined the Attlee government as parliamentary secretary in the Ministry of Pensions. However, the following year Adamson was named deputy chairman of the Assistance Board, a nonpolitical position incompatible with a parliamentary career, and therefore had to leave the House of Commons.

Two widows of members of Parliament killed through enemy action arrived during the war. Both were Conservative, and both stayed only until the next general election. Beatrice Rathbone hailed from the United States. She was the mother of two children and in 1942 married another officer to become Beatrice Wright. A year later, she gave birth to a daughter, the first sitting member to do so. She decided against seeking reelection in 1945.

While Rathbone had no opposition in her by-election, Lady Viola Apsley had to fight hard in her successful attempt to take her late husband's seat. This she did though confined to a wheelchair. Apsley was less successful, however, in 1945 and never did return to Parliament, despite a further effort in 1950.

The Parliament of 1945

With the end of World War II, a new era dawned. The long-delayed general election was held shortly after the war ended in Europe. A record number of 87 women competed, and a record number of 24 were elected. Lady Davidson, Megan Lloyd George, and Edith Summerskill continued as members. So did Wilkinson and Eleanor Rathbone, who were to die before the end of that Parliament, and Adamson, who was to resign. Three former Labour members (Noel-Buxton, Lee, and Manning) made up for their 1931 defeats by returning in triumph, while 15 new female Labourites came in for the first time. All but one had captured a former Conservative seat.

Clarice McNab Shaw, 63 years old, had the briefest tenure because ill health forced her into retirement in the fall of 1946, one month before her death.

Six others were in the House just one term, until the next general election in 1950. Grace Colman (1892-) was the daughter of a canon. In 1950, she was defeated by Irene Ward.

Barbara Ayrton Gould was a suffragette who had fought for election since 1922. She finally succeeded in 1945 but met with defeat again in 1950. [23]

Also victorious in 1945 and unsuccessful in 1950 were Muriel Nichol (1893-), who was the daughter of a former M.P. and who had been active in local government; Florence Paton, a magistrate and the wife of a member of Parliament, the first woman to sit on the Speaker's Panel of Chairmen of Committees;[24] and Mabel Ridealgh (1898-), who exclaimed in the House that "the splendid job of the housewife is not fully recognized."[25]

Edith Wills (1892-1970) had gained local government experience as member of the Birmingham City Council. She did not seek reelection in 1950.

Lady Astor had retired in 1945, and her seat was captured by Lucy Middleton (1894-), a schoolteacher, worker in the Labour movement, and the wife of a former national secretary of the Labour party. In 1950, she won reelection by 924 votes over Lady Astor's son but in 1951 lost to the same opponent by 710 votes.

Caroline Ganley was born in 1879 and was the oldest woman to enter Parliament in 1945. She had sat on local county and borough councils. She won again in 1950 and lost in 1951.

Jean Mann (1890-1964) was of working-class background and had repeatedly tried to get into Parliament. She had served on the Glasgow City Council. A mother and grandmother, she served as M.P. for 14 years before her retirement. Brookes calls her "the housewife's M.P."[26] and the "woman-next-door."[27] When she wrote her memoir, <u>Woman in Parliament</u>, she bemoaned that homemakers were underrepresented in Parliament, a sentiment frequently echoed elsewhere.

Bessie Braddock (1899-) was also the "woman next door," if one happened to live in a working-class area. She and her husband had at one time been Communists and been expelled from the party. After sitting on the Liverpool City Council, she served in Parliament for 25 years, fighting for the interests of working men and women.

Two other women who entered in 1945 served 25 years each before their retirement in 1970. Margaret Herbison (1907-) and Alice Bacon (1911-) were both miners' daughters who had become schoolteachers and ardent Labour supporters. Both reached ministerial rank. Herbison was joint undersecretary of state in the Scottish Office from 1950 to 1951, and when Labour returned to office in 1964, she became minister of pensions and national insurance, later called social security. Harold Wilson appointed Bacon minister of state at the Home Office and then put her in charge of Education and Science. Upon retirement, she accepted a life peerage.

Freda Corbet (1900-) was fortunate in representing a safe Labour seat and therefore was able to accumulate 29 years of service until her retirement in February 1974. She is listed as farmer, teacher, lecturer, and barrister[28] and had served on the London County Council.

Barbara Castle (1911-) won the seat of Blackburn in 1945 and held it until she retired in 1979, after having spent exactly half of her life in Parliament. She holds the record for consecutive service by a woman and is surpassed in total service only by Irene Ward. After being appointed P.P.S. to the president of the Board of Trade in the Attlee government, she later headed consecutively the Ministries of Overseas Development, Transport, Employment and Productivity, and Social Services. She was one of the very few women to achieve cabinet rank. On leaving the House, she was elected a member of the new, popularly chosen European Parliament.

Two more women were added to this Parliament when vacancies developed. In 1946, Lady Priscilla Grant (1915-1978), a widow with two small daughters, won a seat in Scotland after an unsuccessful attempt to enter the House a year earlier. In 1948, she married again and became Lady Tweedsmuir and in time gave birth to a daughter while an M.P. She held a junior position in the Scottish Office from 1962 to 1964, was defeated for reelection in 1966, and in 1970 went to the House of Lords, where she served as minister of state, Scottish Office, during the Heath administration.

A by-election in Glasgow in 1948 brought into Parliament its first Roman Catholic woman, Alice Cullen (1892-1969). A widow who later remarried, she won repeated reelection and was the oldest woman in Parliament at the time of her death in 1969.

The Parliament of 1950

A record number of 126 women competed in the general election of 1950, and 21 got elected.[29] A number of Labour members were defeated as the pendulum swung back to the right, allowing the Attlee government a bare majority. Five new women arrived, three Labourites and two Conservatives. Dorothy Rees (1898-), a Labourite, was a widow, schoolteacher, and alderman. She served as P.P.S. to newly appointed Minister of National Insurance Edith Summerskill and was defeated for reelection in 1951.

Another Labour supporter was Elaine Burton (1904-), who was an athlete and interested in consumer protection.[30] She remained in Parliament until defeated in 1959 and later accepted a life peerage and moved to the House of Lords.

Labour's third newcomer was Eirene White (1909-). The daughter of a deputy secretary to the cabinet of another generation, she was a journalist who married a journalist. "A distinct acquisition to the Labour benches . . . independent, self-confident" is how Kann described her and her constant fight for a better deal for widows.[31] She held important government posts in the Colonial, Foreign, and Welsh Offices until she decided to retire in 1970.

Evelyn Hill (1898-) was new on the Conservative side. She had had city council experience and was also a company director. She stayed in Parliament until defeated in 1964.

Conservative Patricia Hornsby-Smith (1914-) captured a seat in Kent. From 1951 to 1961, she held junior government posts in the Ministry of Health, the Home Office, and the Ministry of Pensions and National Insurance. She lost her seat in 1966, won it back in 1970, but failed to return to Parliament in February 1974. She had become Dame Patricia by that time.

The Parliament of 1951

No new women were added in the 1951 general election, which brought the Conservatives back into power. Only 17 female M.P.s were returned. However, four more arrived as the result of by-elections in 1953. Harriet Slater (1903-) began a 13-year stretch in the Commons, lasting until her retirement in 1966. A Labour member, she served as a lord commissioner of the treasury, a parliamentary whip, which was another first for a woman.

Death by drowning on a ferry boat led to a by-election in Northern Ireland.[32] The victim's daughter, Patricia Ford, at the age of 31 took her father's place as an Ulster Unionist, a Northern Ireland associate of the Conservatives. She shares with Beatrice Rathbone (Wright) the rare distinction of not being opposed in the by-election. She was also the first woman from an Irish constituency. The mother of two small children, she decided against re-election in 1955.

Next to arrive was Edith Pitt (1906-1966), who, despite her working-class background, ran as a Conservative. She had had local government experience and for seven years served as parliamentary secretary, first to the Ministry of Pensions and National Service, and then the Ministry of Health. She became Dame Edith when she was dropped from the government during a reshuffle in 1962. She died suddenly in 1966 while still a member of Parliament.

Lena Jeger (1915-) barely managed to hold for Labour the seat previously occupied by her late husband. She won again in 1955, lost in 1959, won again in 1964, and held on to the constituency until her retirement in 1979, after having served a total of 21 years in the House of Commons.

The Parliament of 1955

Four new faces appeared among the women in the Commons after the 1955 general election. Greatest longevity was displayed by Joyce Butler (1910-), a widow who held her seat for Labour until retiring 24 years later. For a short time, she served as P.P.S. to the minister of land and natural resources.

From Northern Ireland came Ulster Unionist Patricia McLaughlin (1917-), daughter of a clergyman, married, and mother of three children. Always interested in the welfare of Northern Ireland, she had the courage not to support the Conservative government when such action seemed necessary to her. Reelected in 1959, she decided to retire in 1964 because of ill health.

Joan Vickers (1907-), later Dame Joan, was a lecturer and welfare officer. She had the distinction to defeat Michael Foot in 1955 and to hold her marginal constituency until February 1974, when she was beaten by David Owen, later Labour's foreign secretary. A Conservative, she was unable to win in a rematch the following October.

The oldest of the 1955 quartet was another Conservative, Evelyn Emmet (1899-). She retained her seat until after the 1964 general election, when she accepted a peerage and departed for the House of Lords.

Four more women joined the House of Commons during by-elections between 1956 and 1958. We have already mentioned Megan Lloyd George and her return to Parliament after her conversion from the Liberal to the Labour party. Also winning a by-election during that period was Mervyn Pike (1918-), a managing director of a pottery concern. Brookes reports that it was a rarity for an agricultural seat to nominate a woman and also that a group of Conservatives "thought it unwise to put up a woman 'in these times to deal with Nasser, Dulles and those sort of people. '"[33] Pike ultimately was "adopted" and won the seat, getting reelected repeatedly until she retired in 1974. Meanwhile, she served as a P.P.S., and was assistant postmaster general and joint undersecretary of state at the Home Office. However, Mann reports that some unkind souls regarded her original appointment as "the most remarkable . . . since Emperor Caligula made his horse a consul."[34]

In 1957, Lady Muriel Gammans (1898-) retained for the Conservative party the seat held by her late husband for many years. She won reelection until her retirement in 1966.

The last by-election during that period featured another widow, who was, however, frustrated in her attempt to hold on to her late husband's seat in Glasgow. Another woman, Mary McAlister, succeeded in winning the district for Labour by a handful of votes, only to be defeated the very next time in that marginal constituency.

The Parliament of 1959

Of the three women who first entered Parliament in 1959, the most prominent is undoubtedly the youngest of the group, Margaret Thatcher (1926-). The daughter of a grocer, she twice fought for a practically hopeless constituency before her marriage, then gave birth to her children before being "adopted" in Finchley, a seat she still holds.* She made her maiden speech in support of her own private member's bill. "Mrs. Thatcher does not believe in taking two bites at a cherry," writes her one-time parliamentary colleague and political opponent, Jean Mann. "She takes two cherries in one bite." Mann cites as examples the facts that Thatcher gave birth to twins and that she is both a qualified chemist and a barrister.[35]

---

*See the beginning of this chapter for further details.

Thatcher was a junior minister in the Ministry of Pensions and National Insurance from 1961 to 1964 and became secretary of state for education and science with a seat in the cabinet in 1970. After her party was defeated twice in 1974, she successfully challenged the leadership of Edward Heath and was chosen to replace him as leader of Her Majesty's opposition, although her governmental service experience was pretty slim by British standards. As leader of her party, she was instrumental in defeating the Labour government in the House of Commons by one vote on March 28, 1979, thus precipitating a general election the following May. When her party emerged victorious from this contest, she became Britain's (and Europe's) first female prime minister.

Another Conservative to arrive in 1959 was Betty Harvie Anderson (1915-), a veteran of several previous campaigns. She was married soon after her election. Anderson served as deputy speaker and deputy chairman of the Ways and Means Committee and became the first woman to sit in the Speaker's chair.[36] After 20 years in the House, she retired in 1979.

The last of the 1959 trio was Labourite Judith Hart (1924-). Hers was a marginal constituency in Scotland that she took from the Conservatives and managed to keep ever since. She began her ministerial career as undersecretary at the Scottish Office, became minister of state in commonwealth relations, minister of social security, and paymaster general with a seat in the cabinet, and was repeatedly put in charge of Overseas Development.

The 1959 Parliament lasted for five years; yet, only one woman entered through a by-election, Joan Quennell (1923-). She was a Conservative, served briefly as a P.P.S., and was reelected several times until her retirement in October of 1974.

The Parliament of 1964

The general election of 1964 brought the number of women in Parliament to an all-time and so far unsurpassed high of 29, though the figure was reduced by two through Emmett's elevation to the House of Lords and the death of Pitt. After an absence of five years, Jeger returned to the House. Five newcomers appeared, all members of the Labour party, which had attained a bare majority.

Two remained only until 1970. Margaret McKay (1911-) took a seat away from the Conservatives, retained it in 1966, but retired in 1970.

Anne Kerr (1925-) performed a similar feat and in so doing joined her husband in the Commons. She also was victorious in 1966 but in 1970 was defeated by another woman, Peggy Fenner.

Renée Short (1919-), a journalist, had to combat another woman in order to gain entry into the House of Commons. Despite her leftist leanings, she has succeeded in retaining her seat since that time.

Shirley Summerskill (1931-) followed in the footsteps of her mother in both medicine and politics. In 1974, she was named undersecretary at the Home Office. She held that office until her party lost the election in 1979, though she herself was reelected.

The "other Shirley" was Vera Brittain's daughter, Shirley Williams (1930-). Her governmental experience included service as P.P.S., parliamentary secretary to the minister of labour, minister of state in education and science and in the Home Office, secretary of state for prices and consumer protection, paymaster general, and most recently secretary of state for education and science in the James Callaghan administration. She was in the cabinet for several years and had been mentioned as a possibility for a future prime minister. However, her defeat in 1979 made her one of the most talked-about casualties of the Conservative victory. In addition to the general anti-Labour sentiment in the country (or at least the southern part of it), she was unpopular among teachers because of her decision as minister of education to postpone salary negotiations until after the election. At the same time, a strongly Conservative source referred to her as having "earned the respect of all concerned with education by her sincerity and conviction," calling her defeat "a disaster for the moderates of her party."[37] Immediate speculation was that she would soon return to Parliament.

The Parliament of 1966

The election in 1966 gave the Labour party a stronger majority. On the Conservative side, another woman replaced the late Dame Edith Pitt. Jill Knight (1927-) lists herself as housewife, lecturer, and broadcaster.[38] Thus far, she has been successful in defending her seat.

New on the Labour side was Joan Lestor (1931-), a schoolteacher. She served as undersecretary in the Ministry of Education and Science and later in Foreign and Commonwealth Affairs. She has remained in Parliament since her first victory.

Gwyneth Dunwoody (1930-) comes from a prominent Labour family. Her father, Morgan Phillips, had been general secretary of the Labour party. Her mother accepted a peerage in the mid-1960s and, as baroness in waiting, became the first woman in the House of Lords to hold ministerial rank.[39] Dunwoody arrived in

the House of Commons with her husband in 1966, and she became
parliamentary secretary at the Board of Trade. In 1970, they both
were defeated, but she staged a comeback in February 1974 and
retained her seat in October of that year and in 1979.

In 1966, 26 women had entered Parliament. During the next
four years, the figure remained unchanged. Two women died during the period and both were replaced by men. Two women won
by-elections and caused quite a stir, partly because of their personalities and partly because they were not major-party candidates.
In April 1969, a seat in Northern Ireland was won by Bernadette
Devlin (1948-), who became Parliament's youngest member. "So-
cially my father was the bottom Cookstown could produce," she
writes in her autobiography. "He was the road sweeper's son."[40]
The North Irish, Catholic young woman of very poor background
had "antiestablishment" written all over her. Her election was a
sensation, and so was her reelection in 1970. She ran on an
"Independent Unity" label, winning the first time against the widow
of the former Ulster Unity incumbent. Within the next few years
she gave birth to a daughter, then married, and as Bernadette
McAlister tried to defend her seat in February 1974 but came in
third among the four candidates with only 25 percent of the vote.
This time her ticket was that of an "Independent Socialist," and
she describes herself as a Marxist while still continuing on her
militant political course. [41]

Also an individualist but much less of a "loner" was the
second female by-election winner, Winifred Ewing (1929-). She
and her husband were ardent believers in independence for Scotland.
"Do you wish to be rich Scots or poor British?" their party asked
in its election manifesto in 1974. [42] Ewing turned a Labour majority of 18,000 in the Scottish constituency of Hamilton into a Scottish
Nationalist majority of 1,800, but in 1970 she failed to repeat her
success. At the next general election, she tried in another Scottish district. In February 1974, she was one of seven and in
October one of 11 members of her party to be elected, each time
with rather small majorities. But when in May 1979 only two
Scottish Nationalists managed to be victorious, Ewing was not
among them. However, the following month she was elected to the
European Parliament, the only non-major party candidate from
Britain to be successful.

The Parliament of 1970

The general election of 1970, which returned the Conservatives to power, brought nine nonincumbent women into the House of

Commons, eight of whom were Conservatives. The one Labourite
was Doris Fisher (1919-), a homemaker and long-time Birmingham
City Council member. She had fought this former Labour seat in a
by-election in 1969 but lost to a Liberal. In 1970, she competed
for it again and won. Fisher did not seek reelection in 1974.

Among the Conservatives, Dame Patricia Hornsby-Smith
returned after four years. Others included Janet Fookes (1936-),
a teacher who had previously served on a borough council, and
Elaine Kellett (1924-), a barrister, farmer, and social worker,
who after remarriage became known as Elaine Kellett-Bowman.
Both Fookes and Kellett-Bowman were successful in the two 1974
elections and in 1979. A member of the European Parliament since
1975, Kellett-Bowman and her husband, now Edward Kellett-
Bowman, were both elected to the European Parliament in June 1979.

Sally Oppenheim (1928-), like Kellett-Bowman, had to capture
a previously Labour-held seat and was able to retain it in the elections that followed. She was prominently mentioned for inclusion in
a future Conservative cabinet. But when the Thatcher administration took office, Oppenheim became minister of state for consumer
affairs in the Department of Trade, a position that did not entail
cabinet rank.

Joan Hall (1935-), a secretary, won her seat from Labour by
fewer than a thousand votes but lost it by the same margin four
years later.

Mary Holt (1924-) was a barrister whose success was equally
short-lived. She tried again in October 1974, after being defeated
in February, but to no avail.

Constance Monks was born in 1911 and was therefore a little
older than most newcomers in recent years. She had competed
unsuccessfully for her seat in 1966, won in 1970, and met with
defeat again in 1974.

Peggy Fenner (1922-), a homemaker, transformed a 48 percent Conservative deficit in 1966 into a 55 percent victory in 1970.
She survived the February 1974 election by a handful of votes but
failed in October. In 1979, she tried the same constituency again
and was triumphant. During the Heath administration, Fenner became parliamentary secretary at the Ministry of Agriculture,
Fisheries, and Food.

By-elections brought two more women into the House. Betty
Boothroyd (1929-) finally succeeded in May 1973 after trying several times. She won during the two 1974 elections, thus competing
successfully three times within one and one-half years. In 1979, she
was again able to retain her seat. She became an assistant government whip in 1974. It should also be noted that at the same time a
woman became government chief whip in the House of Lords for the

first time; Lady Llewelyn-Davies of Hastoe was given the ancient, if not exactly feminine, title of captain, gentlemen at arms!

The second by-election in 1973 was in Glasgow, which quite naturally was a battleground for the Scottish Nationalists and which was won at the expense of the Labour party by Margo Macdonald (1944-), a teacher. She was unable, however, to extend her victory beyond the by-election, losing both times in 1974 and in a subsequent by-election.

The Parliament of February 1974

Prime Minister Heath called a general election for late February 1974 because of the industrial crisis. This resulted in the Labour party's forming a minority government in March. Another general election was held in October, enabling Labour to consolidate its position. More women than ever participated in these contests.

There were 143 female candidates in February and 161 in October. Four newcomers arrived in the spring and were all reelected in the fall. Lynda Chalker (1942-), a Conservative, is a statistician and market researcher. After the successful defense of her seat in 1979, Margaret Thatcher named her joint parliamentary undersecretary for health and social security.

Of the three Labourites new in February, only Josephine Richardson (1923-), an export manager, was able to withstand the 1979 Conservative tide. Going down to defeat that year were Audrey Wise (1935-), a lecturer who had joined her borough council at the age of 21, and Maureen Colquhoun (1928-). She had made headlines earlier when her constituency refused to renominate her because allegedly she is a lesbian. [43] Although she eventually did run again as the official Labour candidate, she was not successful in retaining her seat in 1979.

The Parliament of October 1974

Six new women arrived in October. The Scottish Nationalists won another victory when Margaret Bain (1945-) polled 31.2 percent of the vote in her district and took a seat away from the Conservatives by a 22-vote margin. In February, she had placed third with 22.3 percent of the vote. But in 1979, Labour took the seat, and Bain was again third, with 20.6 percent of the total vote cast.

The other five newly elected women were all members of the Labour party. Millie Miller (1923-1977), who died in October 1977, was in Parliament for only three years. Like three other female newcomers, she had captured a previously Conservative-held seat. Again, like her three colleagues, she had done so by a majority of under 1,000 votes.

The other women included Margaret Jackson (1943-), a Labour party research assistant who was defeated in 1979; Helene Middleweek (1949-), soon to marry and become Helene Hayman, national director of one-parent families, who also was unsuccessful in 1979; and Ann Taylor (1947-), a teacher who was able to withstand the Conservative sweep five years later.

Joan Maynard (1921-) contested a safe Labour seat. Her victory was by no means assured, since she had to fight the incumbent, a Labourite himself until he ran into difficulties with the local constituency party, which dismissed him. This motivated him to run as an Independent Labour candidate, thus actually splitting the Labour vote. With no such problems in 1979, Maynard won very comfortably.

One woman was involved in a by-election victory in 1976. Conagh McDonald (1938-), a university lecturer, had previously attempted to get into Parliament. She succeeded in retaining her seat for Labour in 1979.

The Parliament of 1979

By the time the 1979 general election was called, there were 27 women in the House. The same number of women had been elected in October 1974, one had died, and one had come in as a result of a by-election. The immediate cause of the election was the defeat of the Labour government in the House of Commons, and this, together with a variety of problems at home, put the administration on the defensive.

A major source of excitement during the campaign was due to the fact that in 1975 the Conservative members of Parliament had replaced former Prime Minister Heath with Margaret Thatcher as their leader. This meant that a Conservative victory would lead to a woman occupying 10 Downing Street in her own right and not just as her husband's spouse. A record number of women candidates were in the field: 50 Labourites, 31 Conservatives, and 51 Liberals, together with 76 others from minor parties and groups. The right-wing National Front alone had 35 female candidates, the Ecology party nine, and the Workers' Revolutionary party eight. The result was most disappointing, since only 19 women were successful.

Of the 27 incumbents, four decided to retire after long periods of service. On the Conservative side, Anderson called it
quits after 20 years. Jeger had added 15 consecutive years to her
previous six. Butler had been in the House since 1955, and the
dean of them all, Castle, had first been elected with the Attlee government at the end of World War II. (As mentioned before, she
did not really retire, since she immediately ran for and won a seat
in Europe's first elected Parliament.)

All the other 23 incumbent women stood again, seven of them
unsuccessfully. The six Conservatives were reelected, but the two
Scottish Nationalists lost and so did five of the 15 Labourites
(Colquhoun, Hayman, Jackson, Williams, and Wise). Two new
Conservatives brought their number up to eight, one new Labour
member swelled their ranks to 11. Not since Churchill's victory
in 1951, when 17 women were elected, had the number of women in
the House been so low. True, a woman now was prime minister of
Britain for the first time in history, but there was no other woman
in the cabinet, and only three others held government positions:
Oppenheim, Chalker, and Baroness Young, who, as a member of
the House of Lords, was given the post of minister of state for
education. Of course, a woman in the prime minister's spot was
an important "first," but none of the other positions were break-
throughs in any way. As to the casualties, the disappearance of
Macdonald and Bain meant that only the two major parties were
represented by women in Parliament, and Williams's defeat deprived Labour of one of its most prominent female members.

Regarding the newcomers, one was not a newcomer at all.
Fenner again contested her constituency of Rochester and Chatham,
which had elected her twice but rejected her the last time; now she
was successful once more. This left only two real neophytes, Sheila
Faith (1928–), a dental surgeon who captured a Derbyshire constituency by fewer than 1,000 votes for the Conservatives, and
Sheila Wright (1925–), a veteran of a number of unsuccessful campaigns, who was able to retain the Birmingham district for Labour.

DISCUSSION

Thus, by 1979, 108 women have sat in the House of Commons.
Many more have tried to get there. Table 4.1 lists the number of
female candidates in each election. The table indicates that 20.58
percent of the female candidates were successful, roughly one in
five. Of course, there were fewer than 1,686 candidates because
the same person frequently ran on more than one occasion. An
approximate count shows that at least 40 percent of the successful

TABLE 4.1

Women Candidates in British General Elections

Type of Election	Date	Candidates	Number Elected
General election	December 1918	17	1
By-elections	1918-22	4	2
General election	November 1922	33	2
By-elections	1922-23	1	1
General election	December 1923	34	8
By-elections	1923-24	0	0
General election	October 1924	41	4
By-elections	1924-29	12	6
General election	May 1929	69	14
By-elections	1929-31	9	2
General election	October 1931	62	15
By-elections	1931-35	5	0
General election	November 1935	67	9
By-elections	1935-45	25	6
General election	July 1945	87	24
By-elections	1945-50	6	2
General election	February 1950	127*	21
By-elections	1950-51	1	0
General election	October 1951	77	17
By-elections	1951-55	8	4
General election	May 1955	92	24
By-elections	1955-59	11	4
General election	October 1959	81	25
By-elections	1959	6	1
General election	October 1964	90	29
By-elections	1964-66	2	0
General election	March 1966	81	26
By-elections	1966-70	10	2
General election	June 1970	99	26
By-elections	1970-74	7	2
General election	February 1974	143	23
By-elections	February-October 1974	0	0
General election	October 1974	161	27
By-elections	1974-79	12	1
General election	May 1979	206	19
Total		1,686	347

*Florence Horsbrugh is counted twice. She was defeated in 1950 in one constituency but immediately adopted in another where the sudden death of the Conservative candidate necessitated postponing of the election by a few days.

Source: F. W. S. Craig, British Electoral Facts, 1885-1975 (London: Macmillan Press, 1976), pp. 96-97; and The Times Guide to the House of Commons, 1979 (London: Times Books, 1979).

women candidates served an apprenticeship by contesting a parliamentary seat and failing to win it before they eventually succeeded. Slightly fewer than half of these "apprentices" lost at least twice before winning.

A woman is far more likely to be "adopted" for a hopeless seat than for a safe one. This is borne out by the fact that whenever there is a sharp swing toward one party, a number of women are elected, and many of them do not survive when their party becomes less popular. Since more of the female M.P.s have been associated with the Labour party than with the Conservative, a swing away from Labour has sometimes resulted in the election of fewer women. The election of 1951 is one example of this. Another example is the election of 1979, when five incumbent Labourites among the women were defeated. The decline of the Scottish Nationalists wiped out their female contingent in the House. Together with the voluntary retirement of four veteran members and only three newcomers, female representation was down to about two-thirds of its previous strength.

The major parties seem to be less than enthusiastic about women candidates, even though this is, of course, officially denied. The scarcity of female candidates is attributed by the Labour party to the difficulty of finding "sufficient women to stand because of conflicting domestic or professional ties."[44] The Conservatives say that the local constituency selection committees are at fault, because they "persist in the idea that women make poor candidates and unpopular members."[45] The older men on these committees are blamed in particular, for they allegedly "tend to fear a woman if she appears to be very able. . . . if she is young and attractive, middle-aged women tend to distrust their influence on their menfolk."[46]

The inheritance syndrome, so important in the United States, where 32 female representatives followed their husbands into the House, is much less apparent in Britain. Only six M.P.s succeeded their late husbands immediately (Wintringham, Hardie, Rathbone-Wright, Apsley, Jeger, and Gammans), four took over when their husbands moved to the House of Lords (Astor, Iveagh, Noel-Buxton, and Davidson), three kept constituencies warm for their husbands (Philipson, Runciman, and Dalton), one won a constituency represented by her husband six years earlier (Atholl), and one (Ford) was elected to take the place of her father when the latter perished in a drowning accident. (Ford and Lady Gammans are the only two cases where a woman was returned unopposed in a by-election.) Instances of benefiting from direct family connections are thus much rarer in Britain than in the United States. Moreover, while the first few women clearly came in on their husbands' coattails, the last wife to follow her spouse into Parliament was Lady Gammans in 1957. It is too early to say that the practice is now dying out in Britain, but it certainly is not the often-used stepping stone that it still is in the United States.

A smaller number of women left the House of Commons voluntarily than did those in the House of Representatives, 36 (including the duchess of Atholl, who resigned in order to fight for her old seat in a by-election) as compared to 48. But whereas only 25 female U.S. House members went down to defeat, 59 of the British women M.P.s had this unpleasant experience. It will be noted that while in the U.S. House of Representatives only two women had their service interrupted, 14 in British politics staged a comeback and therefore have to be counted twice in Table 4.2.

TABLE 4.2

Termination of Service of Women M.P.s

Reason	Number
Voluntary retirement	36
Death while serving	8
Defeat for reelection	59
Still serving	19

Note: The data reflect the situation as of 1979.
Source: Compiled by the author.

As to party affiliation, while the first few women were Conservative and Liberal, the Labour party soon made up for a late start. Of the women in Parliament, 55 percent belonged to the Labour party and 35 percent to the Conservative. Table 4.3 shows the breakdown.

The Liberals elected their four women M.P.s in the 1920s, with Megan Lloyd George retaining her seat for 22 years. After her defeat, the only way back for her was on the Labour party label. The Independents scored with outstanding personalities. Eleanor Rathbone represented the English universities from 1929 until her death in 1946, and Devlin sat for her Northern Irish constituency for five years. Three women were at one time or another M.P.s for the Scottish Nationalists.

TABLE 4.3

Party Affiliation of Women Members of the British House of Commons

Party	Number
Labour	60[a]
Conservative	38
Liberal	4[a]
Scottish Nationalist	3
Ulster Unionist	2
Independent Unionist	1
Independent	1
Total	109[b]

[a]Megan Lloyd George is counted twice, among Liberals and Labourites.

[b]The countess of Markievicz, elected on the Sinn Fein label, is not included.

Source: Compiled by the author.

By and large, it is true that chiefly candidates affiliated with the two major parties get elected. Indeed, in 1979, all victorious female candidates ran on either the Conservative or the Labour tickets. This is not to say that others did not try, however, as Table 4.4 shows. Interestingly, next to the Ecologists, the Communists and the National Front had, in terms of percentages, the highest number of women among their list of candidates. When we discuss the German Weimar Republic, we will note that leftist parties never hesitated to have many female candidates but that the Right was reluctant—Hitler's Nazi party, for example, denounced the entire concept of women in public life. The National Front has quasi-fascist tendencies. Yet in 1979, they fielded the same number of women candidates as the Conservative party. But this did not save them from disaster. Like the Communists, they lost all their deposits, which means that nowhere did they poll 12.5 percent of the total vote.[47] Other fringe groups did not do any better. For example, Vanessa Redgrave, who has repeatedly stood for Parliament, this time received .7 percent of the vote in a Manchester constituency where she represented the Workers Revolutionary party.

TABLE 4.4

Women Candidates for Parliament
during the 1979 Election

Party	Total Number of Candidates	Number of Women Candidates	Percent of Women Candidates
Conservative	622	31	5.00
Labour	622	52	8.36
Liberal	576	51	8.85
National Front	303	31	10.23
Scottish Nationalist	71	6	8.45
Welsh Nationalist	36	1	2.78
Communist	38	4	10.53
Ecologist	54	7	12.96
Other	254	23*	9.06
Total	2,576	206	

*Includes eight candidates from the Workers Revolutionary party.

Source: The Times Guide to the House of Commons, 1979 (London: Times Books, 1979).

As we have seen, a British woman in Parliament is much more prone to defeat than a female U.S. representative, for there is in general a greater turnover. If this leads us to believe that more members serve shorter time periods than in the United States, we would be wrong. Looking at those women who have completed their service in the British House of Commons, we find their average length of stay to be well over ten years, about three years more than for a U.S. female representative. In all, 16 women have served 20 years or more:

Irene Ward, 38 years, 1931-45, 1950-74
Barbara Castle, 34 years, 1945-79
Megan Lloyd George, 31 years, 1929-51, 1957-66
Freda Corbett, 29 years, 1945-74
Jennie Lee, 27 years, 1929-31, 1945-70
Lady Astor, 26 years, 1919-45
Alice Bacon, 25 years, 1945-70

Bessie Braddock, 25 years, 1945-70
Margaret Herbison, 25 years, 1945-70
Joyce Butler, 24 years, 1955-79
Florence Horsbrugh, 23 years, 1931-45, 1950-59
Lady Davidson, 22 years, 1937-59
Alice Cullen, 21 years, 1948-69
Lena Jeger, 21 years, 1953-59, 1964-79
Lady Tweedsmuir, 20 years, 1946-66
Betty Anderson, 20 years, 1959-79

Moreover, 13 others served longer than ten years each. Of those still in the House of Commons after the 1979 election, two have been there continuously since 1959, two since 1964, and two since 1966, which demonstrates once more that every third or fourth female M.P. is accumulating more than a decade of service in Parliament.

As to location, while we have been unable to identify six or so constituencies represented by women along rural-urban lines, it is clear that the vast majority of women M.P.s come from urban districts. However, at least ten were classified as rural.[48] Table 4.5 shows where the constituencies are located that were represented by women. The areas with the greatest population centers, such as London, Lancashire (which includes Liverpool and Manchester), Lanarkshire in Scotland (which includes Glasgow), and Warwickshire (which includes Birmingham and Coventry), are among those represented by the largest contingent of women. There is a slight reapportionment taking place in Britain every few decades and in order to make the table meaningful, we have added the number of seats each area was allocated in the mid-1960s.

As previously indicated, the ages of women M.P.s present a problem, because in some instances the year of birth is just not available. Sometimes not even the obituary columns in the Times divulge that information. The British seem to have a sense of chivalry that permits a woman not to disclose her age if she does not want to, and we must respect this sentiment. Table 4.6, therefore, deals with only 97 women M.P.s. Even these incomplete figures show that the youngest female M.P.s were not Conservative, that the bulk of the newcomers were under 50, and that, among those over 51, the Labour members outnumber the Conservatives almost three to one. This last statistic may result from recognition finally being given to older union leaders or to women who had most of their family obligations out of the way. Two of the three Scottish Nationalists and Devlin were under 30, a rather sparsely represented age group. On the other hand, Eleanor Rathbone was among the oldest, but this was perhaps to be expected from a university constituency, where maturity was a factor, at least in those days.

TABLE 4.5

Geographic Distribution of Seats Held by Women

	Seats	Women M.P.s
England	511	94
Greater London	102	22
Buckinghamshire	5	2
Cheshire	16	1
Cornwall	5	2
Derbyshire	10	1
Devon	10	4
Durham	18	3
Essex	12	3
Gloucestershire	12	2
Hampshire	14	1
Hertfordshire	7	3
Kent	13	4
Lancashire	62	10
Leicestershire	8	1
Lincolnshire	9	2
Norfolk	8	3
Northamptonshire	5	2
Northumberland	10	4
Nottinghamshire	10	1
Shropshire	4	1
Somerset	4	1
Staffordshire	19	7
Sussex	12	1
Warwickshire	23	7
Yorkshire	56	6
Wales	36	4
Anglesey	1	1
Carmarthenshire	2	1
Flintshire	2	1
Glamorganshire	16	1
Scotland	71	17
Aberdeenshire	4	1
Angus & Kincardine	4	1
Ayrshire & Bute	5	1
Berwick & E. Lothian	1	1
Dumbartonshire	2	1
Lanarkshire	22	10
Perth & Kinross	2	1
Renfrewshire	4	1
Northern Ireland	12	3
Antrim	6	1
County Down	2	1
Mid-Ulster	1	1

Source: Compiled by the author.

99

TABLE 4.6

Ages of Women Entering British Parliament

Party	21-30	31-40	41-50	51-60	61-70
Conservative	0	18	12	6	0
Labour	3	18	13	15	2
Liberal	1	1	1	0	0
Scottish Nationalist	2	0	1	0	0
Ulster Unionist	0	2	0	0	0
Independent	1	0	0	1	0
Total	7	39	27	22	2

Source: Compiled by the author.

As might not be surprising, the female members of Parliament came from a variety of backgrounds. In Britain, this means that they originated from the several layers of the class structure. Lady Astor, despite the fact that she was born in the United States, perhaps best represented the aristocracy that, as a rule, found its natural home in the Conservative party. Other members of that class, however, sometimes were imbued with a desire for social justice and reform and therefore became active in the Labour party, as did Lady Mosley, no matter how short-lived her alliance with democratic socialism may have been. The working classes, quite obviously, were more inclined to side with Labour. Here we find at least two distinct types. On the one hand, there were those who knew poverty and found themselves fighting against it from a very early age, perhaps as members of the trade union movement in which they and their families played leading parts. The names of Bondfield and, later on, Braddock come to mind. Then there were also the university-educated women. Indeed, university education is far more noticeable among Labour members. For them, it was a sure way to the top, whereas Conservatives, who often were economically better situated, did not really need it. Lee and Wilkinson were among those receiving a university education that they felt they had to use for the good of the working people. As far as the middle class is concerned, the picture is more confused. Lawrence, a solicitor's daughter, started out as a Conservative before her conversion to socialism. Although Thatcher's father was a grocer, she was never anything but a Conservative. Pitt, despite her working-class origin, became a Conservative. Thus, class lines did not always determine party allegiance.

In the U.S. Congress, longevity in the legislature brings seniority and with it power and influence in a highly developed committee structure. Nothing like this exists in Britain. The reward a member of the British Parliament can look to lies in a different direction. The conferring of knighthood and elevation to the peer-ave are age-old practices from which women in their own rights were barred until relatively recently. Only since 1958 have women been admitted to the House of Lords, thus overcoming the objections of one noble lord. "Many of us do not want women in this House. We do not want to sit beside them on those benches nor do we want to meet them in the Library."[49]* But a title with or without membership in the upper chamber, although now available to members of both sexes, has lost in importance, and its attainment can hardly be regarded as fulfillment of a lifetime's ambition. Besides, membership in Parliament is not the only and not even the most traveled road to receiving such honors.

What is obtainable through election to the House of Commons is a government position and with it executive powers and authority. So far, not many women have achieved this. The Labour party has been more obliging in this respect than the Conservative. A number of females have been able to climb the first rung of the ladder by being named parliamentary private secretary. Others were promoted to junior ministerial rank, beginning with Bondfield in 1924. Five years later, she became the first woman not only to head a department but to sit in the cabinet as well. Membership in the cabinet (the small, inner circle around the prime minister that is the real center of power) has been held by only a handful of women. After Bondfield, it took a world war and the formation of the Attlee government in 1945 before another woman, Wilkinson, reached a cabinet-level appointment as minister of education. Horsbrugh headed the Ministry of Education under Churchill in 1951 but had to wait three years before she was admitted to the cabinet. The only other Conservative woman to attain cabinet rank was

---

*Brookes relates many other "problems" that arose with the admission of women to the House of Lords, such as how they should be addressed, what robes they should wear, and what would happen to their hairdos if they had to raise their hats three times to the lord chancellor. It is good to know that in the end such "problems" did not prove insurmountable. For example, it was decided that the women did not have to take off their hats at all (Pamela Brookes, Women at Westminster [London: Peter Davies, 1967], pp. 211-12).

TABLE 4.7

Women Members of the British House of Commons

M.P.	Dates	Party	In Office	Reason(s) for Departure
Countess Constance Markievicz	1884–1927	Sinn Fein	1918–22	not sworn in
Lady Nancy Astor[a]	1879–1964	Conservative	1919–45	retired
Margaret Wintringham[a]	–b	Liberal	1921–24	defeated
Mabel Philipson[a]	–1951	Conservative	1923–29	retired
Katherine, duchess of Atholl	1874–1960	Conservative	1923–38	resigned
Lady Vera Terrington	—	Liberal	1923–24	defeated
Dorothy Jewson	—	Labour	1923–24	defeated
Susan Lawrence	1871–1947	Labour	1923–24, 1926–31	defeated, defeated
Margaret Bondfield	1873–1953	Labour	1923–24, 1926–31	defeated, defeated
Ellen Wilkinson	1891–1947	Labour	1924–31, 1935–47	defeated, died
Countess Gwendolyn Iveagh[a]	1881–1966	Conservative	1927–35	retired
Hilda Runciman	–1956	Liberal	1928–29	retired
Ruth Dalton	—	Labour	1929	retired
Jennie Lee	1904–	Labour	1929–31, 1945–70	defeated, defeated
Edith Picton-Turbervill	1872–1960	Labour	1929–31	defeated
Ethel Bentham	1861–1931	Labour	1929–31	died
Marion Phillips	1881–1932	Labour	1929–31	defeated
Mary Agnes Hamilton	1884–1966	Labour	1929–31	defeated
Lady Cynthia Mosley	–1933	Labour	1929–31	retired
Eleanor Rathbone	1872–1946	Independent	1929–46	died
Megan Lloyd George	1902–1966	Liberal	1929–51	defeated
		Labour	1957–66	died

Name	Dates	Party	Term	Status
Lady Noel–Buxton[a]	-1960	Labour	1930-31, 1945-50	defeated, retired
Leah Manning	—	Labour	1931, 1945-50	defeated, defeated
Mary Pickford	-1934	Conservative	1931-34	died
Ida Copeland	-1964	Conservative	1931-35	defeated
Marjorie Graves	1884-1961	Conservative	1931-35	defeated
Sarah Ward	-1969	Conservative	1931-35	defeated
Norah Runge	1884-	Conservative	1931-35	defeated
Helen Shaw	—	Conservative	1931-35	defeated
Thelma Cazalet (–Shaw)	1899-	Conservative	1931-45	defeated
Mavis Tate	-1947	Conservative	1931-45	defeated
Florence Horsbrugh	1889-1969	Conservative	1931-45, 1950-59	defeated, retired
Irene Ward	1895-	Conservative	1931-45, 1950-74	defeated, retired
Lady Joan Davidson[a]	1894-	Conservative	1937-59	retired
Agnes Hardie[a]	-1951	Labour	1937-45	retired
Edith Summerskill	1901-	Labour	1938-55	retired
Jennie Adamson	1882-1962	Labour	1938-46	resigned
Beatrice Rathbone (–Wright)[a]	—	Conservative	1941-45	retired
Lady Viola Apsley[a]	-1966	Conservative	1943-45	defeated
Clarice Shaw	-1946	Labour	1945-46	resigned
Grace Colman	1892-	Labour	1945-50	defeated
Barbara Gould	-1950	Labour	1945-50	defeated
Muriel Nichol	1893-	Labour	1945-50	defeated
Florence Paton	—	Labour	1945-50	defeated
Mabel Ridealgh	1898-	Labour	1945-50	defeated
Edith Wills	1892-1970	Labour	1945-50	retired

(continued)

Table 4.7, continued

M.P.	Dates	Party	In Office	Reason(s) for Departure
Lucy Middleton	1894–	Labour	1945–51	defeated
Caroline Ganley	1879–	Labour	1945–51	defeated
Jean Mann	1890–1964	Labour	1945–59	retired
Bessie Braddock	1899–	Labour	1945–70	retired
Margaret Herbison	1907–	Labour	1945–70	retired
Alice Bacon	1911–	Labour	1945–70	retired
Freda Corbet	1900–	Labour	1945–74	retired
Barbara Castle	1911–	Labour	1945–79	retired
Lady Priscilla Grant-Tweedsmuir	1915–1978	Conservative	1946–66	defeated
Alice Cullen	1892–1969	Labour	1948–69	died
Dorothy Rees	1898–	Labour	1950–51	defeated
Elaine Burton	1904–	Labour	1950–59	defeated
Eirene White	1909–	Labour	1950–70	retired
Evelyn Hill	1898–	Conservative	1950–64	defeated
Patricia Hornsby-Smith	1914–	Conservative	1950–66, 1970–74	defeated, defeated
Harriet Slater	1903–	Labour	1953–66	retired
Patricia Ford[c]	–	Ulster Unionist	1953–55	retired
Edith Pitt	1906–1966	Conservative	1953–66	died
Lena Jeger[a]	1915–	Labour	1953–59, 1964–79	defeated, retired
Joyce Butler	1910–	Labour	1955–79	retired
Patricia McLaughlin	1917–	Ulster Unionist	1955–64	retired
Joan Vickers	1907–	Conservative	1955–74	defeated

Name	Born	Party	Years	Status
Evelyn Emmet	1899–	Conservative	1955–64	retired
Mervyn Pike	1918–	Conservative	1956–74	retired
Lady Muriel Gammans[a]	1898–	Conservative	1957–66	retired
Mary McAlister	—	Labour	1958–59	defeated
Margaret Thatcher	1926–	Conservative	1959–	n.a.
Betty Anderson	1915–	Conservative	1959–79	retired
Judith Hart	1924–	Labour	1959–	n.a.
Joan Quennell	1923–	Conservative	1960–74	retired
Margaret McKay	1911–	Labour	1964–70	retired
Anne Kerr	1925–	Labour	1964–70	defeated
Renée Short	1919–	Labour	1964–	n.a.
Shirley Summerskill	1931–	Labour	1964–	n.a.
Shirley Williams	1930–	Labour	1964–79	defeated
Jill Knight	1927–	Conservative	1966–	n.a.
Joan Lestor	1931–	Labour	1966–	n.a.
Gwyneth Dunwoody	1930–	Labour	1966–70, 1974–	defeated, n.a.
Bernadette Devlin	1948–	Independent Unity	1969–74	defeated
Winifred Ewing	1929–	Scottish Nationalist	1967–70, 1974–79	defeated, defeated
Doris Fisher	1919–	Labour	1970–74	retired
Janet Fookes	1936–	Conservative	1970–	n.a.
Elaine Kellett (–Bowman)	1924–	Conservative	1970–	n.a.
Sally Oppenheim	1928–	Conservative	1970–	n.a.
Joan Hall	1935–	Conservative	1970–74	defeated
Mary Holt	1924–	Conservative	1970–74	defeated

(continued)

105

Table 4.7, continued

M.P.	Dates	Party	In Office	Reason(s) for Departure
Constance Monks	1911–	Conservative	1970–74	defeated
Peggy Fenner	1922–	Conservative	1970–74, 1979–	defeated, n.a.
Betty Boothroyd	1929–	Labour	1973–	n.a.
Margo Macdonald	1944–	Scottish Nationalist	1973–74	defeated
Lynda Chalker	1942–	Conservative	1974–	n.a.
Josephine Richardson	1923–	Labour	1974–	n.a.
Audrey Wise	1935–	Labour	1974–79	defeated
Maureen Colquhoun	1928–	Labour	1974–79	defeated
Margaret Bain	1945–	Scottish Nationalist	1974–79	defeated
Millie Miller	1923–1977	Labour	1974–77	died
Margaret Jackson	1943–	Labour	1974–79	defeated
Helene Middleweek (Hayman)	1949–	Labour	1974–79	defeated
Ann Taylor	1947–	Labour	1974–	n.a.
Joan Maynard	1921–	Labour	1974–	n.a.
Ooonagh McDonald	1938–	Labour	1976–	n.a.
Sheila Faith	1928–	Conservative	1979–	n.a.
Sheila Wright	1925–	Labour	1979–	n.a.

aFollowed husband into office.   bData not available.   cFollowed father into office.

Note: n.a., not applicable.

Source: Compiled by the author.

TABLE 4.8

The British House of Commons and Female Members

Election	Number of Women	Names
December 14, 1918	1	Markievicz
By-elections	2	Astor (November 1919), Wintringham (October 1921)
November 15, 1922	2	Astor, Wintringham
By-elections	1	Philipson (May 1923)
December 6, 1923	8	Astor, Wintringham, Philipson, Atholl, Terrington, Lawrence, Bondfield, Jewson
October 29, 1924	4	Astor, Atholl, Philipson, Wilkinson
By-elections	6	Lawrence (April 1926), Bondfield (July 1926), Iveagh (November 1927), Runciman (March 1928), Dalton (February 1929), Lee (March 1929)
May 30, 1929	14	Astor, Atholl, Iveagh, Wilkinson, Lawrence, Lee, Bondfield, Bentham (died January 1931), Hamilton, Mosley, Picton-Turbervill, Lloyd George, Phillips, Rathbone
By-elections	2	Noel-Buxton (July 1930), Manning (February 1931)
October 27, 1931	15	Astor, Atholl, Iveagh, Lloyd George, Rathbone, Cazalet, Ward, Horsbrugh, Copeland, Runge, Shaw, Tate, Ward, Graves, Pickford
November 14, 1935	9	Astor, Atholl (resigned November 1938), Cazalet, Ward, Horsbrugh, Tate, Lloyd George, Rathbone, Wilkinson
By-elections	6	Davidson (June 1937), Hardie (September 1937), Summerskill (August 1938), Adamson (November 1938), Rathbone-Wright (March 1941), Apsley (February 1943)
July 5, 1945	24	Davidson, Wilkinson (died February 1947), Rathbone (died January 1946), Summerskill, Adamson (resigned May 1946), Bacon, Braddock, Castle, Colman, Corbet, Ganley, Herbison, Middleton, Nichol, Gould, Mann, Paton, Ridealgh, Shaw (resigned October 1946), Wills, Lloyd George, Noel-Buxton, Lee, Manning

(continued)

Table 4.8, continued

Election	Number of Women	Names
By-election	1	Grant (-Tweedsmuir) (November 1946)
February 23, 1950	21	Mann, Ward, Corbet, Lee, Middleton, Burton, Rees, Lloyd George, White, Hill, Hornsby-Smith, Horsbrugh, Bacon, Braddock, Castle, Ganley, Herbison, Cullen, Tweedsmuir, Davidson, Summerskill
October 25, 1951	17	Davidson, Summerskill, Bacon, Braddock, Castle, Lee, Corbet, Herbison, Mann, Tweedsmuir, Cullen, Ward, Burton, Hill, White, Hornsby-Smith, Horsbrugh
By-elections	4	Slater (March 1953), Ford (April 1953), Pitt (July 1953), Jeger (November 1953)
May 26, 1955	24	Davidson, Summerskill, Bacon, Braddock, Castle, Lee, Corbet, Herbison, Mann, Tweedsmuir, Cullen, Ward, Burton, Hill, White, Hornsby-Smith, Horsbrugh, Slater, Pitt, Jeger, Butler, Emmet, McLaughlin, Vickers
By-elections	4	Pike (December 1956), Lloyd George (February 1957), Gammans (May 1957), McAlister (March 1958)
October 8, 1959	25	Summerskill (peerage January 1961), Bacon, Braddock, Castle, Lee, Corbet, Herbison, Tweedsmuir, Cullen, Lloyd George, Ward, Hill, Hornsby-Smith, White, Slater, Pitt, Emmet, McLaughlin, Vickers, Pike, Gammans, Butler, Anderson, Hart, Thatcher
By-election	1	Quennell (November 1960)
October 15, 1964	29	Bacon, Braddock, Castle, Corbet, Herbison, Tweedsmuir, Cullen, Lee, Lloyd George, Ward, Hornsby-Smith, White, Slater, Emmet (peerage after election), Vickers, Pike, Gammans, Butler, Anderson, Hart, Thatcher, Quennell, Jeger, Kerr, McKay, Short, S. Summerskill, Williams, Pitt (died January 1966)

Election	Number of Women	Names
March 31, 1966	26	Bacon, Braddock, Castle, Corbet, Herbison, Lee, Cullen (died May 1969), Ward, White, Vickers, Pike, Butler, Anderson, Hart, Thatcher, Quennell, Jeger, Kerr, McKay, Short, S. Summerskill, Lloyd George (died May 1966), Dunwoody, Knight, Lestor, Williams
By-elections	2	Ewing (November 1967), Devlin (April 1969)
June 18, 1970	26	Castle, Corbet, Ward, Vickers, Pike, Butler, Anderson, Hart, Thatcher, Quennell, Jeger, Short, S. Summerskill, Williams, Knight, Lestor, Devlin, Hornsby-Smith, Fisher, Fenner, Fookes, Hall, Holt, Kellett-Bowman, Monks, Oppenheim
By-elections	2	Boothroyd (May 1973), Macdonald (November 1973)
February 28, 1974	23	Castle, Butler, Anderson, Hart, Thatcher, Quennell, Jeger, Short, S. Summerskill, Williams, Knight, Lestor, Fenner, Fookes, Kellett-Bowman, Oppenheim, Boothroyd, Dunwoody, Ewing, Chalker, Colquhoun, Richardson, Wise
October 10, 1974	27	Castle, Butler, Anderson, Hart, Thatcher, Jeger, Short, S. Summerskill, Williams, Knight, Lestor, Fookes, Kellett-Bowman, Oppenheim, Boothroyd, Dunwoody, Ewing, Chalker, Colquhoun, Richardson, Wise, Bain, Hayman, Jackson, Maynard, Miller (died October 1977), Taylor
By-election	1	McDonald (July 1976)
May 3, 1979	19	Hart, Thatcher, Short, S. Summerskill, Knight, Lestor, Fookes, Kellett-Bowman, Oppenheim, Boothroyd, Dunwoody, Chalker, Richardson, Maynard, Taylor, McDonald, Wright, Faith, Fenner

Note: Unless otherwise indicated, dates in parentheses show when M.P.s entered the House of Commons.

Source: Compiled by the author.

Thatcher under Prime Minister Heath. On the Labour side, Castle and Williams were cabinet members, at one time even serving together. Although in 1979 Thatcher became the first woman prime minister, no other woman was appointed to the cabinet by her.

It will be noted that, to start with, women were mostly associated with such departments as Labour, Education, Health, Pensions, and Food, departments that are closest to women's alleged main interests of home and children. Apart from Wilkinson, who during the war was in charge of air raid shelters and other home security problems closely related to military affairs, it was not until the mid-1960s that the interests of women in far wider aspects of life were finally recognized by giving some of them responsibilities in matters relating to overseas development, transportation, and, above all, colonial, commonwealth, and foreign affairs.

All in all, therefore, while progress is certainly visible, it has been and still is very slow. There is still truth in Edith Summerskill's remark that "a woman has to be better than a man to be adopted by a constituency."[50] Williams gives as a reason for so few women in politics

> that absolutely no concessions are made for the special problems of being two things at once, in most cases a wife and mother. . . . I can see the argument, why should women ask for concessions when they want equality, but it's no good pretending if you're the person who's supposed to take the kids to the dentist or get the meat at weekends that you're in the same position as someone who has a wife to do all these things for them.[51]

Wilkinson expressed a similar sentiment even more bluntly when she uttered the cry, "Oh! for a wife!" She explained: "If I had a wife, she might have collected these [her letters which she had just claimed at the House Post Office], drafted answers and finally typed them. She would help with the women's section, give a hand with the bazaar, and when I get home, fagged out, have a delicious meal ready for me."[52] (For a concise listing of the women members of the British House of Commons, see Tables 4.7 and 4.8.)

NOTES

1. Pamela Brookes, Women at Westminster (London: Peter Davies, 1967), p. 5 (Admiral of the Fleet Sir Hedworth Meux in opposing the Representation of the People Act, which was to give women the right to vote).

2. Cited in Melville Currell, Political Woman (London: Croom Helm, 1974), p. 2.

3. Ruth Ross, "Tradition and the Role of Women in Great Britain," in Women in the World, ed. Lynne B. Iglitzen and Ruth Ross (Santa Barbara: CLIO Books, 1976), p. 165.

4. Brookes, op. cit., pp. 4-6.

5. Sir J. A. R. Marriott, Modern England, 1885-1945 (London: Methuen, 1946), pp. 328-29.

6. The Times Guide to the House of Commons, October 1974 (London: Times Books, 1974), p. 282.

7. For a more detailed, if not entirely unbiased, account, see Russell Lewis, Margaret Thatcher: A Personal and Political Biography (London and Boston: Routledge & Kegan Paul, 1975).

8. Peter G. Richards, Honorable Members (New York: Frederic A. Praeger, 1959), p. 30.

9. Congressional Quarterly 32 (1974): 3057.

10. Brookes, op. cit., p. 14.

11. Jean Mann, Woman in Parliament (London: Odham Press, 1962), p. 42.

12. Brookes, op. cit., p. 33.

13. Ibid., p. 37.

14. Ibid., p. 67.

15. Ibid., p. 48.

16. Ibid., p. 72.

17. Jennie Lee, This Great Journey (New York: Farrar & Rinehart, 1942), p. 266.

18. Mann, op. cit., p. 51.

19. Ibid., p. 19.

20. Brookes, op. cit., p. 98.

21. Ibid., p. 202.

22. Ibid., pp. 136-37.

23. Ibid., p. 154.

24. Ibid., p. 166.

25. Ibid., p. 163.

26. Ibid., p. 215.

27. Ibid., p. 239.

28. The Times Guide to the House of Commons, 1964 (London: Times Office, 1964), p. 111.

29. Brookes, op. cit., p. 171.

30. Mann, op. cit., p.29.

31. Ibid., p. 27.

32. Brookes, op. cit., p. 186.

33. Ibid., pp. 195-96.

34. Mann, op. cit., p. 43.

35. Ibid., p. 31.

36. The Times Guide to the House of Commons, 1974 (London: Times Books, 1974), p. 212.

37. David Fletcher in the Daily Telegraph, May 5, 1979.

38. Guide to the House of Commons, 1974, p. 56.

39. Brookes, op. cit., p. 235.

40. Bernadette Devlin, The Price of My Soul (New York: Alfred A. Knopf, 1969), p. 1.

41. New York Times, March 23, 1975.

42. Guide to the House of Commons, 1974, p. 326.

43. International Herald Tribune, October 10, 1977.

44. Times (London), September 21, 1964.

45. Kenneth Hudson, Men and Women (Newton Abbot: David & Charles, 1968), p. 111.

46. Times (London), September 21, 1964.

47. Guide to the House of Commons, 1979, p. 252.

48. B. R. Mitchell and Klaus Boehm, British Parliamentary Election Results, 1950-1964 (London: Cambridge University Press, 1966).

49. Brookes, op. cit., p. 210.

50. Mann, op. cit., pp. 16-17.

51. New York Times, September 2, 1976.

52. Currell, op. cit., p. 16.

5

THE CANADIAN HOUSE OF COMMONS

HISTORY

Canada has many close connections with the United States and with Britain. Stretching for several thousand miles between the Atlantic and the Pacific, the easily crossed border between the two giant North American nations separates and at the same time unites two peoples that for the most part have the same roots and speak the same language (with the notable exception of Quebec). The British heritage, a colonial past, and a quest for self–determination are part of the history of both. Independence came much later to the North, which, thus far at least, has never completely broken its ties with the British mother country and continues to recognize the queen of Britain not merely as head of the commonwealth of which Canada is a member, but as queen of Canada as well.

Democratic principles have been adopted and developed for quite a while in all three countries, and Canada has borrowed from Btitain and from the United States. From the "old country," Canada adopted the parliamentary system, the division into a large number of election districts, each of which sends one member to the House of Commons. The majority party forms the government and is responsible for the conduct of national affairs as long as it retains the confidence of Parliament. The prime minister has the right to call a general election whenever he deems it necessary or politically advantageous, which means that parliaments are elected for irregular and unpredictable periods. From its southern neighbor, Canada borrowed the federal system, the right of local units (that is, the provinces) to have their own governments and to make their own decisions, although, unlike the U.S. Constitution, Canadian law provides that all powers not specifically granted to the provinces remain within the domain of the federal government.

With regard to the extension of suffrage to women, the relationship of provincial to federal law in Canada differs from that in the United States. As in the United States, where some of the western states allowed women to vote before the Nineteenth Amendment was passed, several of the Canadian provinces preceded the Parliament in Ottawa in allowing women to participate in political life (see Table 5.1). In the United States, no further restrictions could be placed in the political path of women once the Constitution had been changed to include the provision that "the right of citizens of the United States to vote shall not be denied or abridged by the United States or by any State on account of sex." Obviously this included every level of government, federal, state, and local. But the law that went into effect in Canada in 1919 merely stipulated that "every female person" could vote in dominion elections,[1] and this clearly did not affect the individual provinces. The net result was that only gradually was the franchise extended to women beyond the federal level. In May 1922, when Prince Edward Island gave its female population the right to vote and hold office, woman suffrage had been achieved throughout Canada with two notable exceptions.* In New Brunswick, where women were allowed to vote in 1919, they had to wait until 1934, 15 years, before they were eligible to be elected to the provincial legislature.[2] Still further behind, however, was the French-speaking province of Quebec, where women could not vote or hold office until 1940. (It should be remembered that in France itself women were not enfranchised until the end of World War II.) This reluctance to give women full civil rights is illustrated by the fact that only in 1972 were the first women from Quebec elected to the House of Commons in Ottawa. On the other hand, four of the 12 women elected in 1979 represent Quebec districts.

As in the United States, the western provinces led the way. Manitoba, Saskatchewan, and Alberta took the plunge in that order in 1916, followed by British Columbia in 1917. Although giving women the right to vote also extended to them the right to be elected, women were not immediately sent to the House of Commons. Not until 1963 did a woman from Manitoba take her seat in the House of

---

*In 1922, Newfoundland was an independent dominion and not part of Canada, which it joined in 1949. Women in Newfoundland achieved the franchise in 1925. Although one woman, Lady Squires, sat in the Newfoundland House of Assembly from 1928 until 1932, Newfoundland is the only part of Canada never yet to have been represented in Parliament in Ottawa by a woman (Catherine L. Cleverdon, The Woman Suffrage Movement in Canada [Toronto: University of Toronto Press, 1974], p. 212).

TABLE 5.1

Woman Suffrage in Canada

	Right to Vote	Right to Hold Office	First Woman Elected to House of Commons	Number of Women Elected to Commons by 1979
Alberta	1916	1916	1941	1
British Columbia	1917	1917	1965	6
Manitoba	1916	1916	1963	1
New Brunswick	1919	1934	1964	1
Newfoundland	1925	1925	n.a.[a]	0
Nova Scotia	1918	1918	1974	1
Ontario	1917	1919	1921	13
Prince Edward Island	1922	1922	1961	1
Quebec	1940	1940	1972	5
Saskatchewan	1916	1916	1940	3
Northwest Territories			1962	1
Yukon	1917–18	1920	1935	1
Dominion of Canada	1917–18[b]	1920	1921	34[c]

[a]Not applicable.

[b]Female relatives of members of the armed forces were granted voting rights in 1917. These rights were extended to all women in 1918.

[c]By the time the 1979 election was over, 33 women had held membership in the House. Jewett had to be counted twice, since she has sat for Ontario as well as most recently for British Columbia.

Source: Part of the material in the first two columns is taken from Catherine L. Cleverdon, The Woman Suffrage Movement in Canada (Toronto: University of Toronto Press, 1974).

Commons, and then it was only for two years. Saskatchewan and
Alberta did not wait quite that long, electing their first female
M.P.s in 1940 and 1941, respectively.

A milestone was reached when Ontario allowed woman to vote
in 1917 and to be elected in 1919. This most important province
had been in the forefront of the struggle for equality for women.
The developments in the city of Toronto in a sense provided a pat-
tern. Women were first allowed to vote for school board trustees.
The right to participate in municipal elections followed. Usually
unmarried women were enfranchised first, because a voting wife
was said to be disrupting the peace at home! By 1884, there was
full municipal franchise in Toronto, and a few years later the first
woman was elected to the school board.

Various groups championed the cause of woman suffrage
throughout Canada, with the Women's Christian Temperance Union
playing a leading part. Labor was generally positive as were many
Protestant clergymen, while the Catholic church, especially in
Quebec, was opposed.

The wartime circumstances that in Ontario and elsewhere led
to increased female participation in the economic life of the country persuaded a previously reluctant government to advocate the extension of the franchise to women. This was achieved in 1917. At
the same time, women became eligible to vote in municipal elections.

However, while getting the vote was one thing, being able to
sit in the elective body was quite another. The government was not
about to be rushed into such a venture, and it took another two years
of agitation before the situation was remedied.

In 1921, Agnes Macphail became the first woman to enter the
House of Commons. She held office for almost two decades.
Macphail was followed by 12 others also from Ontario, by far the
largest contingent from any part of the country. Except for the
decade between 1940 and 1950 and a four-year period between 1968
and 1972, there was always at least one woman from Ontario in the
House of Commons. Before Parliament was dissolved in 1979,
there were four women from Ontario. With one defeated and a new
one elected, the figure remained unchanged by the election. However, as previously mentioned, the Quebec contingent, while arriving late, was brought up to four in 1979, thus equaling Ontario in
the number of women sent to the House of Commons.

Quebec had come a long way. The conservative attitude of
the Catholic church was a hindering factor in early years, as was
the fact that women in France did not vote until 1944. Since federal
laws applied to the whole country, women in Quebec could vote in
federal elections and even be candidates themselves, which happened
as early as 1930. But provincial elections were another matter.

Only in 1927 was an attempt made to give women voting rights in the province. It failed, as did efforts allowing women to practice law. The prevailing attitude can perhaps best be illustrated by Catherine Cleverdon's mention of a bill that reached the Quebec legislature in 1935 that would have prohibited women from working anywhere but in homes, fields, and forests. This proposal was actually supported by 16 of 63 legislators voting![3] Only in 1940 were women in Quebec finally fully enfranchised—on the fourteenth try.

Most important was the action by the dominion Parliament itself. Franchise bills in the 1880s were concerned with females, at least widows and unmarried females, but no emancipation took place. Indeed, a federal act in 1885 defined a person as "a male person, including an Indian and excluding a person of Mongolian or Chinese race."[4]

Eventually, however, the winds of change were irresistible. The Military Voters Act of 1917 dealt with voting rights of all British subjects in the armed forces, and this included some women, especially nurses. Later that year, female relatives of servicemen were enfranchised. The new law specifically stated:

> Every female person shall be capable of voting and qualified to vote at a Dominion election in any province or in the Yukon Territory, who, being a British subject and qualified as to age, race and residence, as required in the case of a male person in such a province or in the Yukon Territory, as the case may be, is the wife, widow, mother, sister or daughter of any person, male or female, living or dead, who is serving or has served without Canada in any of the military forces, or within or without Canada in any of the naval forces, of Canada or Great Britain in the present war.[5]

The principle was now established that some women could indeed vote, and extending it to all could not be long delayed. This was done on January 1, 1919. Henceforth, "every female person" that had the same qualifications as a male person was treated equally for election purposes. But not quite. Women still could not be elected, and it took another measure a few months later to remedy that situation.

There were still some efforts to put the clock back. Thus, in 1922 a proposal was introduced in the Senate that would have disenfranchised unmarried women under the age of 30. It failed but received 19 votes out of 52 votes cast.[6]

Canadian women have been eligible for membership in the Canadian House of Commons since the end of World War I. This puts them in a position similar to the women in Britain and in the United States. If one maintains that far too few women entered the British House of Commons and the U.S. Congress, one finds the Canadian situation even more dismal. In the six decades since Canadian women were granted full citizen rights on the federal level, 18 general elections have been held. The size of membership in the House of Commons varied between 235 and 282, and of those only a very small number were women. A total of 33 women have been elected up to 1979. From 1921 until 1935, from 1945 until 1949, and from 1968 until 1972, only one woman sat in the House, and there was even a brief period between the general election of 1949 and a by-election in 1950 when no woman was in the House of Commons. The general election of 1979 resulted in an all-time high of 12, the first time a two-digit figure was reached. But this still represents little more than 4 percent of the total membership.

WOMEN MEMBERS OF THE CANADIAN HOUSE OF COMMONS

The Parliament of 1921

The fourteenth general election in Canada took place in 1921. With women voting for the first time, the number of votes cast jumped from 1,885,000 to beyond the 3 million mark.[7] Four women offered themselves as candidates, and one won.[8] Agnes Macphail (1890-1954), whose cradle stood in a log cabin, came from a poor family and was of Scottish background.[9] Born and bred in the country, she identified with the rural farm scene throughout her life, whether as schoolteacher or as member of Parliament. She became involved in farm organizations and joined the United Farmers of Ontario (UFO), on whose behalf she contested and won the rural constituency of South-East Grey in Ontario province. She was 31 years old at the time.

The Parliaments of 1925, 1926, and 1930

Macphail was successful in the next three general elections and was again the only woman to win. While affiliated with the Progressives, she was, nevertheless, an Independent in every sense of the word and championed such causes as agricultural improvements and prison reforms. She wanted equality for women but not special privileges. "I think women just want to be individuals, no more and no less."[10] She developed expertise in budgetary and defense matters. In 1929, she was part of an all-party delegation to the League of Nations at Geneva. When she was put on a committee dealing with welfare, women, and children, she protested because this was "where they stow women away."[11] She wanted to discuss disarmament, and when informed that no woman had ever been on the pertinent committee before, she suggested, "Then we may as well make a start."[12] She won the assignment. Her biographers report that on several occasions she came close to becoming a cabinet member, but Macphail either was unwilling to pay the political price, or her affiliates were unable to come up with the necessary parliamentary majority. In 1940, a number of factors, including a deteriorating grass-roots organization, less of a need for an Independent in times of war, and a snowstorm that kept many of her supporters away from the polls, led to her defeat. She contested a by-election without success. She did serve for several years as member of the provincial legislature in Ontario and was apparently about to be named to the Canadian Senate when she died.[13]

The Parliament of 1935

In 1935, Macphail once more won reelection. But she no longer was the only woman in the House of Commons. With 20 women competing in the general election, one more was elected. Martha Louise Black (1866-1957) was a Conservative from the Yukon Territory. Born in Chicago, she had gone to the Yukon as part of the gold rush and eventually became an expert on Yukon flowers. Her speeches and other activities won her membership in the Royal Geographical Society and the Order of the British Empire (O.B.E.). Her husband reportedly had occupied the seat "as though by divine rights," and it was said of her that she was "a lady of considerable spunk and talent but with no knowledge of public affairs."[14] However, she did show special concern for the Yukon, pensions, and unemployment.[15] She stepped in for her husband when he was too ill to run and stepped out again five years later upon his recovery and resumption of his parliamentary career.

The Parliament of 1940

In 1940, with Black's retirement and Macphail's defeat, it fell to another woman, Dorise Nielsen (1902-), to represent her sex in Parliament. Nielsen had emigrated from her native England to Saskatchewan. A schoolteacher before her marriage, she became involved in farming with her husband. At first her political ties were with the Cooperative Commonwealth Federation (CCF), but it was under the Unity or United Reform party label that she entered the House of Commons. Incidentally, it was that party that offered Macphail a chance to return to Parliament in a by-election in Saskatchewan, a contest she lost by 741 votes.[16] Nielsen lost her bid for reelection in 1945, and the National Library of Canada publication of 1975 lists her as at present living in China.[17]

However, Nielsen was not to remain the only woman in that Parliament. The Liberal member for Edmonton East in Alberta had died, and in a by-election in June 1941 his widow, Cora Casselman (1888-1964), was chosen to take his place. She was the holder of a university degree, had taught high school, and was a nurse during World War I. As member of Parliament, Casselman was an advisor to the Canadian delegation of the International Labour Organization in Philadelphia and a delegate to the United Nations Conference in San Francisco. But none of these accomplishments could prevent her defeat in the general election of 1945.

The Parliament of 1945

The only woman to enter Parliament in 1945 was Gladys Strum (1906-) from the CCF, who represented a Saskatchewan district. Married and a schoolteacher, she was widely traveled and had newspaper experience. She had previously unsuccessfully attempted to get into the provincial legislature. In Ottawa, Strum took a special interest in agriculture, housing, family allowances, and similar matters. She lost her bid for reelection four years later.

The Parliament of 1949

With Strum's defeat and no new woman elected in 1949, there was a gap in female representation in Parliament. Once more, the House of Commons consisted exclusively of males. However, the situation changed in May 1950, when a by-election in Ontario resulted in victory for Ellen Fairclough (1905-). She was an accountant and had served on the Hamilton City Council. She had unsuccessfully contested the seat in 1949, but after she won it, she was able to retain it for several elections. It was not until 1963 that she was defeated, and her service of 13 years is surpassed only by the record set by Macphail. Unlike Macphail, however, she belonged to a party that from time to time has had a majority in Parliament and thus been in charge of the government. A progressive Conservative, Fairclough had represented her country at the United Nations and at NATO meetings and in 1957 became Canada's first female cabinet member, holding successively the positions of secretary of state of Canada, minister of citizenship and immigration, and postmaster general.

The Parliament of 1953

For three years, Fairclough was the only woman among 262 members of Parliament. Then lightning struck, for, in addition to her own reelection, three other women were successful. They were all members of the two major parties. Indeed, with the notable exception of Grace MacInnis a decade later, only Progressive Conservative and Liberal women were able to secure entrance into the House of Commons until the 1979 general election.

Although 1953 was a Liberal year in Canada, only one of the three female newcomers was a Liberal. This was Marie Ann Shipley (1899–). She was a civil servant and after her marriage became active in school board and municipal affairs. Like all the other female M.P.s in the 1953 Parliament, she represented an Ontario constituency. She was defeated for reelection in 1957, and another bid for Parliament five years later was also unsuccessful.

On the Progressive Conservative side was Sybil Bennett (1904–1956). She was a lawyer who had previously attempted to enter Parliament. However, her tenure was short; she died while still a member.

The other Conservative newcomer was Margaret Aitken (1908–). She was a journalist by profession. Capital punishment, education, and pensions were among her main interests.[18] She was reelected in 1957 and 1958 but defeated in 1962.

The Parliament of 1957

The general election of 1957 brought about a minority Progressive Conservative administration. No new women were elected, leaving only Fairclough and Aitken as the female "survivors."

The Parliament of 1958

After taking his cause to the country in a general election, Prime Minister John Diefenbaker was given a huge majority in the House of Commons, although he soon ran into political difficulties. The Parliament of 1958 lasted four years. Again, Fairclough and Aitken were the only women to be returned in the general election. However, three more women were elected in by-elections, bringing the total to an unprecedented five.

First to arrive was Jean Wadds (1920-). She was married to a Progressive Conservative member of Parliament, and after his death, she contested a by-election for his Ontario seat. She won and was subsequently reelected three times. She was a delegate to the UN General Assembly for several months and served as parliamentary secretary to the minister of national health and welfare. In 1964, she remarried and became Jean Wadds, having first entered politics as Jean Casselman. She remained in Parliament until defeated in 1968 after ten years of service.

In 1960, a Liberal woman from Niagara Falls, Ontario, Julia LaMarsh (1924-), entered Parliament. A lawyer, she did not remain a "back-bencher" very long. In April 1963, she became a member of the cabinet as minister of national health and welfare. Two years later, she was appointed secretary of state, a post she occupied until her voluntary retirement in 1968, after which she remained active in the fields of writing, reporting, and teaching.

Margaret MacDonald (1910-), a teacher and secretary before her marriage, succeeded her late husband in Parliament. A Progressive Conservative, she provided Prince Edward Island with its first and so far only female M.P. She was reelected in 1962 but defeated the following year.

The Parliament of 1962

In 1962, Prime Minister Diefenbaker received a mere plurality in the House of Commons and had to form a minority government. All five sitting female M.P.s sought reelection, all but Aitken succeeding. The number was brought up to five again, however, because Isabel Hardie contested a seat held until his death by her husband, a Liberal from the Northwest Territories. This was the first time that this area had had a woman M.P., and no other has been elected thus far. In the general election the following year, Hardie was defeated.*

---

*Hardie is the only former Canadian female M.P. for whom no birth date seems available.

The Parliament of 1963

In 1963, the Liberals just missed getting control of the House of Commons. Among the women, only Wadds and LaMarsh were returned. But two new ones came in. Both were Liberals, both had unsuccessfully run for election the previous year, and both were defeated in 1965. Margaret Konantz (1899-1967) was elected from Winnipeg. "Active in volunteer work throughout her life,"[19] she was awarded the O.B.E. and represented Canada on several UN bodies. While in Parliament, she paid special attention to the Canadian flag and the Bank of Western Canada.

Pauline Jewett (1922-) represented an Ontario constituency. She studied at Radcliffe, Queen's University, and the London School of Economics and became a professor of political science and a university president. She won her seat in 1963 by 505 votes and lost it again two years later by a 563-vote margin. But this was not the end of her political career. In 1979, she staged a comeback. She had switched parties and was now very active in New Democratic ranks. Running in a district in British Columbia, she was successful in the election that ended the Pierre Trudeau regime. She thus became the first and thus far the only woman in Canadian history to return to Parliament after an earlier defeat.

In 1964, two by-elections resulted in two widows' succeeding to seats previously held by their late husbands. Eloise Jones (1917-) took her place on the Progressive Conservative benches. She was a physician and psychiatrist who had married a lawyer. Jones served in Parliament from a Saskatchewan district for a year and did not seek reelection in 1965.

The other newcomer was Margaret Rideout (1923-), New Brunswick's one and only female M.P. to date. She, however, did seek reelection and won, remaining in Parliament until 1968 when she did not stand again. She was a Liberal and for more than two years held the office of parliamentary secretary to the minister of health and welfare.

The Parliament of 1965

The 1965 election, like the one two years earlier, presented Canada with a Liberal minority government. Konantz and Jewett were defeated, and Jones was not a candidate, leaving Wadds, LaMarsh, and Rideout as the remaining women in Parliament. One newcomer joined their ranks, Grace MacInnis (1905-). She and her husband were prominent in the Cooperative Commonwealth Federation, which later became the New Democratic Party (NDP). Angus

MacInnis was a member of the Canadian Parliament for over 25 years until his retirement in 1957. His wife served in the provincial legislature and unsuccessfully attempted to join her husband in the House of Commons in 1949. She won, however, in 1965 in his old constituency of Vancouver South in the province of British Columbia and was reelected twice until she retired in 1974.

The Parliament of 1968

Not only was MacInnis the first minor-party female M.P. in two decades; from 1968 until 1972, she was the only woman in the House of Commons. The 1968 election was a triumph for the Liberal party and its newly chosen leader, Pierre Trudeau. It was a disaster for female representation, with MacInnis alone preventing the House of Commons from reverting to its all-male status.

The Parliament of 1972

In 1972, however, she was joined by four more women, one Progressive Conservative and three Liberals, even though Trudeau's Liberal government could barely muster a plurality over the Progressive Conservatives. What made the addition of the three Liberal women M.P.s even more remarkable under these circumstances was that all three came from Quebec, which, until that time, had gone without any female representation in the House of Commons.

Youngest among the newcomers was Monique Begin (1936-). Born in Italy, of a French-Canadian father and a Belgian mother, she is a sociologist, having studied in Montreal, Paris, and at McGill University. She is interested in broadcasting, is a member of the External and National Defence Committee, and is also concerned with abortion and the status of women. She was reelected in 1974 and became consecutively parliamentary secretary to the secretary of state for external affairs, minister of national revenue, and minister of national health and welfare. In 1979, she was able to retain her seat in Parliament.

The second female member from Quebec was Albanie Morin (1921-1976). Both she and her husband had been strongly identified with the Liberal party. Her election to Parliament in 1972 was followed by her reelection two years later. Illness forced her to be absent from Parliament for quite a while before her death in 1976. She was only the second female member to die in office. Jeanne Sauvé (1922-) was also new to the House of Commons in 1972. Married to a former federal minister of forests and rural development, she is a journalist and has been described as "magnetic, taut . . . beautifully coiffed and garbed" and as possessing "class."[20] Her leading positions on numerous committees and commissions were recognized upon her arrival in the House of Commons. She was appointed minister of state for science and technology and, after her reelection in 1974, minister of the environment. She later became minister of communications. She was successful in retaining her seat in 1979.

The Progressive Conservative newcomer in 1972 was Flora MacDonald (1926-). Her election from Kingston, Ontario, was the culmination of many years of party work, both on the provincial and on the federal level. MacDonald was associated with Queen's University, worked on studies dealing with political behavior, and acted as consultant when electoral expenses and the status of women were examined on the federal level. In 1975, she made a bid for the leadership of her party that, had it been successful, would have made her prime minister a few years later. Although she failed in that endeavor, it practically assured her of an important position upon her party's next victory. After the 1979 election in which she retained her seat, Prime Minister Joe Clark named her minister of external affairs, another very significant "first" for a woman.

The Parliament of 1974

When the thirtieth general election was held in 1974, MacInnis retired, but the four women of the "class of 1972" were all reelected. In addition, five new female M.P.s entered Parliament. They were all Liberals, helping Prime Minister Trudeau to his working majority. The nine women amounted to only 3.41 percent of the 264-member body. Nevertheless, this was an unprecedented high for Canada. Another woman was to join them in 1976 as a result of a by-election, but her election occurred two weeks after the death of Morin, so that a two-digit figure was not yet reached.

Ursula Appoloni (1929-) was born in Ireland, immigrated to Canada, then lived in Rome where she married. On her return to Canada, she and her husband became active in the Liberal party. She won her Ontario constituency by defeating NDP leader David Lewis. Five years later, she was returned to Parliament.

Also Irish-born was another Ontario Liberal, Aideen Nicholson (1927-). Educated at Trinity College and the London School of Economics, she worked as a psychiatric social worker and taught. After an unsuccessful attempt to enter Parliament in 1972, she won her seat two years later. Nicholson was named parliamentary secretary to the minister of supply and services and was able to win reelection in 1979.

Until 1974, Nova Scotia had been without a woman representative, but this was remedied when Liberal Coline Campbell (1940–) was elected. She had taught school, added a law degree to her arts and education degrees, and entered into legal practice before coming to Ottawa. She was named parliamentary secretary to the minister of national health and welfare. In 1979, she also won reelection.

The remaining two newcomers both represented British Columbia constituencies. Iona Campagnolo (1932–) worked in broadcasting, was a school board member and president, and served as city alderwoman. After her election to Parliament, she became parliamentary secretary to the minister of Indian affairs and northern development and then minister of state for fitness and amateur sports. The opposition called her "Minister for Gambling" since she was in charge of the national lottery,[21] which is quite a controversial subject. The relative unpopularity of the Trudeau administration in 1979 contributed to her defeat at that time.

Simma Holt (1922–) was another Liberal, representing a Vancouver district. She is a journalist and writer. Holt has appeared on radio and television and has often commented on social issues, including legalization of soft drugs, which she opposes. She was unsuccessful in 1979 in retaining her seat.

The one Progressive Conservative newcomer to the 1974 Parliament entered the House in October 1976 from Ontario as the result of a by-election. Jean Pigott (1924–) had been active on the Council of Christians and Jews, the Hospital Planning Council, and the Health Council. She was unable to secure reelection in 1979.

The Parliament of 1979

The 1979 election marked the end of the Liberal administration of Prime Minister Trudeau, whose party received fewer seats in Parliament than did the Progressive Conservatives (though outpolling their principal opponents by 4 percent). As already indicated, two Liberal and one Conservative female M.P.s were forced into retirement by the voters. Six of the incumbents won reelection. In addition, Jewett returned after an absence of 15 years, representing a new province and a new party, and five entirely new faces appeared among the women in Ottawa, bringing their total to an all-time high of 12. The parties were evenly represented among the newcomers. Pat Carney from British Columbia and Diane Stratas from Ontario came to the Progressive Conservative side, Therese Killens and Celine Hervieux-Payette from Montreal both contributed to the strong Liberal tide that was sweeping Quebec but no other province, and Margaret Mitchell joined Jewett in representing the New Democratic party from British Columbia.

In 1972, there had been 71 female candidates and five were elected (7 percent). In 1974, 137 women competed and nine were successful (6.57 percent). In 1979, out of 195 female candidates, 12 won (6.15 percent). Having more women candidates obviously does not guarantee success. What is important is whether or not they are in a contest where they have at least a fighting chance. Table 5.2 indicates the party affiliations of the female candidates in the 1979 general election.

TABLE 5.2

Women Candidates in the Canadian Election of 1979

Party	Number of Candidates	Number Elected	Percent Elected
Marxist-Leninist	48	0	0
New Democrat	46	2	4.35
Liberal	21	7	33.33
Communist	19	0	0
Progressive Conservative	14	3	21.43
Rhinoceros	14	0	0
Union Populaire	11	0	0
Libertarian	10	0	0
Social Credit	7	0	0
Independent	5	0	0
Total	195	12	6.15

Source: Canadian Wire Service.

It is obvious that the two major parties do not put up enough female candidates. Their rate of success is fairly high; every third female Liberal candidate won as did every fifth female Progressive Conservative. More women candidates put up by the major parties in constituencies that are not hopeless might well lead to more women being elected.

DISCUSSION

Although the newly reached figure of 12 out of 282 compares favorably with the situation in Britain and the United States, it is still far too small. Moreover, in six out of 18 parliaments since 1921, there has been only one woman at a time, and the maximum number was five or six until the early 1970s. Only 33 women have been elected so far. One served 19 years; one, 13 years; two, nine years; one, eight years; and the rest fewer than this. The 21 women who have completed their parliamentary service have together accumulated 120 years in the House of Commons, for an average stay in office of 5.7 years, a figure much lower than in the countries previously discussed. Of those who were in Parliament after the 1979 election, three have served seven years; three, five years; five are newcomers; and one had previously served two years. The latter, as mentioned before, is the only female M.P. to stage a successful comeback, an event equally rare in the United States but quite common in Britain.

There have been seven cases where wives replaced their husbands. Such events occurred frequently until 1964. Indeed, all seven were among the first 17 women elected. Since 1964, not one woman came in as her husband's replacement. Eight women first entered the House of Commons as a result of by-elections, five of whom were widows competing for their late husbands' seats.

As can be imagined in a system where the political pendulum swings from one party to another in parliamentary elections and where the government is tied to a majority in the House of Commons, defeat is a common occurrence for individual members. Two-thirds of the female M.P.s who are no longer in Parliament had their careers terminated in that way—which is a very high proportion. Five retired of their own volition, two died in office, and 15 were defeated. From these statistics, one can conclude that rather than having many women occupy safe seats, a large number seem to represent swing districts, where the national party fortunes may well make or break the incumbents.

In terms of party affiliations, the Liberals accounted for 17 or 50 percent of all female M.P.s. The Conservatives elected only one-third or 11, even counting Black, who in one source is listed as Independent Conservative (with stress on the first word).[22] The CCF and its successor, the NDP, supplied the remaining six, which is quite a lot for such a small party. It has been noted that after the 1979 election, which left the Progressive Conservatives with a plurality in the House of Commons, only three of the women M.P.s supported the Clark administration. Seven others were members of the Liberal opposition, and two more belonged to the New Democratic party.

Since Ontario possesses about one-third of all the seats in the House of Commons, it is not surprising that 13 of all the female M.P.s came from that province (see Table 5.1). With the metropolitan center in Toronto and other fairly large towns, Ontario claims to be progressive as far as the acceptance of women in politics is concerned. This trait is apparently especially noticeable among voters of Jewish and English backgrounds.[23] Quebec, the second most populated province, made a late start in sending women to Ottawa. However, it seems determined to rectify the situation and between 1972 and 1979 has elected five women to the House of Commons. British Columbia (which in 1968 had 23 seats in the House of Commons as compared to 88 from Ontario and 74 from Quebec) is showing its pioneer spirit by having elected a total of six female M.P.s. (In 1979, two of its incumbents were defeated, but three others were elected.) Saskatchewan has been represented by three women in the past. All the other provinces and territories have at one time or another sent a woman to Ottawa, with the single exception of Newfoundland, which thus far has not chosen a woman for Parliament.

With data on the ages of the women M.P.s not complete, we find that of the 27 women about whom we have information, the youngest (and first) was 31 years old when she initially was elected. Six others were under 40, 11 were between 41 and 50, seven were between 51 and 60, and two were 64 and 69 years old, respectively.

Considering that only 33 women have sat in the House of Commons, it is remarkable that as many as ten have achieved governmental positions.* Fairclough in 1957 became the first woman to hold cabinet rank, and it is recorded with apparent pride[24] that in 1958 she was acting prime minister for two days! Four women (Wadds, Rideout, Campbell, and Nicholson) never did advance beyond the office of parliamentary secretary, which is a position below cabinet level. Bégin and Campagnolo started in that somewhat lowly post and advanced to full ministerial rank. LaMarsh and Sauvé both held high office under different Liberal administrations, and in 1979 Clark made Flora MacDonald minister of external affairs. These may not be many positions compared with the number held by men, but they must be viewed in connection with the few women available as members of Parliament.

---

*Excluded from our discussion are members of the Senate, who are appointed but are also eligible to be named to the government.

TABLE 5.3

Women Members of the Canadian House of Commons

M.P.	Dates	Party	Province	In Office	Reason(s) for Departure
Agnes Macphail	1890–1954	UFO/CCF	Ontario	1921–40	defeated
Martha L. Black[a]	1866–1957	Conservative	Yukon	1935–40	retired
Dorise Nielsen	1902–	Unity (New Dem.)	Saskatchewan	1940–45	defeated
Cora Casselman[a]	1888–1964	Liberal	Alberta	1941–45	defeated
Gladys Strum	1906–	CCF	Saskatchewan	1945–49	defeated
Ellen Fairclough	1905–	Prog. Cons.	Ontario	1950–63	defeated
Marie Ann Shipley	1899–	Liberal	Ontario	1953–57	defeated
Sybil Bennett	1904–1956	Prog. Cons.	Ontario	1953–56	died
Margaret Aitken	1908–	Prog. Cons.	Ontario	1953–62	defeated
Jean Casselman Wadds[a]	1920–	Prog. Cons.	Ontario	1958–68	defeated
Julia LaMarsh	1924–	Liberal	Ontario	1960–68	retired
Margaret MacDonald[a]	1910–[b]	Prog. Cons.	Prince Edward Island	1961–63	defeated
Isable Hardie[a]		Liberal	Northwest Territory	1962–63	defeated
Pauline Jewett	1922–	Liberal	Ontario	1963–65	defeated
		NDP	British Columbia	1979–	n.a.
Margaret Konantz	1899–1967	Liberal	Manitoba	1963–65	defeated
Eloise Jones[a]	1917–	Prog. Cons.	Saskatchewan	1964–65	retired

Name	Born/Years	Party	Province	Term	Status
Margaret Rideout[a]	1923–	Liberal	New Brunswick	1964–68	retired
Grace MacInnis	1905–	NDP	British Columbia	1965–74	retired
Monique Bégin	1936–	Liberal	Quebec	1972–	n.a.
Albanie Morin	1921–1976	Liberal	Quebec	1972–76	died
Jeanne Sauvé	1922–	Liberal	Quebec	1972–	n.a.
Flora MacDonald	1926–	Prog. Cons.	Ontario	1972–	n.a.
Ursula Appoloni	1929–	Liberal	Ontario	1974–	n.a.
Aideen Nicholson	1927–	Liberal	Ontario	1974–	n.a.
Coline Campbell	1940–	Liberal	Nova Scotia	1974–	n.a.
Iona Campagnolo	1932–	Liberal	British Columbia	1974–79	defeated
Simma Holt	1922–	Liberal	British Columbia	1974–79	defeated
Jean Pigott	1924–	Prog. Cons.	Ontario	1976–79	defeated
Pat Carney	—	Prog. Cons.	British Columbia	1979–	n.a.
Diane Stratas	—	Prog. Cons.	Ontario	1979–	n.a.
Therese Killens	—	Liberal	Quebec	1979–	n.a.
Celine Hervieux-Payette	—	Liberal	Quebec	1979–	n.a.
Margaret Mitchell	—	NDP	British Columbia	1979–	n.a.

[a]Followed husband into office.
[b]Data not available.

Note: Abbreviations used: UFO, United Farmers of Ontario; CCF, Cooperative Commonwealth Federation; Prog. Cons., Progressive Conservative; NDP, New Democratic Party; n.a., not applicable.

Source: Compiled by the author.

TABLE 5.4

The Canadian House of Commons and Female Members

Election	Number of Women	Names
December 6, 1921	1	Macphail
October 29, 1925	1	Macphail
September 14, 1926	1	Macphail
July 28, 1930	1	Macphail
October 14, 1935	2	Macphail, Black
March 26, 1940	1	Nielsen
By-election	1	Casselman (June 1941)
June 11, 1945	1	Strum
June 27, 1949	0	
By-election	1	Fairclough (May 1950)
August 10, 1953	4	Fairclough, Aitken, Bennett (died November 1956), Shipley
June 10, 1957	2	Fairclough, Aitken
March 31, 1958	2	Fairclough, Aitken
By-elections	3	Wadds (September 1958), LaMarsh (October 1960), MacDonald (May 1961)
June 18, 1962	5	Fairclough, Wadds, LaMarsh, MacDonald, Hardie
April 8, 1963	4	Wadds, LaMarsh, Jewett, Konantz
By-elections	2	Jones (June 1964), Rideout (November 1964)
November 8, 1965	4	Wadds, LaMarsh, Rideout, MacInnis
June 25, 1968	1	MacInnis
October 30, 1972	5	MacInnis, Bégin, F. MacDonald, Sauvé, Morin
July 8, 1974	9	Bégin, F. MacDonald, Sauvé, Morin (died October 1976), Appoloni, Nicholson, Campbell, Campagnolo, Holt
By-election	1	Pigott
May 22, 1979	12	Bégin, F. MacDonald, Sauvé, Appoloni, Nicholson, Campbell, Jewett, Carney, Stratas, Killens, Hervieux-Payette, Mitchell

Note: Unless otherwise indicated, dates in parentheses show when M.P.s entered the House of Commons.

This brings us back to the problem of why there are not more women in the Canadian House of Commons. As elsewhere, there appear to be two major problems. The first has to do with family responsibilities. "This problem of home versus career exists all right," said Jeanne Sauvé. "It's very real. But it has to be solved, and it can be, in a variety of ways. If a woman can't solve it, then she should stay at home."[25] Coming to some sort of an arrangement, frequently with a sympathetic husband, who is as essential to a female politician as an understanding wife is to a male aspirant for office, is often mentioned as a prerequisite for a successful career, especially if the female M.P. has a family that includes small children.

The second major problem concerns the prejudice that women still meet, from males and females alike. Hesitancy to "adopt" a woman as a candidate in a constituency where she stands a good chance to be elected, lack of funds, and, after election, the indignity of being treated as a curiosity item are part of that problem. Macphail reports: "The misery of being under observation . . . is what I remember most vividly. . . . I was a curiosity and stared at whenever I could be seen in the House. . . . Eating was the worst, it may be they thought I would eat peas with my knife or cool my tea in my saucer. . . ."[26]

Canada's first female member of Parliament did not want any special privileges. She wanted equal treatment for men and women alike, nothing more and nothing less. At a party convention in 1933, a woman delegate spoke in favor of having a woman on each committee. Macphail retorted:

> All I have to say is this. I'm sick and tired of all this "woman" business. In all the time I've been in the House of Commons, I've never asked for anything on the ground that I was a woman. If I didn't deserve it on my own merit, I didn't want it! That's all I have to say.[27]

And with this, she stalked out of the meeting. (For a concise listing of the women members of the Canadian House of Commons, see Tables 5.3 and 5.4.)

NOTES

1. Catherine L. Cleverdon, The Woman Suffrage Movement in Canada (Toronto: University of Toronto Press, 1974), p. 136.

2. Ibid., p. 197.

3. Ibid., p. 246.
4. Ibid., p. 208.
5. Ibid., p. 124.
6. Ibid., p. 139.
7. J. M. Beck, Pendulum of Power (Scarborough, Ont.: Prentice Hall of Canada, 1968), pp. 148, 161.
8. Cleverdon, op. cit., p. 138.
9. For details on Agnes Macphail's life, see Margaret Stewart and Doris French, Ask No Quarter (Toronto: Longman, Green, 1959).
10. Ibid., p. 69.
11. Ibid., p. 150.
12. Ibid.
13. Ibid., p. 301.
14. Ibid., p. 234.
15. Gwynneth Evans, comp., and Marion C. Wilson, ed., Women in Federal Politics: A Bio-Bibliography (Ottawa: National Library of Canada, 1975), p. 27.
16. Stewart and French, op. cit., p. 260.
17. Evans and Wilson, op. cit., p. 29.
18. Ibid., p. 37.
19. Ibid., p. 49.
20. Globe Gazette, October 19, 1972.
21. New York Times, July 13, 1978.
22. Evans and Wilson, op. cit., p. 78.
23. According to a Toronto woman politician in private conversation several years ago.
24. In an undated handout by the Canadian Consulate in Chicago.
25. Globe Gazette, October 19, 1972.
26. Canada Today/Aujourd'hui, June 1975, p. 6.
27. Stewart and French, op. cit., p. 170.

6
THE GERMAN PARLIAMENT

HISTORY

Turning now to Germany, we can see a number of differences in its historic and constitutional background, differences that have left their impact on the position of women in Parliament. Unlike the Anglo-Saxon countries, where the franchise for women was yet another step on the road toward full democracy, in Germany woman suffrage and democracy arrived at the same time. Moreover, when universal adult suffrage was adopted, it operated under a system that stressed not the individual candidate in his effort to be the "first past the post" but a party list drawn up by the leadership of the party. While the number of votes received by the party determined the number of candidates elected, the place on the list had a lot to do with the electability of the candidate. This put the successful candidate at the mercy of his party to a far greater extent than in the Anglo-Saxon countries.

Once admitted, women in the legislatures of North America and Britain became more and more accepted, and this acceptance was part of a continuous and continuing process. In Germany, however, there was a definite break in this development. It came in 1933 with the end of the Weimar Republic. For the next 12 years, Hitler reigned supreme, with the one-party Reichstag called upon merely to give rousing receptions to the tirades of the Führer. After the latter's demise, another four years passed before nationwide elections could once again take place after all the upheaval and destruction caused by dictatorship and war. When the first democratic Parliament reassembled after 16 years, it was a representative body not of the whole of Germany, which Hitler had taken over in January 1933, but only of the three Western zones of occupation that gradually became independent of Allied control. It should be noted that Austria, which will be discussed in the next chapter, has experienced similar developments, except that the dimensions of Austria after World War II remained unchanged from what they were after World War I.

When Germany was unified by Bismarck in 1871, democracy was far from his mind. He had originally won his position as principal advisor to the king of Prussia by helping the monarch overcome restrictive efforts by the elected legislature on military spending. Throughout the days of the empire (1871-1918), the Reichstag played a relatively minor part. Its approval was necessary for new legislation, and it could criticize the administration, but it could not force the government to resign or to change its policy. Thus, the rulers of Germany were able to ignore completely the famous "Peace Resolution" in 1917, in which the overwhelming majority of the Reichstag called for a negotiated peace without annexations at a time when the fortunes of war were still seemingly on Germany's side.

Nevertheless, it had gradually become clear that determined opposition in the Reichstag could in fact make the government's position untenable and thus bring about its resignation, even if during World War I neither government nor Reichstag had much influence over the military high command.[1] The Reichstag was elected by all men above the age of 25 except those on active military duty at the time of the election. The districts were originally set up with about 100,000 people per representative on an equal basis. However, they had not been reapportioned in the 47 years the empire existed. Thus, by 1912 there were 300,000 voters in one constituency and a mere 12,000 in another.[2]

All this changed with the establishment of the Weimar Republic in 1919. The Reichstag now became not only the law-making chamber but also the representative body of the sovereign people. As such, it exercised control over the government, which it could dismiss at will.[3] Because of commitments to democratic principles, the decision was made as early as mid-November 1918 that voting rights should belong to all men and, for the first time, also to all women over the age of 20. Any voter, regardless of sex, was entitled to be a candidate if over 25 years old.[4] No woman had previously sat in the national legislature, but in the election of 1919, 8.5 percent of the 423 representatives were women, and the figure increased to 9.7 percent through the filling of vacancies by the time the body was dissolved the following year.

Woman suffrage was not achieved overnight in Germany. Demands for voting rights for women had been overshadowed by other

requests for equality that were often of far greater immediate importance to the people than the right to participate in elections.
The extent to which women could play a part in economic life; the right to work and the scale of pay; the protection of working women; their place in trade, commerce, and even the professions; the degree to which educational facilities were available to them—all these and others seemed to be more pressing issues than that of voting privileges. Great injustices existed that left a married woman legally entirely dependent on her husband and that set very clear double standards in the event of divorce. Only when protests in the 1890s brought no results did women turn to demands for suffrage as a remedy, rather than as an end in itself.[5]

When the voting rights were accorded to women, it was apparently quite unexpected.[6] It took a law in 1908 to allow women to participate in public meetings and political associations on an equal basis with men.[7] Until then, women had to sit in a segregated room if they wished to attend such gatherings.[8] There were some organizations advocating woman suffrage. Of the political parties, the Social Democrats were most interested in achieving equality in this as in other spheres of life. Their party program in 1875 called for "general equal and direct suffrage with secret and obligatory voting for all citizens over 20 years of age," a compromise after the phrase "the right to vote for citizens of both sexes" proposed by August Bebel had been rejected by 62 votes to 55. At that conference a warning was issued that women, due to their "inadequate education," might well support reactionary candidates.[9] The party conference in 1891 did support equal suffrage "for all citizens of the Reich over twenty years of age without distinction as to sex,"[10] and in 1894 the Social Democrats attempted to get a law to that effect adopted by the Reichstag but failed.[11] It was therefore quite natural that when the Social Democrats were in positions of leadership at the end of World War I, woman suffrage was finally enacted and more than half of the female contingent in the first prewar national assembly were Social Democrats.

We have already mentioned that Germany adopted a system of proportional representation. Its purpose was to ensure representation of various shades of opinion on as broad a basis as possible.
In effect, this implied that party was competing against party, not individual against individual. The crucial questions were, first, What percentage of the vote would a party get (for this would decide the number of seats allocated to it)? and, second, In what order did the individual candidates appear on the party list? Saying that more Social Democratic women were elected than women from other parties does not necessarily mean that the others put up fewer women or none at all. It does mean that Social Democrats placed their female candidates into positions where they could also be elected.

Before Hitler put an end to all pretense of democracy in Germany, nine elections took place. The first assembly, in January 1919, was to work on a constitution for the newly established republic. In addition, however, it also had to pass the first measures designed to put the country back on its feet after a devastating war and in the process accept a highly unfavorable and unpopular peace treaty. After that assembly, there were a series of Reichstag elections between 1920 and 1933. From the last one, the Communists were excluded, which made it easier for Hitler to get a law passed giving him unlimited powers. Three more times the German people were called upon to vote for Reichstag deputies, but each time only the Nazi party ran a list of candidates, and each time the sole purpose was to put a popular stamp of approval on Hitler's most recent foreign policy successes. On each of these occasions, the German people responded overwhelmingly and with hardly any opposition at all, particularly since opposition was both futile and highly dangerous. The next time democratic elections were held, Hitler's empire had vanished, the Reich was split in two, the country was occupied (with its former enemies speedily becoming its friends and protectors), and the Reichstag had become the Bundestag in the German Federal Republic in the West and the Volkskammer in the Communist-controlled German Democratic Republic in the East.

WOMEN MEMBERS OF THE NATIONAL ASSEMBLY AND THE REICHSTAG

The National Assembly of 1919

The Nationalversammlung, which was elected on January 19, 1919, and first assembled on February 6, contained 423 members.[12] Of its members, 36 were women, a figure that increased to 41 as the year progressed. The Social Democrats had 163 seats, of which 19 were occupied by women.

Seven of these served only in the National Assembly in 1919-20: Anna Blos (1866-1933), a schoolteacher from Stuttgart; Minna Bollmann (1876-1935), a homemaker (eventually driven to suicide); Else Höfs (born in 1876), a homemaker who became a member of the Prussian Landtag ("state parliament"); Frieda Lührs (1869-1941), a welfare officer from Hanover; Ernestine Lutze (1873-1948), a flower-shop worker from Dresden; Elisabeth Röhl-Kirschmann (1888-1930), a homemaker who also became a member of Prussia's state parliament; and Anna Simon (born in 1862), oldest of the group, an industrial worker and labor union official.

Other Social Democratic women continued as members of the Reichstag. Wilhelmine Eichler (1872-1937), a bookbinder, entered the Reichstag in 1921, after a senior Social Democratic member had died, and served until 1924. She later accepted the Communist label. Elfriede Ryneck (1872-1951), a Berlin homemaker, served until 1924. She then served in the Prussian state parliament from 1925 to 1933. Johanna Tesch (1875-1945), a homemaker, served until 1924. She died in a concentration camp. Wilhelmine Kähler (born in 1864) was a dressmaker from East Prussia. (She represented an area claimed by both Germany and Poland. A referendum was eventually held. Meanwhile, no election took place in 1920. Her mandate was consequently continued until February 20, 1921, when it automatically expired.) Frieda Hauke (born in 1890), a homemaker, also automatically lost her seat in East Prussia in 1922. She was later imprisoned by the Nazis. Minna Schilling (1877-1943) worked in the tobacco industry. She served until 1928 with the exception of the period from May to December in 1924. Johanne Reitze (1878-1949), a homemaker from Hamburg, served until November 1932. She was imprisoned by Hitler for several weeks. Klara Bohm-Schuch (1879-1936), a writer, was long associated with the struggle for equality for women. A one-time editor of her party's magazine for women, Die Gleichheit ("equality"), she served until June 1933.* She was also imprisoned by the Nazis. Antonie Pfülf (1877-1933), a schoolteacher, sat in Parliament from 1919 until 1933, when she committed suicide.

Louise Schroeder (1887-1957), who had worked as a secretary and social worker, also served from 1919 until 1933. She was under police supervision under Hitler. Active in Berlin politics immediately after World War II, Schroeder was at one time the governing mayor of Berlin. She was a member of the Bundestag from 1949 until her death in 1957, thus accumulating 22 years in parliamentary service.

Marie Juchacz (1879-1956), who had worked for woman suffrage, became disillusioned with women's lack of involvement in parliamentary life[13] and the fact that women did not all vote for the

---

*On June 22, 1933, the Social Democratic party was dissolved as "subversive and inimical to the State" (William L. Shirer, Decline and Fall of the Third Reich [New York: Simon and Schuster, 1960], p. 201), a step that was followed on July 7 by a decree depriving Social Democrats of their seats in the Reichstag. On July 14, all political parties except the Nazis were outlawed (Arnold Brecht, Prelude to Silence [New York: Oxford University Press, 1944], p. 114).

socialists.[14] She served in parliaments during the entire 14 years of the Weimar Republic and then fled abroad, eventually coming to the United States. She was back in Germany when she died.

In addition to the Social Democrats, there was a leftist splinter party, the Independent Socialists (USPD). The USPD fielded separate lists in 1919 and in 1920 but united with the Social Democrats after that. It was represented in 1919 by Anna Hübler (born in 1876), a homemaker who served only in the National Assembly; Luise Zietz (1865-1922), a party secretary from Berlin who served in the National Assembly and in the Reichstag at the time of her death; and Lore Agnes (1876-1953), a homemaker who sat in all parliaments until 1933 (she was imprisoned by the Nazis).

The Social Democrats (SPD) and the USPD supplied the largest group of women to the National Assembly. Second was the old Liberal party, which, under the name of the German Democratic party (DDP), had 75 seats in 1919, five of which were held by women. Elise Ekke (born in 1877), a high school teacher, served only during the life of the National Assembly. Katharina Kloss (1867-1945), a school principal, also was a member only during 1919-20. Elisabeth Brönner (born in 1880) was a teacher from East Prussia whose seat was automatically vacated in February 1921. Marie Baum (1874-1964), a Hamburg school principal who represented Schleswig-Holstein, also lost her seat in February 1921. Gertrude Bäumer (1873-1954), holder of a doctorate in philosophy and well-known for her activities in the women's movement, took a high civil-service position in the Ministry of the Interior in 1919. She was a member of the legislature until 1932.*

The Center party (Zentrum), another principal supporter of the Weimar Republic, had clerical ties and stressed freedom of worship, civil equality, and as little state control as possible. In 1919, under the label of the Christian People's party, it elected 90 deputies, six of whom were women.[15] Maria Schmitz (1875-1962), a teacher from Aachen, and Marie Zettler (1885-1950), a Bavarian secretary, served only for the duration of the National Assembly. Hedwig Dransfeld (1871-1925), a teacher and writer, remained in the legislature until she died. (Dransfeld had become a teacher in order to escape the orphanage where she was brought up. Otherwise,

---

*By that time, the DDP had changed its name to the German State party, and its membership had fallen to 14, a figure that was to decline even further. It was a supporter of the Republic, and its decline was therefore one of the tragedies of the Weimar democracy.

she would have had to go into domestic service.)[16] Agnes Neuhaus (1854-1944), a homemaker, was a member of the legislature until 1930. Christine Teusch (1888-1968), a schoolteacher, sat in the National Assembly and then in the Reichstag until 1933. She was imprisoned by Hitler in 1944-45. After World War II, she supported the Christian Democratic Union party (CDU) and was minister of education (Kultusminister) in North Rhine-Westphalia. Helene Weber (1881-1962), a teacher, worked in the Prussian Ministry for Social Welfare, was a member of the Prussian state parliament, and served in the National Assembly and Reichstag from 1924 to 1933. After the war, she was active in establishing a Catholic women's organization and the CDU. Weber helped draw up the new constitution and served in the Bundestag from 1949 until her death. Clara Mende (born in 1869) held one of the 22 seats of the German People's party (DVP), the more conservative wing of the old Liberal movement. She stayed on until 1928.

The right-wing German National People's party (DNVP) opposed the Weimar Republic from the start and helped Hitler to power. It sent three women to the National Assembly. Anna von Gierke (1874-1943), a well-known feminist, headed the party's women's committee, but was denied nomination for the Reichstag because of anti-Semitic pressure (her mother was Jewish, though she was Protestant). Gierke and her father, a well-known legal authority and author and a leader in the party, left the DNVP after this incident.[17] Käthe Schirmacher (1865-1930) was a writer and a board member of the German Association for Women Suffrage, which in 1902 became the first such organization with a political aim. Some of her ideas were shaped at a world congress she attended in Chicago.[18] Schirmacher advocated a greater Germany and was thus opposed to the Weimar Republic. Margarethe Behm (1860-1929), a schoolteacher and holder of a medical degree, sat in Parliament until 1928, the year before her death.

These 36 women in the National Assembly, which sat until May 1920, were joined by five more who filled in for departed colleagues. (It should be pointed out that under the list system the party simply designates someone to fill an unexpired vacancy, and this is usually the person in the runner-up position.) Gertrud Lodahl (born in 1878), a Social Democrat, had worked in the graphic industry. She sat from February 1919 until May 1920. Hedwig Kurt (born in 1877), also a SPD member, was a hatmaker. She filled the unexpired vacancy only. Marie-Helene Behnke (1880-1944), Social Democrat and homemaker, served from August 1919 until the assembly was dissolved. Marie-Elisabeth Lüders (1878-1966), the successor to Pastor Friedrich Naumann, was a teacher and social worker. She sat in the legislature until 1930 and was mainly involved in penal reform and legislation affecting women, children, and families.[19] Lüders was imprisoned by the Nazis and then was a member of the Bundestag from 1953 until 1961. A DDP member during the Weimar Republic, she was a Free Democrat in Bonn. Helene Grüneberg (1874-1928) was a dressmaker and union secretary. An Independent Socialist, she sat for only a few months.

The First Reichstag (1920-24)

Elections were held on June 6, 1920, and 466 deputies were chosen, including 37 women. Of these 37, 21 had been members of the National Assembly, and 16 were newcomers, with Wilhelmine Eichler having to wait for a vacancy the following year. The Social Democrats still supplied the largest number of women, although their total membership in Parliament had been drastically reduced. The Independent Socialists on the left and the German Nationalists on the right showed gains in total membership as well as in female representation. While this growth of the extremist parties was a bad omen for the health of the young democracy, it does show that at least at this stage the Right was not discriminating against women.

Franziska Eschholz (born in 1886), a Socialist, was a homemaker who resigned within a week after the Reichstag opened. Berta Schulz (1878-1950), another SPD homemaker, did not win immediate reelection in May 1924. She returned in December and served until the summer of 1933. Adele Schreiber-Krieger (1872-1957), also a Socialist, was a writer. Concerned with the protection of mothers, she founded a mother's home in Berlin as early as 1903.[20] She was forced into exile by Hitler. Maria Ansorge (1880-1955), a Socialist, served until Hitler came to power except for the May-December period in 1924. She was repeatedly put in prison and concentration camps by the Nazis. Ansorge served in the Bundestag as a replacement from 1951 to 1953. War victims were among her chief concerns.

The differences between the SPD and the Independent Socialists were settled in 1922. Six women are listed as SPD/USPD,[21] but those who returned in 1924 did so under the Socialist label. Three others served only from 1920 until May 1924: Marie Wackwitz (born in 1865), a writer; Anna Ziegler (1882-1942), a domestic employee; and Frieda Wulff (1876-1952), a party secretary.

Tony Sender (1888-1964), an office worker and editor of the paper Die Frauenwelt, served until 1932. She emigrated to the United States. Anna Franziska Nemitz (1873-1962), a dressmaker, served until 1933. Mathilde Wurm (1874-1935), a writer, stayed in the Reichstag until 1933. She then went to England and died there.

Marie Karch (born in 1877), a homemaker, served until 1924. She preferred the Communist rather than the Socialist label after the disappearance of the USPD.

Clara Zetkin (1857-1933), a Communist member from 1920 to 1933, taught girls "so that husbands would not be bored by their own firesides."[22] A close collaborator of Lenin and associated with Die Gleichheit, she "developed the socialist theory of women's emancipation to its purest form and gave the most effective direction to the agitation and organization of women."[23] Zetkin presided briefly over the first session of the Reichstag in the summer of 1932 as its oldest member and expressed the hope for the coming of Soviet Germany.[24] She was reelected in March 1933, when no Communist was allowed to be seated. She died in Russia.

Two women arrived from the German People's party (DVP). Katharina von Kardoff-Oheimb (1879-1962), a factory owner, stayed only for the one session. Elsa Matz (1881-1959), a university-trained educator, served until 1933, except for the May-December period in 1924.

Two other parties sent women into the Reichstag for the first time. Paula Mueller-Otfried (1865-1946), a writer, represented the DNVP, serving until November 1932. Thusnelda Lang-Brumann (1880-1953), a schoolteacher, was a member of the conservative, church-oriented Bavarian People's party (BV). She remained in the Reichstag until late 1933.

These 16 newcomers brought the number of women in the Reichstag to 37. Before the next election, four more arrived, in addition to Eichler. Hedwig Hoffmann (born in 1863), a homemaker from the DNVP, served from December 1921 until the end of the term. Elise Bartels (1880-1925), a homemaker and Socialist, stayed in Parliament until her death in October 1925. Maria Schott (born in 1878), a professional gardener from the DNVP, served until 1928. Finally, Milka Fritsch (born in 1867), a homemaker representing the DVP, came in March 1923 and stayed a year.

The Second Reichstag (May-December 1924)

The new elections in May 1924 returned seven new women in addition to 22 incumbents, bringing the total to a low of 29. Anna Stegmann (born in 1871), a medical doctor and native of Zurich who served until 1930, was the only Socialist newcomer. Else von Sperber (born in 1881), a homemaker from the DNVP, served until 1928. Frances Magnus (born in 1882), holder of a philosophy degree, came from the DVP and served only until the end of the year.

Of the four Communist newcomers, three served merely until
the next election in December 1924: Maria Backenecker (1893-1931)
and Anna Reitler (1894-1948), both homemakers; and Hedwig Krüger
(born in 1882), an employee who served briefly in the Prussian <u>land</u>
parliament. Elfriede Gohlke (1895-1961), however, stayed until
1928. Under the name of Ruth Fischer, she was a well-known writer
and outspoken critic (she called the League of Nations, for example,
"a consortium of bandits for the purpose of sugar-coating war with
idealism").[25] Expelled from the party for "deviation,"[26] Gohlke left
Germany in 1933, which gave Hitler the excuse to deprive her of
German citizenship and confiscate her property.[27] She lived in
France and the United States.

The Third Reichstag (December 1924-28)

New elections in December 1924 were supposed to bring more
economic stability. The extremists on both sides lost support, and
the Socialists and the Nationalists gained. Of the former women
deputies, 29 returned, together with only four new ones. Two others
joined before the next election, by which time two of the incumbents
had died. Martha Arendsee (1885-1953), a Communist, was a Berlin bookkeeper. A member of the Reichstag until 1933, she emigrated to the Soviet Union and played a leading part in Communist
affairs in East Germany after the war. Marie Arning (born in 1887),
a Socialist, sat in the Reichstag until 1930. She emigrated to
Holland, was imprisoned by the Nazis, and eventually returned to
Germany. Luise Schiffgens (1892-1954), a homemaker, was a member of the Prussian Landtag and then sat in the Reichstag until 1930.
Persecuted by Nazis, Schiffgens spent more than a year in a concentration camp. Ulrike Scheidel (born in 1886), a DNVP representative, was a professional educator who served only until the next
election.

The two women who came in during the life of the parliament
were Agnes Plum (1869-1951), a homemaker and Communist who
served for the remaining two and one-half years, and Klara Philipp
(1877-1949), a homemaker from the Center party, who remained in
the Reichstag for two years. However, with the deaths of Dransfeld
and Bartels, the total number of women in this Reichstag was back
to the original 33.

The Fourth Reichstag (1928-30)

In the general election of May 1928, 25 women were reelected
and eight newcomers arrived, most of them from the Left. Before

the session ended two years later, three more had come in. Maria Reese (1889-1958), a writer, was elected as a Socialist but became a Communist. She remained in Parliament until expelled by Hitler. Reese then emigrated to Sweden, was extradited, but somehow survived the Nazi period. She later converted to Catholicism. Wilhelmine Kurfürst (1892-1945), a homemaker and Socialist, remained only until 1930. Anna Siemsen (1882-1951), a Socialist and educator, also served only until 1930. She emigrated to Switzerland in 1933. Klara Weich (born in 1883), listed as employee, remained in the legislature until July 1932. She was also a Social Democrat. Marie Kunert (1871-1957), a SPD member, stayed until Hitler made it impossible and then escaped to Switzerland. A writer, she had previously been in Prussia's land parliament. Helene Overlach (born in 1894), a Communist employed in Berlin, stayed in the Reichstag even after Hitler came to power. She was imprisoned and, after the war, lived in East Berlin. Doris Hertwig-Bünger (born in 1882), a DVP representative and high school teacher, was a member of the Reichstag until 1930. Annagrete Lehmann (1877-1954), from the DNVP, was a professional educator and a former member of Prussia's legislature. She served in the Reichstag until Hitler dispensed with services of even his one-time Nationalist allies.

Three more women entered to fill vacancies. None of them served beyond the end of the current Reichstag. Hedwig Fuchs (1864-1944) came in 1929 to represent the Zentrum. Karoline Dettmer (1867-1939), a homemaker and SPD member, entered in January 1930. Emilie Kiep-Altenloh (born in 1888) was a member of the German Democratic party. She became a Free Democrat after World War II and served first as senator from Hamburg for 12 years and then from 1961 to 1965 in the Bundestag.

The Fifth Reichstag (1930-May 1932)

In the elections of September 1930, with the economy going from bad to worse, the Nazis received 6.5 million votes and 107 seats, the Communists 4.5 million votes and 77 seats, while the Socialists, like the other moderate and democratic parties, declined. Joining the 24 women who were returned to their seats were 15 new female members. Among the newcomers, there were only two Socialists, bringing their total to 16. But nine new Communists were added to three holdovers. The Nazis, as will be explained later, did not believe in women in public life and included no women among their deputies.

Three of the Communist newcomers served only until the next election: Barbara Esser (1902-1952), a bookbindery worker; Grete Mildenberg (born in 1902), listed merely as Arbeiterin ("worker");[28] and Roberta Gropper (born in 1897), a worker in the tobacco industry.

Gropper later emigrated to the Soviet Union. She became a leading member of the Communist-run Socialist Unity party in the German Democratic Republic and a member of the Volkskammer as
representative of the trade union movement. [29]

Olga Körner (born in 1887), a cook, sat in the Reichstag until
Hitler excluded the Communists. She spent several years in concentration camps. Active in Communist and Socialist Unity party
affairs in East Germany after the war, Körner became a member
of the party's central committee. [30]

Other Communists who served until forcibly excluded by
Hitler were Marie Ahlers (born in 1898), a homemaker and city
council member, and Elise Augustat (born in 1889) and Johanna
Himmler (born in 1894), both homemakers who were later sent to
concentration camps by the Nazis. Himmler was active in Communist circles in East Germany after the war.

Other Communists included Maria Blum (born in 1890), a
worker who served in the Fifth and Seventh Reichstags, and Lotte
Zinke (born in 1891), a homemaker who served until the end of the
Seventh Reichstag.

Two Social Democratic women arrived who both served until
their party activities were terminated by Hitler. Margarethe Starr-
mann (born in 1892) was an educator. Anna Zammert (born in 1898)
was a union secretary who, after repeated imprisonment, emigrated to Sweden.

Serving until the Nazis made it impossible for them were two
women from the Zentrum: Else Peerenboom-Missong (1893-1958)
and Elisabeth Zillken (born in 1888), a teacher of commercial subjects.

Magdalene von Tiling (born in 1877) represented the DNVP.
A high school teacher and former member of the Prussian state parliament, she served for the next three years in the Reichstag.

Gertrud Eitner (1880-1955), a teacher, served one legislative
term for a Protestant-oriented splinter party, the Christlich-
Sozialer Volksdienst (literally, "Christian-Social People's Service").

Before the Fifth Reichstag was dissolved in the spring of 1932,
four more women replaced outgoing members. Helene Driessen
(1876-1938), a homemaker from the Zentrum, was elected in July
1932 and served from January 1931 until November 1932. Selma
Lohse (1883-1937), a homemaker representing the SPD; Hanna
Sandtner (1900-1958), a shorthand-typist and Communist; and Frieda
Fiedler (born in 1885), a homemaker from the SPD who had sat in
the state parliament of Anhalt, merely served out the unexpired
terms.

The Sixth Reichstag (July-November 1932)

The July 1932 elections returned 33 former members and
four newcomers among the women. There were 15 Social Democrats, 11 Communists, including three newcomers, and six members of the Zentrum, one of whom was new.

The new Zentrum member, Clara Siebert (1873-1949), a
schoolteacher and former member of the Baden land parliament,
was not reelected in November but came back in March 1933.

The three Communist newcomers included the following women.
Helene Fleischer (1899-1941), a textile worker, served until 1933
when she was imprisoned. She died in a concentration camp.
Franziska Kessel (1906-1934), a saleswoman, was also reelected in
November. She eventually committed suicide in a prison cell. Lisa
Ullrich (born in 1900) stayed in the Reichstag as long as it was possible and then was sentenced to three years hard labor, after which
she went to a concentration camp. Somehow she survived and lived
in East Berlin after the war.

The Seventh Reichstag (November 1932-March 1933)

July 1932 had brought successes to the Nazis on the right and
the Communists on the left. It somewhat weakened the Social Democrats but in no way helped the minority government of Franz von
Papen, who therefore proceeded to call for new elections in November. These showed a decline in Nazi strength but an increase in
Communist support. Returned were 33 previously elected women,
including 13 Social Democrats and 12 Communists. There were
only two newcomers, a Communist, Helene Kirsch (born 1906), who
served only until the following election, and a Nationalist, Anna
Rawengel (1878-1932), a high school teacher who had hardly been
elected when she died in December 1932.

The Eighth Reichstag (March 1933)

As leader of the largest single party in the Reichstag, Hitler
was appointed chancellor on January 30, 1933, with the understanding that new elections would be called. These were held in March
1933. Of the former female representatives, 28 were returned,
and only one newcomer appeared, Else Meier (born in 1901), a
Communist homemaker.

Under the pretext of their having set the parliament building on fire, the Communists were outlawed even before the election took place. Formally, nine Communist women were elected, but none was permitted to take her seat. Among the Socialists, 12 women won election, but the party immediately came under violent attack. The SPD courageously voted against Hitler's Enabling Act and faced persecution when the party was dissolved in June 1933. Even the non-Marxist parties, including the Nationalists, who supposedly were allied to Hitler, soon found themselves outlawed as Germany became a one-party state.

The Reichstag under Hitler

"Elections" were held in November 1933, March 1936, and April 1938. Each time, the Nazi party list was the only one presented to the voters. Each time, the so-called election was tied to a recent foreign policy coup (the withdrawal from the League of Nations, the remilitarization of the Rhineland, and the occupation of Austria). Each time, the German people gave Hitler almost unanimous approval.

In the Nazi-controlled Reichstag, there were no women. Goebbels's wife stated in an interview that German women in Hitler's Reich were excluded from "only three professions: the military (as is the case all over the world), government, and the practice of law. If the German girl is faced with the choice of marriage or a career, she will always be encouraged to marry, since this undoubtedly is best for a woman."[31] Even more pointed is this quotation.

> There is no place for the political woman in the ideological world of National Socialism. . . . The intellectual attitude of the movement on this score is opposed to the political woman. It refers the woman back to her nature-given sphere of the family and to her tasks as wife and mother. The postwar phenomenon of the political woman, who rarely cuts a good figure in parliamentary debates, signifies robbing woman of her dignity.[32]

Hitler himself had this to say in 1934.

> The term Emancipation of Women is a term invented only by the Jewish intellect. The German woman did not have to be emancipated during the really good times of German life. Her world is her husband, her

family, her children and her home. Every child she
bears is a battle which she wages for the existence or
non-existence of her people. Whereas formerly the
liberal intellectual women's movements had many
points in their programs . . . the program of our
National Socialist women's movement consists basically of only one point and this point is called the child.[33]

It is worth noting that this extreme view was held only by the
extreme Right. The moderate, though antirepublican Right, the
German Nationalists, had quite a few women in the Reichstag. This
was also true of the Zentrum, despite its close connections to the
male-dominated Catholic church.

But it was the Left, the moderate Social Democrats and the
extreme Communists, who not only advocated equality for women—
and had done so at a time when this was a very controversial and
often vehemently opposed notion—but also placed women into positions where they could be elected. Table 6.1 gives an indication of
how many women were included in the parliamentary delegations of
each party. The Social Democrats have the best overall record.
In 14 years, at least 10 percent of their representatives in the
Reichstag were always women, and at times the figure was considerably higher. For the Communists, the figure fell as low as 5.5
percent but in 1930 reached almost 17 percent (leaving aside the
1920 figure of 50 percent when one of the two members was a
woman!). The DDP fluctuated between 6 percent and 12 percent,
while the Zentrum reached a low of 4.34 percent in 1920 and a high
of 7.9 percent in 1932. The right-wing German Nationalists always
included some women in their parliamentary delegations and at
times went beyond the 7 percent mark. The Nazis, of course, did
not believe in having women in politics at all.

WOMEN MEMBERS OF THE BUNDESTAG

The Nazi period covered a time span of 12 years. When democratic life in Germany was resumed, a new generation took over.
Of the 111 women who had sat in the legislature between 1919 and
1933, only five became members of the Bundestag in West Germany,
and only one sat in the Volkskammer in East Germany. A handful of
others participated actively in a variety of different ways in the political life of the two Germanys. During the period from 1919 to
1933, only seven of the legislators who were women had been born
in the twentieth century and only 15 in the last decade of the nineteenth. In the Bundestag, the situation was almost entirely reversed, with only 28 having been born before 1900.

TABLE 6.1

Party Affiliations of Women in the German Reichstag
(highest number in each session)

	Communists (KPD)	Social Democrats (SPD)	German Democrats (DDP)	German Nationalists (DNVP)	Center (Zentrum)	Independent Socialists (USPD)	German People's Party (DVP)	National Socialists (Nazis) (NSDAP)
National Assembly June 1919	1 out of 2 (50%)	22 out of 163 (13.5%)	6 out of 75 (8%)	3 out of 42 (7.14%)	6 out of 90 (6.66%)	3 out of 22 (13.63%)	1 out of 22 (4.5%)	n.a.*
1st Reichstag (1920)	1 out of 2 (50%)	16 out of 113 (14.15%)	4 out of 45 (8.88%)	5 out of 66 (7.57%)	3 out of 69 (4.34%)	8 out of 81 (9.87%)	3 out of 62 (4.83%)	n.a.
2nd Reichstag (May 1924)	5 out of 62 (8.06%)	11 out of 100 (11%)	2 out of 28 (7.14%)	4 out of 95 (4.21%)	4 out of 65 (6.15%)	n.a.	2 out of 45 (4.44%)	0 out of 32
3rd Reichstag (Dec. 1924)	4 out of 45 (8.88%)	16 out of 131 (12.21%)	2 out of 32 (6.25%)	5 out of 103 (4.85%)	5 out of 69 (7.24%)	n.a.	2 out of 51 (3.92%)	0 out of 14
4th Reichstag (1928)	3 out of 54 (5.55%)	21 out of 153 (13.72%)	3 out of 25 (12%)	2 out of 73 (2.73%)	4 out of 62 (6.45%)	n.a.	2 out of 45 (4.44%)	0 out of 12
5th Reichstag (1930)	13 out of 77 (16.88%)	18 out of 143 (12.58%)	1 out of 14 (7.14%)	2 out of 41 (4.87%)	5 out of 68 (7.35%)	n.a.	1 out of 30 (3.33%)	0 out of 107
6th Reichstag (July 1932)	11 out of 89 (12.35%)	15 out of 133 (11.27%)	0 out of 4	3 out of 78 (7.89%)	6 out of 76 (7.89%)	n.a.	1 out of 7 (14.28%)	0 out of 230
7th Reichstag (Nov. 1932)	13 out of 100 (13%)	13 out of 121 (10.74%)	0 out of 2	3 out of 52 (5.76%)	4 out of 71 (5.63%)	n.a.	1 out of 11 (9.09%)	0 out of 196
8th Reichstag (1933)	9 out of 81 (11.11%)	12 out of 120 (10%)	0 out of 5	2 out of 53 (3.77%)	5 out of 73 (6.84%)	n.a.	0 out of 2	0 out of 288

*Not applicable.
Source: Compiled by the author.

The election method itself has changed somewhat also. Although the percentage of votes a party receives still determines the number of seats it obtains, there are important modifications. One-half of the representatives are chosen in districts in accordance with the Anglo-American system of "first past the post" and the other half according to lists in each Land. The total number of legislators to be elected is determined beforehand and is not dependent on the total number of voters who participate in an election. West Berlin was given representation. However, since its status is somewhat complicated, West Berlin's deputies are not chosen directly by the people but are named by the elected parliament of the city. Moreover, while these members of the Bundestag have full rights of participation in discussions, their voting privileges are limited and do not include such crucial issues as naming a chancellor, expressing confidence in the government, or replacing the chancellor with a new one. [34]

The First Bundestag (1949-53)

The first Bundestag election, held four years after the end of the war, produced a new group of legislators. Only Schroeder from the SPD and Weber, now representing the Christian Democrats (CDU), continued with the parliamentary activities they had left off in 1933. They were joined in November 1951 by another old SPD colleage of the Weimar Republic days, Ansorge. Two more women who had sat in the Reichstag, Lüders and Kiep-Altenloh, arrived at later dates.

Not counting the representatives from Berlin, the 1949 Bundestag consisted of 402 members, of which the SPD supplied 131, the Christian Democrats (a more broadly based successor to the Zentrum) 115, and their Bavarian allies, the Christian Social Union (CSU), 52. [35] As in the days of the Weimar Republic, the Social Democrats elected more women than any of their opponents. However, as time progressed, the SPD and the combined CDU/CSU, who were to become the two major contenders for power, were close rivals for providing the greatest number of female representatives.

In 1949, 12 SPD women entered the first Bundestag. Anni Krahnstover (1904-1961), a secretary from Schleswig-Holstein, served four years. Public health and Heligoland Island were among her special concerns. [36] Lisa Albrecht (1896-1958), a gymnastics instructor, had been active in Socialist politics before Hitler and spent several years in prison. Reelected several times, she was a member of the Bundestag at the time of her death. Emmy Meyer-Laule (1899-), a homemaker, served until 1961. Frieda Nadig

(1897-1970), a social worker, also served 12 years. She had participated in the parliamentary council that drew up the Grundgesetz, the basic law that is in effect the present-day constitution of West Germany. Irma Keilhack (1908-), a homemaker, also suffered Gestapo imprisonment. She remained in the Bundestag until January 1961, when she resigned to become Senatorin (a member of the executive) of Hamburg. Both Clara Döhring (1899-) and Liesel Kipp-Kaule (1906-) were union secretaries, and both served until 1965. Luise Albertz (1901-1979) had previously served on a city council. She stayed in the Bundestag for 20 years. Lisa Korspeter (1900-), a homemaker, had been an SPD supporter before 1933. A member of the Bundestag for two decades, she paid special attention to financial and insurance matters. Elinor Hubert (1900-1973) was the daughter of a high-level bureaucrat and the wife of a physician, both of whom had opposed Hitler and suffered for it. When her husband died in 1942, Hubert completed her own medical studies and became a practicing physician. In the Bundestag for 20 years, she was concerned with medical and health problems and penal reform.[27] Martha Schanzenbach (1907-) was interested in welfare and social work. She stayed in Parliament for 23 years. Käte Strobel (1907-) also was in the Bundestag for 23 years. Daughter of a shoemaker and wife of a painter, she was persecuted by Hitler because of her Socialists convictions. From 1966 until 1969, she was minister of health and from 1969 until 1972, minister of youth, family, and health.

Ten women in the 1949 Bundestag sat on the CDU benches. Margarete Gröwel (1889-), a schoolteacher, served one four-year term. Annemarie Heiler (1889-1979) was a homemaker. She also sat in Parliament for just one term. Maria Dietz (1894-), a homemaker and educator active in Catholic women's circles before 1933, served until 1957. Maria Niggemeyer (1888-1968), a homemaker, taught in Catholic schools. Formerly associated with the Zentrum, she was one of the founding members of a local CDU organization. She served 12 years in the Bundestag. Else Brökelschen (1890-1976), a homemaker and candidate for the Reichstag on the People's party label, was a CDU representative for 12 years. Viktoria Steinbiss (1892-1971), a physician married to a physician, was a local town council member and was interested in Christian movements. She sat in the Bundestag for 12 years. Julie Rösch (1902-), a homemaker, served a dozen years. Helene Weber's career in the Bundestag has been detailed in the discussion of the National Assembly. Luise Rehling (1896-1964), a homemaker married to a Protestant minister, was a member of her party's executive committee in the Bundestag at the time of her death. Aenne Brauksiepe (1912-), a homemaker married to a journalist who was missing in action for several years during the war,[38] was a city council member. In the Bundestag until 1972, she was minister for family affairs from 1968 until 1969.

The Christian Social Union, affiliated with the CDU, elected only one woman in the first Bundestag, Maria Probst (1902-1967). A schoolteacher and daughter of a Reichstag deputy, she was married to a Bavarian state legislator who was imprisoned by the Nazis and killed in the war. She remained in the Bundestag until she died, serving as vice-president of that body.

Grete Thiele (1913-), a homemaker, was the only woman among the 15 members representing the Communist party, a party that received 5.7 percent in this election. She served one term, since in 1953 and in every election thereafter the Communists were unable to obtain any seats at all.

Thea Arnold (1882-1966), elected under the old Zentrum label, saw her party disintegrate, and she eventually sat as an Independent until the end of the term.[39] Helene Wessel (1898-1969) led the Zentrum in the Bundestag in 1949. She concerned herself not only with issues involving health, the family, and children, but also with foreign policy. Wessel became unaffiliated with any party when she left the Bundestag in 1953. Like Gustav Heinemann, she was in search of a party until she joined the SPD. She returned to Parliament in 1957 and remained until she died. She had been a member of the Parliamentary Council.

Margot Kalinke (1909-) originally represented the German party, a minor political group that gradually disappeared. She was absent from Parliament between 1953 and 1955, and then came in as a replacement. She changed over to the CDU in 1960 and remained in the Bundestag until 1972.

Berlin supplied quite a few women deputies for every Bundestag session, and despite the limited scope of activities of these representatives, they must be included in our listing. The city was at first allocated eight seats. This was later changed to 19 and is now fixed at 22. The first group had one woman among its members, Louise Schroeder, who has already been mentioned as a member of the Reichstag. Three more women from Berlin came in 1952. Friederike Mulert (1896-) was a physician representing the Free Democratic party (FDP), successor to the old Liberals. She remained only until the 1953 election. Agnes Maxsein (1904-), an educator from the CDU, sat in the Bundestag until 1969. Jeanette Wolff (1888-1976), a prominent Jewish Socialist, was imprisoned by the Nazis and sent to concentration camps, where she lost her husband and two daughters. After the war, Wolff fought hard against merging the SPD with the Communists in the East and was a leader in Berlin's fight for survival.[40] She stayed in Parliament until 1961.

In addition to the 27 female members and the four female representatives from Berlin, seven other women came in as replacements. Margarete Hütter (1909–), a homemaker and member of the
FDP, replaced Theodor Heuss when he became federal president.
She stayed until 1953, and in 1955 she again became a replacement
until 1957. Herta Ilk (1902–1972), a jurist from the FDP, served
from November 1949 until 1957. Gertrud Lockmann (1895–1962),
an SPD representative from Hamburg, had been persecuted by the
Nazis. She was a member of the Bundestag between 1950 and 1957.
Gertrud Strohbach (1911–) served from 1951 until the end of the
legislative period. She was a Communist and temporarily brought
the number of Communist female members to two. Maria Ansorge,
a former Reichstag member who filled a vacancy between 1951 and
1953, has already been mentioned. Elfriede Jaeger (1899–1964), an
Independent, served in 1952–53. Anna-Maria Bieganowski (1906–)
stayed from March 1952 until the 1953 election. She changed from
a member of the small German party to an Independent while in the
legislature.

The Second Bundestag (1953–57)

In the September 1953 elections, 25 incumbent women were
reelected, including three from Berlin. Two others (Kalinke and
Hütter) came later as replacements. There were 18 female newcomers, in addition to two more from Berlin and six replacements
during the term. Numerically, the combined CDU/CSU group now
had as many female members as their Socialist rivals.
    The following women were all SPD newcomers. Trudel Meyer
(1922–), a union secretary, served until 1957. Franziska Benne-
mann (1905–), a homemaker, sat in the Bundestag until 1961. Alma
Kettig (1915–), a secretary, served a total of 12 years. Lucie
Beyer (1914–), later Lucie Kurlbaum-Beyer, worked in households
and offices. She subsequently became a social worker and municipal councillor before serving 16 years in the Bundestag. Margaret
Rudoll (1906–) was active in politics before Hitler. A union secretary, she served 16 years in the Bundestag.
    The sixth SPD newcomer, Annemarie Renger (1919–), was
the youngest child of "one of Berlin's leading Social Democrats."[41]
Married at age 18, she lost her husband and three of her four
brothers during the war. She became secretary and companion to
Socialist leader Kurt Schumacher after the collapse of Hitler's
Reich. Schumacher died in 1952, and a year later Renger entered
the Bundestag, where she steadily advanced in Social Democratic
councils. When her party held a plurality of seats (from 1972 to

1976), she was president of the Bundestag, a position equivalent to
Speaker of the House of Representatives. After 1976, she became
one of its vice-presidents. In 1979, Renger was nominated for the
office of federal president, although this was obviously a lost cause
from the beginning. She remains one of West Germany's most outstanding women. Her attitude toward the position of women in
society is probably best expressed in this statement. "As long as
women topics are 'in' and fully shared political responsibility for
women is 'out,' women have not yet become fully integrated into our
society."[42]

The CDU, who in 1953 had captured 191 seats in the Bundestag
to the SPD's 151, had seven women among its newcomers. Hedwig
Jochmus (1899–), a chemist, served a four-year term. She led
women members in pressing for legislation designed to prevent
harmful chemicals from being added to foodstuffs.[43] Gisela
Praetorius (1902–), a homemaker who taught in a vocational school
before her marriage, served until 1957. Elisabeth Vietje (1902–
1963), an educator, remained until 1957. She returned as a replacement for a deceased colleague in 1960 and stayed in Parliament
until her own death in 1963. Hildegard Bleyler (1899–), university
educated, served a dozen years. She was particularly concerned
with pensions, especially for widows.[44] Annemarie Ackermann
(1913–), born in what is now Yugoslavia, served until 1961 and sat
an additional few months in 1965 as a replacement. Elisabeth Pitz-
Savelsberg (1906–), a social scientist, teacher, and member of the
Committee on Youth, stayed on for 16 years. Elisabeth Schwarzhaupt (1901–), daughter of a German People's party deputy in the
Prussian legislature, had written against Hitler's attitude toward
women and was therefore on the Nazi blacklist.[45] She was a lawyer
by profession. In 1961, Konrad Adenauer yielded to the pressure of
his female colleagues to appoint a woman to a cabinet post and
named Schwarzhaupt minister of health. She held this newly created
position for five years and retired from the Bundestag in 1969.

The CSU, the close ally of the CDU from Bavaria, added two
newcomers to the Bundestag in 1953, both of whom remained for 19
years. Ingeborg Geisendörfer (1907–) was a homemaker who was
trained as a teacher and married to a Protestant clergyman.
Edeltraud Kuchtner (1907–) had trained as a lawyer.

Lotte Friese-Korn (1899–1963) represented the Free Democrats. She served for eight years.

Ernie Finselberger (1902–) was a social worker who had to
flee from the eastern part of Germany. She represented the
Gesamtdeutscher Block/Bund der Heimatvertriebenen und En-
trechteten ("All German Bloc/League of Refugees"—literally,
those who had been driven from their homes and were deprived of

all rights), which, with 1.5 million votes, had received 27 seats. She stayed for one term only, after which her party was no longer in the Bundestag. Gräfin Eva Finckenstein (1903–) also sat for the refugee group but, after some hesitation, joined the CDU until her term expired in 1957.

From Berlin, two newcomers arrived: Marie-Elisabeth Lüders, former National Assembly and Reichstag member now representing the FDP, who stayed until 1961, and Margarete Heise (1911–) (Margarete Berger-Heise after her marriage) from the SPD, who served 16 years.

One of the causes of irritation for German female politicians is that a considerable number of them are placed in nonelectable positions on the party lists. They reach the Bundestag when vacancies develop. Grabspringer ("grave jumpers") is the term used, because they leap into office only after their predecessors are in their graves. However, it must be added that of those who begin their parliamentary careers in this way, quite a few stay on beyond the unexpired term. In the first Bundestag, seven women entered as replacements. In the second, there were six newcomers, in addition to Hütter and Kalinke. Emmi Welter (1887–1971), a homemaker, served from 1954 until 1965. A member of the CDU, she was interested in assistance to the physically handicapped and those suffering from tuberculosis.[46] Elisabeth Ganswindt (1900–), a CDU member, stayed from November 1955 until the next election in 1957. Also representing the CDU, Mathilde Gantenberg (1889–1975) served between 1956 and 1961. Pia Kaiser (1912–1968), a CDU deputy, remained barely a year. Luise Herklotz (1918–), a Socialist editor, was a Bundestag member for 16 years. Luise Peter (1906–), a homemaker, represented the SPD only from July until September 1957.

The Third Bundestag (1957–61)

The elections of September 1957 saw 40 women representatives reelected, including three from Berlin. One other, Elisabeth Vietje, came in as a replacement in May 1960. Eight newcomers appeared in 1957, including one from Berlin: five CDU members, two SPD representatives (counting the Berliner), and one from the FDP. One more replacement arrived in 1959. Cläre Schmitt (1915–), a homemaker from the CDU, served one term. Elfriede Hamelbeck (1924–), who preferred to be known as Elfriede Klemmert after her marriage, was a notary and member of the CDU. She stayed until 1961. Margarete Engländer (1895–), a homemaker of the CDU, served until 1961. However, in 1962, Helene Weber died, and Engländer filled in for her until 1965—one of the very few occasions when a woman replaced another woman. Maria Pannhoff (1902-), a physician from the CDU, sat for eight years in Parliament. Irma Blohm (1909-), a CDU member and medical technician, stayed on for 12 years. Elfriede Eilers (1921-) was a social worker and SPD representative. She has been reelected ever since, making her second in seniority among female members (after Renger). Emmy Diemer-Nicolaus (1910-), a lawyer and homemaker, served as a FDP representative until 1972. Edith Krappe (1909-), a bookkeeper from Berlin representing the SPD, stayed in Bonn for 15 years. Elfriede Seppi (1910-1976), an SPD replacement in 1959, remained until 1972.

The Fourth Bundestag (1961-65)

In 1961, 34 of the women previously in the Bundestag were reelected, including three from Berlin. Two more former incumbents entered during the session, but four dropped out. There were nine newcomers (three each from the CDU, SPD, and FDP), and eight more came in as Grabspringer.

The CDU members who arrived in 1961 included Maria Jacobi (1906-), a homemaker active in women's organizations (especially Catholic ones), who remained in the Bundestag until 1972; Marie-Elisabeth Klee (1922-), a homemaker who also served until 1972; and Christa Schroeder (1913-), who served until 1976.

On the Socialist side, there were Else Zimmermann (1907-), who stayed for only one term; Hedwig Meermann (1913-), a homemaker who served until 1976; and Ilse Elsner (1910-), a journalist who was twice reelected. Elsner resigned in 1970 in order to become Senatorin from Hamburg and a representative with the federal government in Bonn.

The Free Democrats included the following women. Hedi Flitz (1900-), a homemaker, served a four-year term. Emilie Kiep-Altenloh has already been mentioned as a member of the old Reichstag. In 1961, at the age of 73, she returned to the national legislature for a four-year period. Liselotte Funcke (1918-) has become a member of the executive of the FDP in the Bundestag and a vice-president of that body, a position she has held since 1969. She continually needles the government about the small number of women in high places[47] but also stresses the partnership among the sexes, not the importance of one over the other.[48]

The eight newcomer replacements included these women. Brigitte Freyh (1924-), an SPD member, served from December 1961 until 1972. During her last three years in Bonn, she was parliamentary secretary of state at the Ministry of Economic Co-operation, thus becoming one of the very few women to hold junior government rank. Hedda Heuser (1926-), holder of a medical degree, filled a vacancy for the FDP between 1962 and 1965 and again between 1968 and 1969. Dorothea Lösche (1906-), an SPD home-maker from Berlin, also served twice, between April 1963 and the 1965 election and between July 1966 and the 1969 election. Centa Haas (1908-1976), an educator from the CSU, served during the two years preceding the 1965 elections. Gräfin Marlis von Hagen (1911-), representing the CDU, arrived in January 1964 and stayed until the fall of 1965. Ingeborg Kleinert (1926-) represented the SPD from November 1964 until the elections of 1965 and again between December 1967 and the 1969 elections. Maria Stommel (1914-) sat for the CDU from December 1964 until 1976 and made problems dealing with family and youth her special concern. Annemarie Griesinger (1924-) also arrived in late 1964 as a CDU representative and stayed on until 1972, when she resigned in order to assume the office of minister for labor and social affairs in Württemberg-Baden.

The Fifth Bundestag (1965-69)

The elections, held in September 1965, seemed to signal the continuation of the CDU/CSU administration in alliance with the FDP. Before the four years were over, however, the Grand Coalition between the Christian parties and the Socialists had been formed, and the Free Democrats were alone in opposition. None of the other parties has been able to elect anyone since 1961. The women in Parliament were hardly affected by this—only three new ones were elected into the Fifth Bundestag. Ursula Krips (1933-), a Social Democrat, resigned in January 1969, shortly before the expiration of her term. Hildegard Schimschok (1913-), an SPD homemaker, stayed on for several more terms until 1976. Erika Wolf (1912-), a member of the CDU, was a lawyer and active in the affairs of the Protestant church. She remained in Parliament until 1976.

Five more women came in to fill vacancies during this four-year period. All of them were CDU representatives. Elisabeth Enseling (1907-) served from April 1966 until the next election in 1969. Helga Wex (1924-), a homemaker, inherited the seat vacated by Adenauer's death. She served from April 1967 until 1969. In 1972, she returned and was reelected in 1976. Wex is a vice-chairwoman of her party's parliamentary group. Anna Monikees (1905-), a homemaker, served in the Bundestag between October 1967 and the fall of 1969. Lieselotte Holzmeister (1921-) served between February 1968 and the 1969 general election. Lieselotte Pieser (1917-), a leading CDU figure in Berlin, went to the Bundestag in June 1968 and has remained there since.

The Sixth Bundestag (1969-72)

In the election for the Sixth Bundestag, 12 Socialist, nine CDU, two CSU, and two FDP female incumbents (including two from Berlin) were returned. Ten newcomers (three from the CDU and seven from the SPD) were elected. One of the Socialists came from Berlin, as did the one woman who filled a vacancy. The CDU, now in opposition for the first time since the establishment of the Bonn regime, included these newcomers among its women members. Maria Henze (1926-1972), a high school teacher interested in youth and family affairs, died while in the Bundestag. Hanna Walz (1918-), a lawyer, journalist, and member of the European Parliament, was reelected in 1972 and in 1976. Irma Tübler (1922-) has been in the Bundestag since 1969. She is interested in modern social questions. [49]

Among the seven new Social Democrats were Ellen Lauterback (1923-), who served only one, three-year term, and Elisabeth Orth (1921-1976), a holder of a degree in agriculture who was a member of the Bundestag at the time of her death.

The following five Social Democrats were reelected in 1972 and in 1976. Lenelotte von Bothmer (1915-) for a long time believed that politics was for men only. She joined the Social Democrats several years after her husband. She was put on the list for the land parliament but in a nonelectable position. Von Bothmer eventually got in through vacancies, but despite hard work for her constituents, she was not renominated because the party leadership preferred a man. In the Bundestag, she regards herself as an Alibifrau ("token woman"), because she is the only woman on the land list of her party in Bonn. She describes what is essentially a "no win" situation for women. "A female candidate must be intelligent, but not too much so. If she is unmarried, she is suspicious, for she may be interested in catching a man. A housewife is sure to neglect her duties, especially if she is a mother too. It is probable that a woman wants to enter politics because she is disappointed with her life. . . ."[50]

Katharina Focke (1922-) emigrated with her family during the Nazi regime. She has studied, among other places, at the University of Oklahoma and holds a Ph.D. degree in political science. Focke was parliamentary state secretary in the federal chancellery from 1969 until 1972 and then minister of family, youth, and health for the next four years.

Antje Huber (1924-), a journalist and newspaper editor married to an editor, has been minister of family, youth, and health since 1976. She is a strong advocate of equal educational opportunities for boys and girls and of equal pay for equal work regardless of sex.

Helga Timm (1924-), an educator, is a leader of the SPD parliamentary group. She is the head of a commission studying women's place in society. Its 1977 intermediary report states:

> . . . the small representation of women in the political parties is merely a reflection of the fact that equality has not yet been realized in other spheres of society as well. At the same time, this is also one of its causes. The exclusion of women from the political decision-making process also prevents taking the measures necessary to catch up. Legal equality cannot become a social reality as long as there is such a small participation in political decisions on the part of women, which is a factor partially responsible for social remedies still being missing. [51]

Marie Schlei (1919-) represents Berlin. Married in 1940, her husband was killed in the war. She fled to the West from East Germany with her three-year-old son. She is a teacher and has married again. From 1974 until 1976, Schlei was parliamentary secretary of state in the Chancellor's Office and from 1976 until 1978, minister for economic cooperation.

Lieselotte Berger (1920-) entered the Bundestag as a CDU member from Berlin in August 1971 and has remained a member since then. A journalist, she became the head of the Committee on Petitions, a position which traditionally goes to a woman (Albertz, Wessel, and Jacobi, for example, have held it). When asked what makes women different from men, Berger answers that they have to visit the hairdresser more frequently, they have bigger wardrobes, and, occasionally, they are tougher. She maintains that for a successful career in Bonn, one needs good nerves, still better nerves, the ability to view problems from a distance, the ability to listen, and the willingness to remain in verbal contact with a political opponent. Knowledge of subject matter, she adds, is necessary as a matter of course. [52]

The Seventh Bundestag (1972-76)

The 1972 elections were held a year ahead of the legally provided four years and resulted in the SPD becoming the largest single party in the Bundestag, enabling Renger to assume its presidency. In terms of female representation, 19 former members came back, 11 new ones joined them (six CDU, three SPD, one FDP, and one CSU), and another six came in during the next four years. Agnes Hurland (1926-), a CDU member, stayed for one four-year term. Ursula Benedix (1922-), a vocational school teacher from the CDU, was reelected in 1976. Hanna Neumeister (1920-), a dentist representing the CDU, also returned in 1976 for another term. Roswitha Verhülsdonk (1927-), a CDU member married to an editor and interested in youth and adult education, was reelected in 1976. Waltrud Will-Feld (1921-), a widowed tax consultant from the CDU, also returned to the Eighth Bundestag. Paula Riede (1923-), a CDU member, served until 1976. She did not immediately return to the Eighth Bundestag but came in May 1977 to fill a vacancy. Ursula Schleicher (1933-), a CSU representative from Bavaria, had studied art, music, Italian, and medicine and lists her profession as harpist.[53] She was reelected in 1976.

The three Social Democratic newcomers were all reelected in 1976, are all married and have children, and all hold some kind of doctor's degree. Renate Lepsius (1927-), a homemaker, has studied history, literature, and political science. Anke Martiny-Glotz (1939-) is a journalist and music critic. Her husband, a sales engineer in Munich, does the housework and looks after their three children in his wife's absence. Herta Däubler-Gmelin (1943-), born in Bratislava, Czechoslovakia, is a lawyer.

Helga Schuchardt (1939-), an FDP member from Hamburg, was also reelected in 1976. She is a professional engineer. Schuchardt states that a woman in public life has to take a higher risk with the continuation of her marriage and her family than her male colleagues.[54] Real equality, she maintains, will only be achieved when it will no longer take an exceptionally highly developed sense of self-confidence for a man to say, "I am a househusband and my wife is a member of the Bundestag."[55]

Six women arrived during the 1972-76 period to fill unexpired vacancies. Barbara Lüdemann (1922-), an educator, served from September 1973 until 1976 as an FDP member. Angela Grützmann (1937-), a Socialist from Berlin, sat in Bonn between February 1974 and the 1976 election. Doris Pack (1942-), a Christian Democrat schoolteacher from the Saarland, came in June 1974 and was reelected in 1976. Wiltrud Rehlen (1930-), an economist, filled a two-year vacancy for the SPD from Hamburg. Waltraud Steinhauer (1925-), a Socialist and labor union secretary, arrived in December 1974 and won reelection in 1976. Erna-Maria Geier (1923-), a widow with six children and a professional educator, arrived in March 1976 and was returned from Hesse in the following general election for the CDU.

The Eighth Bundestag (1976-80)

As a result of the 1976 elections, 26 former female members came back (12 CDU, one CSU, 11 SPD, and two FDP). Among the 12 newcomers were five Christian Democrats, one Christian Social, four Social Democrats, and two Free Democrats. By the summer of 1979, two vacancies were filled by women, one by Riede for the CDU and one by a Social Democrat. Interestingly enough, in this Bundestag, the CDU had more women representatives than the SPD, a clear indication that the Left no longer has a monopoly on women in politics.

The five CDU newcomers included Leni Fischer (1935-), an educator and now a homemaker; Ingeborg Hoffmann (1923-), who is trained in the hotel business; Irmgard Karwatzki (1940-), a social worker who had served on the Duisburg City Council; Dorothee Wilms (1929-), who holds a doctorate in political science; and Roswitha Wisniewski (1926-), a linguist and university professor.

The four Social Democrats, all married, include the following women. Liesel Hartenstein (1928-), a high school teacher, is interested in the environment and an advocate of tougher pollution control measures.[56] Brigitte Erler (1943-), also a high school teacher, has studied history, Latin, and political science. Heide Simonis (1943-), married to a professor, is an economist. Brigitte Traupe (1943-), a former schoolteacher, has participated in local politics and served on a municipal council.

Ursula Krone-Appuhn (1936-), a CSU member who first worked for the CDU, has studied law and Russian.

Ingrid Matthäus-Maier (1945-) is the youngest woman in the Eighth Bundestag. An FDP representative, she is a lawyer and was a judge before coming to Bonn.

Hildegard Hamm-Brücher (1921-), a Free Democrat, has been a member of the Munich City Council and the Bavarian land parliament. She has worked in the Foreign Office.

As previously mentioned, there were two female replacements by the summer of 1979. In addition to Riede, a vacancy was filled by Christa Czempiel (1925-), who arrived in January 1979. She represents the SPD from Hesse.

DISCUSSION

Thus, in the 60 years between 1919 and 1979, 245 women have sat in German national legislatures,* 111 until Hitler came to power

---

*Not included is the Volkskammer of the German Democratic Republic.

in 1933 and 139 in the Bundestag (with five obtaining membership in both republics). This is the largest number of women in any of the six countries here under discussion. Table 6.2 gives details about the German legislative periods.

TABLE 6.2

Number of Women at the Start of German
Legislative Periods

Year	Total Membership	Number of Women	Percent of Women
1919	423	36	8.51
1920	466	37	7.94
1924 (May)	472	29	6.14
1924 (December)	493	33	6.69
1928	491	33	6.72
1930	577	39	6.76
1932 (July)	608	37	6.09
1932 (November)	584	35	5.99
1933 (March)	647*	29	4.48
1933 (November)	669	0	0
1936	741	0	0
1938	814	0	0
1949	402 (410)	27 (28)	6.72 (6.83)
1953	487 (509)	40 (45)	8.21 (8.84)
1957	497 (519)	43 (48)	8.65 (9.25)
1961	499 (521)	40 (43)	8.02 (8.25)
1965	496 (518)	33 (36)	6.65 (6.95)
1969	496 (518)	32 (35)	6.45 (6.76)
1972	496 (518)	28 (30)	5.65 (5.79)
1976	496 (518)	36 (38)	7.26 (7.34)

*Included are the 81 Communists, nine of whom were women, who were elected in March 1933 but not allowed to take their seats.

Note: Figures in parentheses include the members from Berlin.

Sources: Max Schwarz, ed., MdR: Biographisches Handbuch der Reichstage (Hanover: Verlag für Literatur und Zeitgeschehen, 1965), pp. 822–24; and Hans Ulrich Behn, Die Bundesrepublik Deutschland (Munich: Günter Olzog Verlag, 1974), pp. 157–65. The last two columns were compiled by the author.

The highest percentage of female membership was reached in the very early days of the Weimar Republic and was never again achieved during that period. The actual number varied between 29 and 39. The lowest percentage, reached in March 1933, can be attributed to the rise of Nazism. That the figure was even that high was due to the relative strength of the Communists. Indeed, if one disregards that party and recognizes that its members were unable to play any part at all in March 1933, one gets a much lower figure, namely, 3.53 percent (20 out of 566).

In the Second Republic, each new election brought a sizable number of women into the Bundestag. The number varied from a low of 27 to a high of 43, averaging 35 per election. If the female members from Berlin are counted, the figures are still higher. Moreover, quite frequently women were called upon to fill vacancies (see Table 6.3). Such replacements were numerically much more significant in the Second Republic than in the First, probably because of the longer intervals between elections under the Bonn regime. In the seven completed legislative periods between 1949 and 1976, an average of six women came in to fill vacancies in each parliament. The 42 instances between 1949 and 1976 compare with 19 between 1919 and 1933. Therefore, the complaint of being reduced to Grabspringer is justified, although a number of outstanding female members, such as Lüders, Berger, and Schlei, first entered the Bundestag as replacements during parliamentary sessions.

Because the Weimar Republic lasted only from 1919 until 1933, tenure in the Reichstag was short for every member. There were five women who served throughout that period. Two, Schroeder and Weber,* added service in the Bundestag after 1949 and sat in the national legislature until their deaths, for a total of 22 and 23 years, respectively. Lüders fell one year short of the two-decade mark, having served 11 years in the Reichstag and eight in the Bundestag. There was quite a turnover because of the frequent elections, and the party situation was very flexible, that is, parties gained and lost much support from one election to the next. Thus, the average length of service of the 111 women in the First Republic was 4.8 years.

---

*There are conflicting reports regarding Weber. Some have her serving continuously from 1919 until 1933; others have an interruption from 1920 to 1924 when she served in the Prussian parliament. I have accepted the latter, because of details in Parlamentarierinnen in deutschen Parlamenten, 1919-1976 (Bonn: Deutscher Bundestag Wissenschaftliche Dienste, 1976), p. 19.

TABLE 6.3

Vacancies Filled by Women

Session	Number
Nationalversammlung (1919–20)	5
First Reichstag (1920–24)	5
Second Reichstag (May–December 1924)	0
Third Reichstag (1924–28)	2
Fourth Reichstag (1928–30)	3
Fifth Reichstag (1930–32)	4
Sixth Reichstag (July–November 1932)	0
Seventh Reichstag	0
First Bundestag (1949–53)	7
Second Bundestag (1953–57)	8
Third Bundestag (1957–61)	2
Fourth Bundestag (1961–65)	10[a]
Fifth Bundestag (1965–69)	8[b]
Sixth Bundestag (1969–72)	1
Seventh Bundestag (1972–76)	6[a]

[a]Includes one from Berlin.
[b]Includes two from Berlin.
Source: Compiled by the author.

The length of service in the Bonn Republic is an entirely different matter. Unlike the Weimar Republic, where nine meaningful elections were held between January 1919 and March 1933 (approximately one every 18 months), the Bundestage have lasted four years each, with the single exception of the Sixth, which was dissolved after three years. Therefore, a woman who took her seat at the beginning of a legislative period would usually remain in office for a full four years, even if she did not return the next time. Among the 42 Grabspringer, there were at least a dozen who returned to full terms at the next election. About 100 served four years or more. The average stay in office comes to approximately eight years and ten months, almost double that of the Weimar Republic. The average time spent in the Bundestag is a little lower for men (seven years and ten months for males in the 1949–75 period).[57] Seven of the women whose service has been completed were in the Bundestag 20 years or more. By mid-1979, there were two women in Bonn who had already reached the 20-year mark: Renger, who came in 1953, and Eilers, who arrived in 1957.

The point has been made repeatedly that, in comparison with single-member districts, it is easier for a woman to be put on a list together with many men and to be elected in that way. This, of course, serves two purposes. One can sneak a woman in, hoping that antifeminists will overlook her presence. At the same time, profeminists will be appeased because a woman is after all on the list. Moreover, if a relatively low position on the list does not elect the woman, the blame can be put on the doorstep of the voters. It is quite true that the vast majority of the female members of the Bundestag entered by way of land lists (or election by the Berlin Chamber of Deputies). But it is patently wrong to say (as does one otherwise very fine work on West Germany's governmental and political structure)[58] that no women are elected from districts.

TABLE 6.4

Female Bundestag Members Elected from Districts

Year	SPD	CDU	FDP	CSU	Others	Total	Total Number of Women Elected*
1949	6	5	0	1	0	12	27
1953	3	5	0	1	0	9	40
1957	4	3	0	1	1	9	44
1961	5	1	0	1	0	7	40
1965	6	1	0	1	0	8	33
1969	5	0	0	0	0	5	32
1972	4	0	0	0	0	4	28
1976	5	2	0	0	0	7	36

*Does not include women elected from Berlin or those filling unexpired vacancies during parliamentary sessions.

Sources: Parlamentarierinnen in deutschen Parlamenten, 1919-1976 (Bonn: Deutscher Bundestag Wissenschaftliche Dienste, 1976); and Kürschners Volkshandbuch: Deutscher Bundestag 8. Wahlperiode (Rheinbreitbach: Neue Darmstädter Verlaganstalt, 1978).

The number of women elected in districts is only a fraction of the total number of elected women, as Table 6.4 clearly shows. Thus, if this were the only way in which people were elected to the Bundestag, there would be far fewer women. The system of electing by land list is clearly largely responsible for the rather high percentage of women we find in the German Bundestag as compared to the U.S. House of Representatives and the British House of Commons.

But two factors ought to be considered. One is that there are a total of 248 districts in the German Federal Republic today. This compares with 635 members of the present British House of Commons, 435 of the U.S. House of Representatives, and 282 of the recently elected Canadian House of Commons. If we prorate these figures, the Germans are still not doing too badly. Also to be taken into account is the fact that a land list, after all, does exist. If single-member constituencies were the only method of electing candidates, it is perhaps reasonable to suggest that more women would be candidates in winnable areas. For example, it is hard to imagine that a way would not be found to get Renger or Wex into the Bundestag. It is a fact that in the past people like Brauksiepe and Schwarzhaupt were elected sometimes in districts and sometimes through the land list. This would still leave open the question about the future of the Free Democrats, but then no FDP candidate, male or female, has been able to win in a district in quite a while anyway.

Turning now to the age of the female parliamentarians, seven women under 30 were elected to the Weimar Republic. All but one of them belonged to the Communist party. The oldest three were in their mid-sixties when they first arrived in the Reichstag, two of whom served short, unexpired terms. In Bonn, on the other hand, only one female representative was under 30 when first chosen, 13 were 61 and over, and three were in their seventies. These three had previously been in the Reichstag, and their return to parliamentary life as veterans of another era was quite understandable, even in view of their advanced ages.

Table 6.5 shows the preponderance of the Communists and Social Democrats among the parties that sent women to the legislature in the days of the Weimar Republic. These parties had been the first to take up the cry of equality; apparently, they practiced what they preached. The leftist groups accounted for fully two-thirds of the female members. Considering that the Communists had only 510 mandates altogether during the Weimar period and that a number of their members were reelected, 23 individual Communist women in the Reichstag was quite an achievement.

TABLE 6.5

Ages of Women Entering Weimar Legislature

| | Age Group | | | | | |
	21–30	31–40	41–50	51–60	61–70	Total
SPD	1	12	18	6	1	38
Communist	6	10	5	1	1	23
Other leftists	0	3	7	2	0	12
Zentrum	0	4	4	2	2	12
DNVP	0	1	3	7	0	11
DDP	0	1	5	1	0	7
DVP	0	1	4	1	0	6
Others	0	1[a]	0	1[b]	0	2
Total	7	33	46	21	4	111

[a]Bavarian People's party.
[b]Christian People's party.
Source: Compiled by the author.

The Communists also came up with the youngest women members; six were under 30, and 16 were not older than 40. No other party had quite such an emphasis on youth among their female members, although this was not necessarily a point in their favor, considering the tradition-conscious mentality of the German electorate at that time. The majority of the women entering the Reichstag were below the age of 50, with the exception of the German Nationalists. We have already commented on the fact that they were present at all, since the Right, especially the extreme Right, did not seem to think that women belonged in politics. But it is probably significant that when the upper-middle and upper classes who supported this movement elected women, the women tended to be older.

When German democracy was reborn after 16 years of Hitler, war, and occupation, the Left had clearly lost its preponderance of female members, as is indicated by Table 6.6. The Left, as a revolutionary force attempting sweeping changes in society, was practically nonexistent in the Bundestag. The Communists were represented only between 1949 and 1953, and the Social Democrats were involved in a process that moved them more to the center, toward respectability and what George Bernard Shaw had called "middle class morality." They elected a large number of female members but have now been overtaken by the CDU. If both Christian

parties are taken together, by mid-1979 they had presented the
Bundestag with eight more female members than the SPD. This has
to be considered in light of the fact that only in 1972 did the Socialists have a plurality of seats. In other words, except for the instance just noted, there have always been more CDU/CSU deputies
than SPD members in the Bundestag, so that a 62-to-54 edge in
female representatives is not quite as impressive as it otherwise
might be. The small Free Democrats have always had a few women
among their handful of delegates. Other small parties have also
been represented by some women, but since 1961 these small parties have disappeared from the Bundestag altogether.

TABLE 6.6

Ages of Women Entering Bonn Legislature

	Age Group						
	21-30	31-40	41-50	51-60	61-70	71-80	Total
SPD	1	13	26	11	2	1	54
CDU	0	7	21	22	6	0	56
CSU	0	2	3	1	0	0	6
FDP	0	4	3	4	1	2	14
Others*	0	3	1	4	1	0	9
Total	1	29	54	42	10	3	139

*Others include two Communists (aged 36 and 40), one German
party (aged 40), two Zentrum (aged 51 and 63), two All German/
Refugee Bloc (aged 50 and 51), one Independent (aged 53), and one
who changed from a splinter party to Independent (aged 46).
Source: Compiled by the author.

As mentioned earlier, in the Bundestag the emphasis does not
seem to be on youth. When Däubler-Gmelin was elected in November 1972, she was still several months away from her thirtieth birthday and thus became the youngest female member in the history of
the Bundestag. Only 30 women were under 40 when first arriving
in Bonn. Socialist women, as a rule, enter the Bundestag at an
earlier age than do those of the CDU.
Although we have precise data about the ages of the deputies,
such statistics are not always available when it comes to marital
status and other family information, which may well be regarded as

a person's private affair. However, in early 1955 a survey was taken of the 47 deputies who were women.[59] Of these women, 19 referred to themselves as homemakers. Most of them (31) were married, and not very many were widowed. All married representatives had children. They had 58 children among them, and several had either stepchildren or adopted ones. A few of the children were under ten years old, several others were teenagers, but a good many were grown up by the time their mothers went to Bonn. One mother, whose children were 26 and 30, commented that she would not have considered entering the Bundestag if the children had still been at home and need of motherly care. However, this opinion was clearly not shared by everybody. It must be emphasized that these data were obtained from one group in one particular year and therefore may or may not be typical. Figures about the Eighth Bundestag list 12 female members as unmarried, 19 as married, and four as widowed, with no specific data on the rest.[60]

We have repeatedly noted the sad fact that quite a few of the deputies of the Reichstag had to suffer during the Nazi period. Unfortunately, undergoing persecution in the Third Reich is part of the biography of many female deputies who were old enough to participate in politics before Hitler came to power. Hitler did not discriminate between the sexes when he had a chance to even the score with his enemies, and women were treated just as inhumanely as men. Practically all the female deputies of the Communist party suffered in one way or another, and many of their Socialist colleagues shared their fate. The brief notations in the preceding pages indicate that a sizable number of prominent German women paid for their political activities and convictions with blood and tears.

When discussing the regional distribution of female legislators, we will concentrate on the Second Republic only. The Germany of the Weimar Republic was much larger, and it contained many states quite different from those in existence today. For example, Prussia has now disappeared altogether, and such Länder as North Rhine-Westphalia are entirely new, post-World War II creations. Therefore, a geographic comparison between Weimar and Bonn would not be too meaningful. However, it may be noted that, with so many women in the First Republic belonging to the Left, a large number of them obviously represented industrial areas, which were leftist strongholds.

Table 6.7 shows that female legislators are fairly widespread throughout the Federal Republic, at least as far as the Bundestag is concerned. The small city state of Bremen alone has never sent a woman to Bonn, although its strong Social Democratic vote attests to its otherwise progressive inclinations. The other city state, Hamburg, on the other hand, has been represented by quite a few

TABLE 6.7

Female Bundestag Members by States and Parties

Land	Total Number of Seats (1976)	SPD	CDU	CSU	FDP	Others	Total
Bavaria	88	3	0	6(1)	2(1)	1(1)	12(3)
Baden–Württemberg	71	10	7(2)	0	2(1)	1(1)	20(4)
Bremen	5	0	0	0	0	0	0
Hamburg	14	4(2)	2	0	2	0	8(2)
Hesse	47	5(3)	6(2)	0	1(1)	0	12(6)
Lower Saxony	62	5	6(1)	0	1	3(1)	15(2)
North Rhine–Westphalia	148	14	20(4)	0	4	3(1)	41(5)
Rhineland–Palatinate	31	2(2)	9(4)	0	0	0	11(6)
Saarland	8	0	1(1)	0	0	0	1(1)
Schleswig–Holstein	22	4	2(1)	0	0	1(1)	7(2)
Berlin	22	7(2)	3(2)	0	2	0	12(4)
Total	518	54(9)	56(17)	6(1)	14(3)	9(5)	139(35)

Notes: The table reflects the situations of female members when first entering the Bundestag. Later changes are not shown.

Figures in parentheses indicate how many of the total filled unexpired vacancies (for example, one out of six CSU in Bavaria).

Source: Kürschners Volkshandbuch: Bundestag 8. Wahlperiode (Rheinbreitbach: Neue Darmstädter Verlaganstalt, 1978), pp. 33–40.

women. Another small Land, the Saar area, has had only one
woman in the Bundestag; she came in to fill a vacancy and was reelected. North Rhine-Westphalia, the state with the largest population and therefore the largest contingent in Bonn, has also had
more female representatives than any other state. Baden-Württem-
berg is second. Bavaria, the second-most populated state, lags a
little behind, which may be due to some rather conservative rural
areas.

Table 6.7 also shows that a large number of women, exactly
25 percent, got their start in Bonn by coming in to fill a vacancy.
However, the widow syndrome, so important in the countries previously discussed, does not seem to exist in Germany. After all,
when the next person on the party list is advanced to fill a vacancy,
it is unlikely to be the wife or widow of the person replaced. Moreover, there is no political need to cash in on the name and reputation of the outgoing member, since no new election is involved.

In our discussion of the United States, Britain, and Canada,
we have stressed how a female legislator's career ended and whether
she retired voluntarily or was defeated. Such a point is most difficult to make where a list system operates. Unless some specific
information is available in a person's biography or through personal
interviews, one can only speculate that on reaching a certain age
and/or after so many years of service, a legislator decided on retirement or that, if someone filled a vacancy on more than one oc-
cation, departure from the Reichstag or Bundestag was not entirely
voluntary. However, in most cases such assumptions must remain
merely assumptions.

We have been concerned with democratic Germany, the Weimar
Republic and its successor, the Second Republic. However, something should be said of the "other Germany," the Communist-
controlled German Democratic Republic. Mention has repeatedly
been made of the fact that in the Weimar Republic the parties of the
Left were very much in the forefront in putting into practice their
demands for equality among the sexes as far as female participation
in political life was concerned. One would therefore expect the German Democratic Republic to continue this tradition by sending a
large number of women into the Volkskammer, East Germany's Parliament. This expectation is fully realized, as Table 6.8 shows.

There is even a special women's organization in the German
Democratic Republic that claims to have its own seats in the People's
Chamber (35), in addition to 229 seats in county assemblies, 1,756
in district and town assemblies, and 17,942 in borough and village
assemblies, for a grand total of 19,962 seats.[61] These figures are
certainly impressive, since they clearly show a far greater degree
of female participation in decision making at various levels in East

Germany than in any of the countries discussed more extensively in this book. But Gabriele Gast notes that equality for women is still far away.[62] Women serve shorter periods in the Volkskammer than men and thus lack the continuity and experience that goes with being in the legislature. Moreover, leadership positions are still overwhelmingly occupied by men, and women's participation is largely concentrated in social, cultural, and commercial committees, thus severely limiting female influence. It also must be added that the entire membership of the Volkskammer is chosen by way of an uncontested slate, nor are there meaningful elections for the other assemblies. The real powers of the rank and file are very minimal indeed, thus largely reducing the Volkskammer and the other councils to exercises in futility. Therefore, while the proportion of women in the Bundestag is much smaller than it is across the border in the Volkskammer, it is of course much more significant.

TABLE 6.8

Women Members of the East German Volkskammer

	Total Number of Deputies	Number of Women	Percent of Women
Provisional Volkskammer, 1949	330	53	16.1
First Volkskammer, 1950	400	92	23.0
Second Volkskammer, 1954	400	92	23.0
Third Volkskammer, 1958	400	95	23.8
Fourth Volkskammer, 1963	434	115	26.5
Fifth Volkskammer, 1967	434	131	30.2
Sixth Volkskammer, 1971	434	133	30.6

Source: Gabriele Gast, Die politische Rolle der Frau in der DDR (Düsseldorf: Bertelsmann Universitätsverlag, 1973), p. 165.

That there is not adequate female representation in West Germany and in many other democratic countries is to be deplored. One commentator traced back this inadequacy to these causes: lack of education and training of women, traditional customs and fashions, lack of time and energy due to women's domestic duties, and men![63]

The Federal Republic of Germany has not given women many of the important positions in government. True, Renger presided

TABLE 6.9

The Weimar Republic's Legislatures and Female Members

	Number of Women	Names
German National Assembly (January 19, 1919)	36	Blos, Bollmann, Höfs, Lührs, Lutze, Röhl-Kirschmann, Simon, Eichler, Ryneck, Tesch, Kähler, Hauke, Schilling, Reitze, Bohm-Schuch, Pfülf, Schroeder, Juchacz, Hübler, Zietz, Agnes, Ekke, Kloss, Brönner, Baum, Bäumer, Schmitz, Zettler, Dransfeld, Neuhaus, Teusch, Weber, Mende, Gierke, Schirmacher, Behm
Vacancies	5	Lodahl (February 1919), Behnke (August 1919), Lüders (September 1919), Kurt (October 1919), Grüneberg (November 1919)
1st Reichstag (June 6, 1920)	37	Ryneck, Tesch, Kähler (to February 1921), Hauke (to December 1922), Schilling, Reitze, Bohm-Schuch, Pfülf, Schroeder, Juchacz, Zietz (to January 1922) Agnes, Brönner (to February 1921), Baum (to February 1921), Bäumer, Dransfeld, Neuhaus, Teusch, Mende, Behm, Lüders, Eschholz (to June 1920), Schulz, Schreiber-Krieger, Ansorge, Wackwitz, Ziegler, Wulff, Sender, Nemitz, Wurm, Karch, Zetkin, Kardoff-Oheimb, Matz, Mueller-Otfried, Lang-Brumann
Vacancies	5	Eichler (September 1921), Hoffmann (December 1921), Bartels (August 1922), Schott (March 1923), Fritsch (March 1923)
2nd Reichstag (May 4, 1924)	29	Reitze, Bohm-Schuch, Pfülf, Schroeder, Juchacz, Agnes, Baumer, Dransfeld, Neuhaus, Teusch, Mende, Behm, Lüders, Weber, Sender, Nemitz, Wurm, Zetkin, Mueller-Otfried, Lang-Brumann, Bartels, Schott, Stegmann, Sperber, Magnus, Backenecker, Reitler, Krüger, Gohlke
3rd Reichstag (December 7, 1924)	33	Reitze, Bohm-Schuch, Pfülf, Schroeder, Juchacz, Agnes, Bäumer, Dransfeld (to March 1925), Neuhaus, Teusch, Mende, Behm, Lüders, Weber, Schilling, Sender, Nemitz, Wurm, Zetkin, Mueller-Otfried, Lang-Brumann, Bartels (to October 1925), Schott, Schulz, Ansorge, Matz, Sperber, Stegmann, Gohlke, Arendsee, Arning, Schiffgens, Scheidel
Vacancies	2	Blum (December 1925), Philipp (April 1926)

4th Reichstag (May 20, 1928)	33	Reitze, Bohm–Schuch, Pfülf, Schroeder, Juchacz, Agnes, Bäumer, Neuhaus, Teusch, Lüders, Weber, Sender, Nemitz, Wurm, Zetkin, Mueller–Otfried, Lang–Brumann, Schulz, Ansorge, Matz, Schreiber–Krieger, Stegmann, Arendsee, Arning, Schiefgens, Reese, Kurfürst, Siemsen, Weich, Kunert, Overlach, Lehmann, Hertwig–Bünger
Vacancies	3	Fuchs (March 1929), Dettmer (January 1930), Kiep–Altenloh (May 1930)
5th Reichstag (September 14, 1930)	39	Reitze, Bohm–Schuch, Pfülf, Schroeder, Juchacz, Agnes, Baumer, Teusch, Weber, Sender, Nemitz, Wurm, Zetkin, Mueller–Otfried, Lang–Brumann, Schulz, Ansorge, Matz, Schreiber–Krieger, Reese, Weich, Kunert, Overlach, Lehmann, Esser, Mildenberg, Gropper, Körner, Ahlers, Augustat, Himmler, Blum, Zinke, Starrmann, Zammert, Peerenboom–Missong, Zillken, Tiling, Eitner
Vacancies	4	Driessen (January 1931), Lohse (March 1931), Sandtner (July 1931), Fiedler (January 1932)
6th Reichstag (July 31, 1932)	37	Reitze, Bohm–Schuch, Pfülf, Schroeder, Juchacz, Agnes, Teusch, Weber, Sender, Nemitz, Wurm, Zetkin, Mueller–Otfried, Lang–Brumann, Schulz, Ansorge, Matz, Schreiber–Krieger, Kunert, Overlach, Reese, Lehmann, Körner, Ahlers, Augustat, Himmler, Zinke, Starrmann, Zammert, Peerenboom–Missong, Zillken, Tiling, Driessen, Siebert, Fleischer, Kessel, Ullrich
7th Reichstag (November 6, 1932)	35	Bohm–Schuch, Pfülf, Schroeder, Juchacz, Agnes, Teusch, Weber, Sender, Nemitz, Wurm, Zetkin, Lang–Brumann, Schulz, Ansorge, Matz, Kunert, Reese, Overlach, Lehmann, Korner, Ahlers, Augustat, Himmler, Zinke, Starrmann, Zammert, Peerenboom–Missong, Zillken, Tiling, Blum, Fleischer, Kessel, Ullrich, Kirsch, Rawengel (to December 1932)
8th Reichstag (March 5, 1933)	29	Bohm–Schuch, Pfülf, Schroeder, Juchacz, Agnes, Teusch, Weber, Nemitz, Wurm, Zetkin, Lang–Brumann, Schulz, Kunert, Reese, Overlach, Lehmann, Körner, Ahlers, Augustat, Himmler, Starrmann, Zammert, Peerenboom–Missong, Zillken, Tiling, Ullrich, Siebert, Meier

Note: Unless otherwise indicated, dates in parentheses show when members entered the Reichstag.
Source: Compiled by the author.

TABLE 6.10

West Germany's Bundestag and Female Members

	Number of Women	Names
1st Bundestag (August 14, 1949)	28 (1)	Weber, Krahnstover, Albrecht, Meyer–Laule, Nadig, Keilhack, Döhring, Kipp–Kaule, Albertz, Korspeter, Hubert, Schanzenbach, Strobel, Gröwel, Heiler, Dietz, Niggemeyer, Brökelschen, Steinbiss, Rösch, Rehling, Brauksiepe, Probst, Thiele, Arnold, Wessel, Kalinke, Schroeder*
Vacancies	7	Hütter (September 1949), Ilk (November 1949), Lockmann (November 1950), Strohbach (May 1951), Ansorge (November 1951), Jaeger (February 1952), Bieganowski (March 1952)
Additions (February 1, 1952)	3 (3)	Maxsein*, Mulert*, Wolff*
2nd Bundestag (September 6, 1953)	45 (5)	Weber, Albrecht, Meyer–Laule, Nadig, Keilhack, Döhring, Kipp–Kaule, Albertz, Korspeter, Hubert, Schanzenbach, Strobel, Dietz, Niggemeyer, Steinbiss, Brökelschen, Rösch, Rehling, Brauksiepe, Probst, Schroeder* (to June 1957), Ilk, Lockmann, Maxsein*, Wolff*, Meyer, Bennemann, Kettig, Kurlbaum–Beyer, Rudoll, Renger, Jochmus, Praetorius, Vietje, Bleyler, Ackermann, Schwarzhaupt, Pitz–Savelsberg, Geisendörfer, Kuchtner, Friese–Korn, Finselberger, Finckenstein, Lüders*, Berger–Heise*
Vacancies	8	Kalinke (June 1955), Hütter (September 1955), Welter (January 1954), Ganswindt (November 1955), Gantenberg (October 1956), Kaiser (October 1956), Herklotz (September 1956), Peter (July 1957)

3rd Bundestag (September 15, 1957)	48 (5)	Weber, Albrecht (to May 1958), Meyer–Laule, Nadig, Keilhack, Döhring, Kipp–Kaule, Albertz, Korspeter, Hubert, Schanzenbach, Strobel, Niggemeyer, Steinbiss, Brökelschen, Rösch, Rehling, Brauksiepe, Probst, Wessel, Maxsein*, Wolff*, Kalinke, Bennemann, Kettig, Kurlbaum–Beyer, Rudoll, Renger, Bleyler, Ackermann, Schwarzhaupt, Pitz–Savelsberg, Geisendörfer, Kuchtner, Friese–Korn, Lüders*, Berger–Heise*, Welter, Gantenberg, Herklotz, Schmitt, Hamelbeck, Engländer, Pannhoff, Blohm, Eilers, Diemer–Nicolaus, Krappe*
Vacancies	2	Vietje (May 1960), Seppi (October 1959)
4th Bundestag (September 17, 1961)	43 (3)	Weber (to July 1962), Keilhack (to January 1962), Döhring, Kipp–Kaule, Albertz, Korspeter, Hubert, Schanzenbach, Strobel, Rehling (to May 1964), Brauksiepe, Probst, Wessel, Maxsein*, Kalinke, Kettig, Kurlbaum–Beyer, Rudoll, Renger, Bleyler, Schwarzhaupt, Pitz–Savelsberg, Geisendörfer, Kuchtner, Welter, Berger–Heise*, Herklotz, Pannhoff, Blohm, Eilers, Diemer–Nicolaus, Krappe*, Seppi, Vietje (to May 1963), Jacobi, Klee, C. Schroeder, Zimmermann, Meermann, Elsner, Flitz, Kiep–Altenloh, Funcke
Vacancies	10 (1)	Ackermann (January 1965), Engländer (August 1962), Freyh (December 1961), Heuser (December 1962), Haas (August 1963), Hagen (January 1964), Kleinert (November 1964), Stommel (December 1964), Griesinger (November 1964), Losche* (April 1963)
5th Bundestag (September 19, 1965)	36 (3)	Albertz, Korspeter, Hubert, Schanzenbach, Strobel, Brauksiepe, Probst (to May 1967, Wessel, Maxsein*, Kalinke, Kurlbaum–Beyer, Rudoll, Renger, Schwarzhaupt, Pitz–Savelsberg, Geisendörfer, Kuchtner, Berger–Heise*, Herklotz, Blohm, Eilers, Diemer–Nicolaus, Krappe*, Seppi, Jacobi, Klee, C. Schroeder, Meermann, Elsner, Funcke, Freyh, Stommel, Griesinger, Krips (to January 1969), Schimschok, Wolf
Vacancies	8 (2)	Lösche* (July 1966), Kleinert (December 1967), Heuser (March 1968), Enseling (April 1966), Wex (April 1967), Monikees (October 1967), Holzmeister (May 1968), Pieser* (June 1968)

(continued)

177

Table 6.10, continued

	Number of Women	Names
6th Bundestag (September 28, 1969)	35 (3)	Schanzenbach, Strobel, Brauksiepe, Wessel (to October 1969), Kalinke, Renger, Geisendörfer, Kuchtner, Herklotz, Eilers, Diemer-Nicolaus, Krappe*, Seppi, Jacobi, Klee, C. Schroeder, Meermann, Elsner (to May 1970), Funcke, Freyh, Stommel, Griesinger (to September 1972), Schimschok, Wolf, Pieser*, Henze (to April 1972), Walz, Tübler, Lauterback, Orth, Bothmer, Focke, Huber, Timm, Schlei*,
Vacancy	1	Berger (August 1971)
7th Bundestag (November 19, 1972)	30 (2)	Renger, Eilers, C. Schroeder, Funcke, Stommel, Meermann, Schimschok, Pieser*, Wolf, Orth, Wex, Bothmer, Focke, Huber, Walz, Tübler, Timm, Berger, Schlei*, Hürland, Benedix, Neumeister, Verhülsdonk, Will-Feld, Riede, Schleicher, Lepsius, Martiny-Glotz, Däubler-Gmelin, Schuchardt
Vacancies	6 (1)	Lüdemann (September 1973), Grützmann* (February 1974), Pack (June 1974), Rehlen (November 1974), Steinhauer (December 1974), Geier (March 1976)
8th Bundestag (October 3, 1976)	38 (2)	Renger, Eilers, Funcke, Pieser*, Wex, Bothmer, Focke, Huber, Walz, Tübler, Timm, Berger, Schlei*, Hürland, Benedix, Neumeister, Verhülsdonk, Will-Feld, Schleicher, Lepsius, Martiny-Glotz, Däubler-Gmelin, Schuchardt, Pack, Steinhauer, Geier, Fischer, Hoffmann, Karwatzki, Wilms, Wisniewski, Hartenstein, Erler, Simonis, Traupe, Krone-Appuhn, Matthäus-Maier, Hamm-Brücher
Vacancies	2	Riede (May 1977), Czempiel (January 1979)

*Member from Berlin.

Notes: Figures in parentheses indicate how many members from Berlin are included. Unless otherwise indicated, dates in parentheses show when members entered the Bundestag.

Source: Compiled by the author.

over the Bundestag for four years and even became her party's candidate for the federal presidency in a belated and hopeless effort to stop Karl Carstens in 1979. Women do serve on important committees and are playing leadership roles in their respective party executives. But not many have reached cabinet rank. It was with great reluctance that Chancellor Adenauer finally agreed to appoint Schwarzhaupt to be minister of health in 1961, a position she retained through Ludwig Erhard's term until the Grand Coalition was formed in 1966. Her post then went to a Socialist woman, Strobel, with family affairs later on entrusted to Brauksiepe of the CDU. In the years of the chancellorships of Willy Brandt and Helmut Schmidt, the now combined Ministry for Youth, Family, and Health was alternately headed by Strobel, Focke, and Huber, so that this ministry has now become almost a woman's domain. Future chancellors may have a difficult time should they decide to put a man in charge of this office. But its responsibilities are those traditionally regarded as "women's subjects." It was, therefore, quite refreshing to find that for two years Schlei was minister for economic cooperation and development, dealing with such matters as aid to developing areas in distant parts of the globe. Women have, over the years, held junior ministerial appointments: Focke and Schlei in the chancellery, Frey in the Ministry of Economic Cooperation, and Hamm-Brücher in the Foreign Office. These are important portfolios, but hardly more than mere tokens.

When asked to comment on the difficulties encountered by women in politics, members of the German Bundestag often remark that in view of the biological functions of the female, partnership between the sexes is really the key to the solution. Getting more women to take an interest in politics and to be willing to become candidates for office is widely recognized as a major problem. But Schuchardt demonstrates the importance of keeping a sense of proportion.

> We have to put an end to prejudices. Politics is not solely something concerning men, but neither will the great perpetual peace and the sublime humanity in politics be assured if more women were to enter Parliament. Even supposing that the good fairy would as her contribution to the Year of the Woman reverse the present relationship at the next Bundestag election and give us 483 female deputies and only 35 male ones: Would this alone be a guarantee for better political conditions?[64]

(For a concise listing of the women members of the West German legislatures, see Tables 6.9 and 6.10.)

NOTES

1. For a brief but excellent account of this period, see Walter Tormin, "Der Reichstag im Kaiserreich," in MdR: Biographisches Handbuch der Reichstage, ed. Max Schwarz (Hanover: Verlag für Literatur und Zeitgeschehen, 1965), pp. 115-36.

2. Ibid., p. 123.

3. Walter Tormin, "Die Volksvertretung der Weimarer Republik," in MdR: Biographisches Handbuch der Reichstage, ed. Max Schwarz (Hanover: Verlag für Literatur und Zeitgeschehen, 1965), pp. 509-28.

4. Ibid., p. 513.

5. Hugh W. Puckett, Germany's Women Go Forward (New York: Columbia University Press, 1930), p. 259.

6. Hildegard Meister-Trescher, "Frauenarbeit und Frauenfrage," in Handwörterbuch der Staatswissenschaften, eds. Ludwig Elster, Adolf Weber, and Friedrich Wieser, 4th ed. (Jena: Gustav Fischer Verlag, 1927), 4:338.

7. Ibid., p. 339.

8. Bericht über die Situation der Frau in Österreich (Vienna: Bundeskanzleramt, 1975), Heft 7:9. Certain parallels are drawn here between Germany and Austria.

9. Werner Thönnessen, The Emancipation of Women, trans. Joris de Bres (London: Pluto Press, 1973), p. 32.

10. Ibid., p. 47.

11. Ibid., p. 52.

12. Figures used in this chapter are those cited in Max Schwarz, ed., MdR: Biographisches Handbuch der Reichstage (Hanover: Verlag für Literatur und Zeitgeschehen, 1965). Unless otherwise stated, the biographical data of the women members are also taken from this work. Also used, particularly in identifying individuals, was Parlamentarierinnen in deutschen Parlamenten, 1919-1976 (Bonn: Deutscher Bundestag Wissenschaftliche Dienste, 1976).

13. Thönnessen, op. cit., p. 107.

14. Ibid., p. 110.

15. For a brief account of the Catholic Centrists, see Arnold Brecht, Prelude to Silence (New York: Oxford University Press, 1944), pp. 10-11.

16. Ortrud Stumpfe, "Lebensbilder deutscher Politikerinnen," Politische Studien, 1959, p. 675.

17. Lewis Hertzman, DNVP: Right-Wing Opposition in the Weimar Republic, 1918-1924 (Lincoln: University of Nebraska Press, 1963), p. 130.

18. Puckett, op. cit., p. 245.

19. Stumpfe, op. cit., p. 678.

20. Puckett, op. cit., p. 305.

21. Schwarz, op. cit.

22. Stumpfe, op. cit., p. 671.

23. Thönnessen, op. cit., p. 155.

24. Erich Eyck, A History of the Weimar Republic (New York: Atheneum, 1970), 2:428.

25. Ibid., p. 13.

26. Ibid., pp. 95-96.

27. Karl Dietrich Bracher, Stufen der Machtergreifung (Cologne: Westdeutscher Verlag, Ullstein Buch, 1974), pp. 410-11.

28. Schwarz, op. cit., p. 715.

29. Gabriele Gast, Die politische Rolle der Frau in der DDR (Düsseldorf: Bertelsmann Universitätsverlag, 1973), p. 302.

30. Ibid., p. 289.

31. Quoted from the Vossische Zeitung of July 6, 1933, in George L. Mosse, Nazi Culture (New York: Grosset & Dunlap, Universal Library, 1968), pp. 42-43.

32. Quoted in Mosse, op. cit., p. 47.

33. Gerda Hollunder, "Gleichberechtigung im Alltag?," in Was haben die Parteien für die Frauen getan?, ed. Carola Stern (Reinbek bei Hamburg: Rowohlt Taschenbuch Verlag, 1976), p. 28. My translation.

34. Friedrich Schäfer, Der Bundestag (Opladen: Westdeutscher Verlag, 1975), pp. 165-66.

35. Hans Ulrich Behn, Die Bundesrepublik Deutschland (Munich: Günter Olzog Verlag, 1974), p. 157. This book has served as a most useful source for various statistics.

36. Parlamentarierinnen in deutschen Parlamenten, p. 92.

37. Walter Henkels, 99 Bonner Köpfe (Frankfurt am Main: Fischer Bücherei, 1965), pp. 129-30.

38. Henkels, op. cit., pp. 54-56.

39. For a brief description of the fate of the Zentrum, see Günter Olzog and Arthur Herzig, Die politischen Parteien (Munich: Günter Olzog Verlag, 1977), pp. 72-73.

40. Fritz Sänger, ed., Handbuch des deutschen Bundestages (Stuttgart: J. G. Cotta'sche Buchhandlung Nachfolger, 1954), p. 330.

41. Information about Annemarie Renger was chiefly obtained from Lore Breuer, Frauen in der Politik: Annemarie Renger, Liselotte Funcke (Koblenz: Frauenverlag, 1975).

42. Ibid., p. 64. My translation.

43. Frauen im deutschen Bundestag: I. bis VI. Wahlperiode (Bonn: Deutscher Bundestag Wissenschaftliche Dienste, 1971).

44. Ibid., p. 27.

45. Henkels, op. cit., p. 231.

46. Frauen im deutschen Bundestag, in Anna Rudolph's article, pp. 26-27.

47. Breuer, op. cit., p. 130.

48. Ibid., p. 136.

49. Frauen im deutschen Bundestag, from Das Parlament, Bonn, November 15, 1969, p. 65.

50. Lieselotte Berger, Lenelotte von Bothmer, and Helga Schuchardt, Frauen ins Parlament? (Reinbek bei Hamburg: Rowohlt Taschenbuch Verlag, 1976), p. 22.

51. Frau und Gesellschaft (Zwischenbericht der Enquete-Kommission, Deutscher Bundestag, 1977), pp. 58-59. My translation.

52. Berger, Bothmer, and Schuchardt, op. cit., pp. 57, 67-68.

53. Kürschners Volkshandbuch: Deutscher Bundestag 8. Wahlperiode (Rheinbreitbach: Neue Darmstädter Verlaganstalt, 1978), p. 168.

54. Berger, Bothmer, and Schuchardt, op. cit., p. 44.

55. Ibid., p. 55. My translation.

56. German Tribune, June 18, 1978.

57. Parlamentarierinnen in deutschen Parlamenten, p. 42.

58. Kurt Sontheimer, The Government and Politics of West Germany (New York: Praeger, 1973), p. 112.

59. Charlotte Lütkens, "Die Familienverhältnisse der weiblichen Bundestagsabgeordneten," Zeitschrift für Politik (Jg. 6, N.F., Heft I, pp. 58-61, 1959). Reprinted in Frauen im deutschen Bundestag, pp. 29-32.

60. Kürschners Volkshandbuch, p. 221.

61. Panorama DDR: Documentation (Auslandspresseagentur, GDR, Berlin, 1976), p. 5.

62. Gast, op. cit., p. 245.

63. Gabriele Strecker, Der Weg der Frau in die Politik, 3rd ed. rev. (Bonn: Eichholz Verlag, 1975), p. 34.

64. Frauen ins Parlament?, pp. 83-84. My translation.

7
THE AUSTRIAN NATIONALRAT

HISTORY

We have seen that in the United States and Britain democracy preceded woman suffrage. In both countries, there existed viable democratic legislatures before the female half of the population was enfranchised at the end of World War I. In Germany and in Austria, democracy and the right of women to vote and to participate actively as candidates were achieved at the same time. In the old Austrian Empire, despite its basically autocratic structure, there was some semblance of popular representation. In addition to the House of Lords, the Herrenhaus of the nobility, there was the House of Deputies, the Haus der Abgeordneten. At first, members were elected to this body by different classes of voters, but after 1907, they were chosen on the basis of equal, direct, and secret suffrage. However, voting was still restricted to men only.[1]

In the second half of the nineteenth century, the right to vote for village and provincial councils was granted to tax-paying citizens, and this sometimes included women. In some instances, they were specifically excluded, while in other cases, their voting rights had to be exercised on their behalf by males, notably their husbands.[2] Probably not too many people would have disagreed with a view expressed at the time that political activities would only divert women from their original tasks of looking after family and home and that it was the calling of the man to represent the state internally and externally. Besides, it was deemed desirable for Parliament to become not feminine, but on the contrary stronger and more masculine.[3]

This was the opinion of a Liberal deputy who did not think much of universal suffrage, male or female, and this attitude was shared by members of the Christian Social party. Only the Social Democrats fought for equality of the sexes, although economic equality and improved working conditions for everybody were subjects of greater interest to them than voting rights. Several women's organizations, however, did fight for female suffrage. Periodicals were devoted to that cause, and there were meetings and conferences of women's groups, though these did not always advocate the idea of woman suffrage. (Erika Weinzierl reports that in 1910 the First Austrian Women's Conference actually came out against woman suffrage and against political activities by women.)[4]

The war changed all this. While opposition had not completely disappeared, a Social Democratic deputy in 1917 demanded full political equality for women "not because they are suffering most in this war, but because of the actual achievements made by women in these difficult times, and because the collaboration of women in the tasks of the administration has proven to be a dire necessity in the interest of the common good."[5] When the empire was on the verge of collapse, the Catholic and the national women's organizations joined in calling for voting rights for both sexes. Sweeping changes were in the offing. The non-German-speaking parts of the old Austro-Hungarian Empire were leaving the sinking ship. The hastily constituted Provisional National Assembly of the remaining German-speaking sections of Austria clamored for fusion with Germany (which the victorious Allies denied) and at the same time extended to all adult citizens the right to vote and the right to be elected. Every man or woman who had reached the age of 21 on January 1, 1919, was entitled to vote. Every eligible voter above the age of 29 had the right to be elected. One deputy was to represent 40,000 voters.[6] The voting system has since been modified. Above all, the minimum voting age has been lowered to 19, and a candidate for office must have attained 25 years of age by the New Year's Day preceding the election.[7]

WOMEN MEMBERS OF THE AUSTRIAN NATIONALRAT

The Election of 1919

On February 16, 1919, the first elections of the Austrian Republic took place. To be chosen were the members of the Constituent Assembly. Women participated in large numbers. Thus, in Vienna, 54.91 percent of the electorate consisted of women, of whom 81.79 percent voted as compared with 87.39 percent of the eligible men. In Salzburg, men and women voted in about equal proportions (about 82 percent), while in Linz, 87.78 percent of the eligible women and 82.62 percent of the eligible men participated.[8]

Two major political parties emerged: the Christian Socials (renamed the People's party [ÖVP] after World War II) and the Social Democrats (SPÖ). It was the latter that put up and elected more female candidates, a state of affairs that has not really changed to this day. The city of Vienna, which contains between 20 and 25 percent of the country's population, was and is a Socialist stronghold. About half of the women who have been elected to the national legislature represented the electorate of this city, and of the first eight women who entered the National Assembly in March 1919, seven came from Vienna.

Hildegard Burjan (1883-1933) was the only non-Socialist among the newly elected women. Born in Silesia of Jewish parentage, she was raised in Berlin and studied in Zurich. She married, converted to Catholicism, moved with her husband to Vienna where she did social work among the poor (especially women), and was instrumental in the establishment of Caritas Socialis, a Catholic welfare organization for women. She served on the city council of Vienna and, from March 1919 until November 1920, in the National Assembly, where she was especially concerned with the protection of mothers and infants and with higher education facilities for girls. She did not run for reelection in 1920 in order to devote more time and attention to her Caritas activities.[9]

The other seven women in the 165-member National Assembly were all Social Democrats and were interested in achieving social reforms through political measures. Therese Schlesinger (1863-1940), a writer and author, had fought hard for woman suffrage[10] and was now instrumental in allowing women to represent clients before law courts. She stayed in the lower house until 1923, then went to the Bundesrat, Austria's upper chamber, for seven years. She died in Paris just a few weeks before Hitler's troops arrived.

Emmy Freundlich (1878-1948) was also a writer deeply involved in the woman question. She was one of the cofounders of the Socialist Women's Organization. In 1928, she was Austria's representative on an economic committee of the League of Nations, the only woman to serve on that committee. She remained in the legislature until Chancellor Engelbert Dollfuss terminated all parliamentary operations in 1934 after a short but bloody civil war. The Socialists were prohibited from functioning, and Freundlich was imprisoned. She went to England in 1939 and died nine years later in New York.

Adelheid Popp (1869-1939), also a journalist, was a fighter for woman's rights who pioneered in achieving equality between husband and wife in family life. She also remained in Parliament until 1934.

Gabriele Proft (1879-1971) was a domestic servant and worker who served in Parliament from 1919 until 1934. Arrested by Dollfuss, she later was again imprisoned by the Nazis. She became one of only two female legislators whose service continued into the Second Republic, serving from 1945 until 1953. At that time, the abolition of the death penalty was one of her concerns; she regarded this step as essential "if human rights are to regain respect and recognition."[11]

Anna Boschek (1874-1957) was a factory worker and the first woman to serve on the executive committee of the Socialist party. She sat in all the parliaments of the First Republic and paid special attention to child labor laws and regulations of disputes of domestic servants.[12]

Marie Tusch (1868-1938), a tobacco worker, came from Carinthia and was thus the first female parliamentarian from outside Vienna. Her education had been confined to the elementary school level only. She served in Parliament until 1934.

Amalie Seidel (1876-1952) was also of working-class origin. Her agitation for election-law reforms had resulted in a three-week jail term in the 1890s. She entered the National Assembly in March 1919, resigned at the end of May, but returned with the 1920 elections and remained until 1934.

Seidel's resignation reduced the number of female legislators to seven, but two other Socialists arrived to fill vacancies in June 1919. Irene Sponner (1867-1922), a schoolteacher, served until 1920 only. Paula Rauscha (1878-1926) came from Lower Austria (the area around Vienna) and had been a local council member. She stayed in Parliament until 1923.

The Constituent National Assembly, as it was officially called, consisted of 72 Socialists, 69 Christian Socials, 26 Pan-Germans, and three others.[13] As has been mentioned, Burjan was the non-Socialist female member. But when a vacancy occurred in the fall of 1920, Lotte Furreg (1873-1961), a homemaker from Vienna, joined the ranks of the Pan-Germans until the 1920 election and was to do so again from April to November 1923. Since no minor party in the Second Republic has ever been represented by a woman, it is worth noting that the right-wing Pan-Germans of the early 1920s were more progressive, at least in this respect.

The Election of 1920

The election for the first Nationalrat returned eight Socialist women, all of whom had served in the previous parliamentary body. Burjan was replaced by Olga Rudel-Zeynek (1871-1948) as the only woman among the Christian Socials. She came from Styria, stayed until 1927, and worked on regulations for midwives and for prohibition of the sale of alcoholic beverages to minors. She later went to the Bundesrat and became the first woman to preside over the upper chamber during the First Republic.

The Pan-Germans elected a regular member, Emmy Stradal (1877-1925), who remained for the three-year term, taking a special interest in furthering the education of girls.[14]

A vacancy in the summer of 1921 brought in a second Christian Social woman in the person of Aloisa Schirmer (1878-1951), a seamstress who stayed until the end of the term.

The Election of 1923

In October 1923, only seven women were elected: Boschek, Freundlich, Popp, Seidel, Proft, and Tusch for the Socialists and Rudel-Zeynek for the Christian Socials.

The Election of 1927

With Rudel-Zeynek no longer in the Nationalrat, only the six Socialist incumbents represented the women of Austria in the lower house.

The Election of 1930

In the elections of November 1930, the six Socialist women were returned. Now, however, they were joined by five others. Three of these were Socialists. Marie Hautmann (1886-1967) was a schoolteacher from Lower Austria, where she worked toward introducing the Montessori method in the kindergartens of the town. She eventually died in England. Marie Köstler was an employee from Styria. She was born in 1879 in Bohemia and emigrated in 1937 to England. (The date of her death is not determinable.)[15] Fernanda Flossmann (1888-1964) had been employed in Vienna. She suffered imprisonment under both Dollfuss and Hitler and spent a total of 17 months in jail. Together with Gabriele Proft, she returned to the Nationalrat after the war, remaining for 14 years. Flossmann came to be regarded as an expert on financial questions[16] and repeatedly chaired parliamentary finance and budget committees.

Emma Kapral, born in 1877, was the director of a secondary school in Vienna. She represented the Christian Socials.

Marie Schneider (1898-) was a Viennese professor. She came from the National Economic Bloc, a small, right-wing splinter group.*

Thus, by the end of the uneasy period of the parliamentary democracy, 19 women had been seated in the Austrian Nationalrat, a figure that compares well with the Anglo-Saxon countries when the much larger size of some of their elected bodies is considered. The Austrian Socialists dominated, accounting for 12 of the 19 women, with the Christian Social party's four a very poor second. As in Germany, the church-dominated party was not yet ready to see many women in public office. More remarkable is the fact that right-wing minorities, the Pan-Germans and the National Economists, saw fit to have almost as many women on their small delegations to the Nationalrat as the Christian Socials. Two-thirds of all female deputies came from Vienna.

The Undemocratic Era

Parliament, for all practical purposes, ended in Austria in March 1933. Ironically, it was destroyed almost exactly at the moment when Hitler assumed dictatorial powers in Germany. Austria now became a "Christian-German federal state on a corporate basis."[17] A popularly elected representative body no longer existed in Vienna, nor did any exist after the Nazis occupied the country in 1938, although some Austrian Hitlerites sat in the impotent Reichstag of "Greater Germany." There were no women among them, in accordance with the Nazi philosophy mentioned previously.

The Election of 1945

In 1945, immediately after the end of World War II, political life resumed in Austria, and national elections were held, despite

---

*Kapral and Schneider have the distinction of being officially listed as having served in the Nationalrat three months longer than their other female colleagues. Whereas the others found their services terminated on February 17, 1934, when the Socialist party was prohibited from functioning, other members of Parliament were listed as such until May 2. They were, therefore, entitled to participate in the April 30 meeting at which the antiparliamentary constitution was adopted by the rump Nationalrat. Austria was now a quasi-fascist state, and Parliament had ceased to exist.

the fact that the four victorious powers occupied the country. Although the two major parties dominated the legislature, a handful of Communists sat in the first few parliaments. Beginning with the second legislative period in 1949, a tiny group of right-wingers, now known as the Freiheitliche ("Freedom party"), also managed to be elected. Neither was ever represented by a woman in the Nationalrat. In striking contrast to the German Communists, Weinzierl points out that "the Austrian Communist Party was preoccupied in its program with the struggle against capitalism and with the advocacy of a people's democracy, so much so that it did not even touch on the problem of women."[18] She further reports[19] that in 1956 there were 44 Communist and 20 Freiheitliche female candidates, but they occupied positions on their lists that really gave them no chance at all. That year, 83.8 percent of all Socialists and 91.8 percent of all People's party female candidates did not get elected, the People's party placing 20 of their 23 women candidates into spots where they could not possibly hope to be successful. The net result is that of the 44 women who got into the Nationalrat by mid-1979, all but 12 were Socialists.

Nine women were elected in November 1945. Two, Proft and Flossmann, had served during the First Republic. The others also had records of anti-Nazi activities, which meant that in most cases they were somewhat older (four were over 50 years old). The only one under 42 years of age was Hilde Krones (1910-1948), who had worked illegally for the Socialist cause during Hitler's rule. A left-winger in the Socialist party, she warned against too much cooperation with the People's party and advocated greater friendship with Communist countries rather than "submitting to the yoke of American capitalism."[20] She was closely associated with Erwin Scharf, and when he eventually broke with the Socialists because of their reluctance to accommodate the Communists, Krones committed suicide.[21]

Paula Wallisch (1893-) was the widow of Socialist leader Koloman Wallisch, whom the Dollfuss regime executed in 1934 for his political activities and part in the civil war. Paula Wallisch, a kindergarten teacher, received a Kerker ("hard labor") sentence and was later apprehended in Prague by the Gestapo and imprisoned. In 1945, she took her husband's place as deputy from Styria and served in the Nationalrat until 1956, paying special attention to the victims of earlier persecutions in Austria.

Wilhelmine Moik (1984-1970) was a seamstress, a union secretary, and a member of Vienna's local government councils. She was imprisoned by Dollfuss and by Hitler. In the Nationalrat from 1945 until 1962, she was interested in social legislation and played a prominent part in the Social Welfare Committee as its deputy chairwoman.[22]

Rosa Jochmann (1901-) was a Socialist like Moik. She was also imprisoned by Austria's quasi-fascists and the Nazis and eventually wound up in a concentration camp. She stayed in the Nationalrat until her resignation in May 1967 and took a special interest in helping victims of Nazi persecution and the war. A union leader, she followed Proft as president of the Socialist Women's Organization and was succeeded in that post by Hertha Firnberg in 1967.[23] Jochmann represented Lower Austria.

Marianne Pollak (1891-1963) was closely associated with her journalist husband, Oscar Pollak, editor of the Socialist Arbeiter Zeitung. When Socialist activities became illegal, they fled to Belgium, Czechoslovakia, France, and eventually Britain. They returned in 1945, and she served in the Nationalrat for 14 years, sitting on committees that dealt with foreign policy, justice, and education and fighting for equality for all.[24] Her husband died in late August 1963; two days later she took her own life.

Nadine Paunovic (1903-) represented the People's party. A high school teacher, she was promoted to principal and in 1938 was fired "summarily and without any financial security for political reasons."[25] She served one term in the Nationalrat and headed her party's women's organization, the Österreichische Frauenbewegung.[26]

Frieda Mikola (1881-1958) was another ÖVP representative. A schoolteacher from Styria, she had served in the provincial legislature before 1934 and was prominent in various Catholic youth and women's organizations.[27] She stayed one term in the lower house and concerned herself with the small pensioner, social welfare, and domestic servants.[28]

Filling a vacancy for a few months in 1949 was Maria Pokorny (1888-1966). She had worked in a flower shop, as a streetcar conductor, and as head of a welfare office. A Socialist, she had been persecuted and imprisoned before and after the German takeover in 1938.

The Election of 1949

In October 1949, six Socialist women were reelected. Three new women joined them, one Socialist and two People's party members. The Socialist was Marie Kren (1892-1966), an industrial worker from Lower Austria. She was Austria's first postwar female mayor and served in the Nationalrat for ten years.[29] Kren took a special interest in the development of the vocational school system.[30]

Margarethe Rehor (1910-), textile worker, played a prominent part in the Christian labor union movement, which is affiliated
with the more conservative People's party. Rehor represented the
ÖVP in the Nationalrat until 1970. She became Austria's first female minister in 1966, when she was called upon to head the Ministry for Social Welfare.

Lola Solar (1904-) was the other People's party newcomer,
and she also stayed until 1970. An educator by profession, she continued her interest in that area while in Parliament. Solar also
advocated changes in marriage laws and measures involving x-ray
protection and cancer prevention.[31] From 1950 until 1969, she
headed the Frauenbewegung as successor to Paunovic.

Rosa Rück (1897-1969), a Socialist from Styria, arrived in
1952 to fill a vacancy and stayed a full decade, during which time
she was particularly concerned with the welfare of youth and the
urgent need for more classroom space.[32] She had previously
served three years in the Bundesrat.

The Election of 1953

Rück brought the number of women in the Nationalrat up to
ten. The same number was elected in 1953. Proft was no longer
a member of the Nationalrat, but there was another Socialist newcomer, Marie Emhart (1901-). A textile worker and the first
female representative from the province of Salzburg, she had been
sentenced to a term of hard labor under the anti-Socialist measures
in the mid-1930s. In 1953, Emhart began 12 years of service in
Parliament, during which time she acted as a consumer advocate.[33]
She resigned in 1965.

Marie Enser (1900-) arrived in February 1954 and stayed for
more than two years. She was a Socialist from Upper Austria.

The Election of 1956

In May 1956, nine female legislators were reelected, seven
Socialists and two People's party members. A vacancy in 1957 was
filled by another woman from the ÖVP. Johanna Bayer (1915-),
born in Berlin, was an agricultural engineer. Representing Styria,
she sat in the Bundesrat for three years and even served as its
president for six months. She remained in the Nationalrat until her
resignation in October 1973.

The Election of 1959

Ten women were elected in May 1959, including three Socialist newcomers. Rosa Weber (1919-1967) was a bookkeeper and
served on the Social Administration Committee of the Nationalrat
until she met with a fatal mountaineering accident in 1967. Anna
Czerny (1902-) had served on the town council of Wiener Neustadt
in Lower Austria before and after the war and in Lower Austria's
land parliament. She served in the Nationalrat until her resignation
in February 1968. Social and health questions were her particular
concerns.[34] Stella Klein-Löw (1904-) remained in the Nationalrat
until 1970. Director of a high school, she was naturally concerned
with education and also advocated reform of penal law.[35]

A vacancy in 1960 brought in Maria Hagleitner, Socialist and
the first female representative from Tyrol. She was a dressmaker
and had been persecuted in the mid-1930s. A member of Innsbruck's
municipal council, Hagleitner had advanced to the Nationalrat,
where she remained until November 1961, when she resigned to
become her province's delegate to the Bundesrat.

The Election of 1962

With the election of November 1962, ten women were again
in the Nationalrat, including two Socialist newcomers. Herta
Winkler (1917-) was from Styria and had been a union secretary.
She had served on the municipal council of Graz. Winkler stayed
in the Nationalrat until her resignation 11 years later. Public
health was her particular concern. Hella Hanzlik (1912-) served
in the Viennese Landtag for several years after three years in the
Bundesrat. She was in the Nationalrat until 1966, when she returned to the Bundesrat for another seven years.

October 1963 marked the arrival of one of the most prominent
female members of the Nationalrat, Hertha Firnberg (1909-).
Firnberg was a university librarian and a leading labor-union official. Higher education and science were among her particular
interests. In 1957, she became head of the Socialist Women's
Organization. She is a major force in the Frauenring, an organization established in 1969, which attempts to coordinate the political
activities of women in all Austrian parties. Since the inception of
the Bruno Kreisky cabinet in 1970, Firnberg has continuously
served as minister responsible for science and research and was
reelected in 1979.

The Election of 1966

The elections of 1966 led to a breakup of the People's party-Socialist coalition that had governed the country for more than 20 years, with the ÖVP left in sole charge of the administration. Although the ÖVP had an absolute majority in the Nationalrat, its female members were outnumbered three to seven by the Socialists.

There was one newcomer, Gertrude Wondrak (1920-1971), a seamstress and union official. She was a former member of the Bundesrat and joined the Kreisky administration in 1970 as secretary of state in the Ministry of Social Affairs. A Socialist, she held that ministerial post and her seat in the Nationalrat until her death in a car accident in July 1971.

In February 1968, Lona Murowatz (1919-) replaced Czerny as Socialist representative from Lower Austria, succeeding to a seat that even before 1945 had been occupied by several women (that is, Rauscha and Hautmann). Murowatz worked in a bookstore and had local government experience in Wiener Neustadt. She has been a member of the Nationalrat since 1968.

The Election of 1970

After four years of ÖVP government, the SPÖ received a plurality in the Nationalrat, and Kreisky formed a Socialist minority government. In 1971, another election was held, and the Socialists obtained an absolute majority of seats, a feat they were able to duplicate in 1975 and 1979. Only eight women were elected in 1970, and this number was to be decreased before the next election through the death of Wondrak. There were three newcomers. Hanna Hager (1916-) is a professional nurse and has been director of a sanatorium. A Socialist, she has worked on a communal council and then on the land parliament of Upper Austria. She was reelected in 1971 but left in 1975. (We have previously mentioned that Firnberg and Murowatz were reelected in 1979. The same is true of all the other women who are listed below, with the single exception of Wilhelmine Moser.) Marga Hubinek (1926-) was the first People's party newcomer in more than a decade. She had served on the municipal and provincial councils of Vienna. She is an expert on family law and education and now is deputy chairwoman of the Committee on Health and Environment. Maria Metzker (1916-) is a union secretary who has worked in several commercial establishments. She is a Socialist and is active on the Social Administration Committee, which she cochairs.

The Election of 1971

In 1971, the membership of the Nationalrat was increased from 165 to 183 (its present number), and 11 women were elected. Before the end of the parliamentary term, two had dropped out, and three had come in, for a net gain of one. Four women were new in 1971. Helga Wieser (1940-) represents the ÖVP from Salzburg province. Daughter of a local mayor, she and her husband are involved in farming and in managing a <u>Gasthof</u>. Always interested in agricultural questions, she once organized a protest trip of farm wives to the Agriculture Ministry in Vienna and in this way gained the necessary reputation to be placed on the ticket. She is still very much concerned with agricultural matters.[36] Anneliese Albrecht (1921-) is a Socialist and journalist who edits a weekly women's magazine. Reform of family law and the penal code are of special concern to her. She eventually became a deputy majority leader and in 1979 was appointed state secretary in the Ministry for Commerce and Industry with consumer protection as her special task. Erika Seda (1923-) lists herself as homemaker, though she has studied chemistry and holds a law degree. She belongs to the SPÖ and had served in the Bundesrat before coming to the Nationalrat. Edith Dobesberger (1925-) is a Socialist teacher from Upper Austria. She previously served in the provincial parliament and is now on committees dealing with judicial and educational questions.

Jolande Offenbeck (1930-) entered the Nationalrat as a replacement in November 1973. Holder of a law degree, she is from Styria and a member of a family that has "always" been politically active, even when it was illegal, as in the mid-1930s and during the Nazi occupation.[37] Offenbeck has also been a member of the Bundesrat, was a high civil servant, and is prominent in Socialist and women's organizations.

Wilhelmine Moser (1930-) also arrived in the fall of 1973. She, too, was from Styria but from the People's party. A shorthand-typist and homemaker, she spent ten years of her life abroad. Ill health forced her to retire in February 1979.

Elfriede Karl (1933-), a Socialist from Salzburg, had commercial training and worked as a secretary for Socialist-affiliated organizations. She was named a secretary of state in the Chancellor's Office, and when a vacancy developed in the Nationalrat late in 1974, she moved into that position as well. Returned to Parliament in 1975 and 1979, she was named secretary of state in charge of family affairs.

The Election of 1975

In 1975, the number of women in the Nationalrat increased to 14, with a fifteenth arriving in 1976. The one Socialist newcomer in 1975 was Beatrix Eypeltauer (1929-). Upper Austria was now represented by two women in the same parliament, which was the direct result of a kind of primary held in the town of Linz when she and Dobesberger led the ticket.[38] Eypeltauer holds a law degree and in 1979 was appointed state secretary in charge of housing in the Ministry for Construction and Technology. Ottilie Rochus (1928-) is a ÖVP member from the Burgenland, giving this province its first female representative. This means that tiny Vorarlberg is the only Austrian province that has never had a woman in the Nationalrat, although Carinthia's history of female representation goes back to the First Republic. Rochus is a teacher and an agricultural expert. She was a member of the provincial parliament before coming to Vienna. Elisabeth Schmidt (1920-) is a homemaker and secretary representing the Lower Austrian ÖVP. She previously served in the Bundesrat. Hilde Hawlicek (1942-) filled a vacancy in 1976. She is a Socialist and has studied and taught German, history, and political science. She went to the Bundesrat in 1971 and switched to the lower house five years later. As previously mentioned, Moser resigned early in 1979. However, another ÖVP woman from Styria arrived, Maria Stangl (1928-). She has studied agriculture and home economics and has local government experience.

The Election of 1979

The election in May 1979 not only enabled the chancellor to increase his parliamentary majority, but it also gave women an unprecedented 18-member contingent—almost 10 percent of the total membership. However, 11 Socialists and 7 People's party adherents somewhat diminished the previous overwhelming SPÖ-ÖVP ratio. There were three female newcomers, one Socialist and two members of the ÖVP. Ingrid Tichy-Schreder (1941-) represents the ÖVP. She heads a family business that deals with agricultural products and was active in commercial associations.[39] Marilies Möst (1925-) is married to a physician and has five children. An agricultural engineer from Upper Austria, she has held leading positions in women's organizations and membership in the local town council. Wanda Brunner (1930-) comes from Tyrol. A member of the Socialist party for many years, she held various party positions and served in the Bundesrat between 1972 and her election to the Nationalrat in 1979.

DISCUSSION

Looking over the group of the 61 women, two facts stand out: the predominance of Vienna and the predominance of the Socialists. Perhaps it is not surprising that the capital city with its cosmopolitan characteristics should have many more female deputies than the rest of the country. In the First Republic, Vienna accounted for 13 out of 19 female representatives and in the Second Republic, for 17 out of 42. While this gives Vienna nearly 50 percent of the total (30 out of 61), it also means that in the Second Republic other parts of the country have become less reluctant to elect women. This is especially true of the provinces of Upper Austria, Lower Austria, and Styria, which together have now overtaken Vienna in terms of the number of women elected to the Nationalrat since 1945. With the exception of Vorarlberg, all provinces have had women among their delegates to the lower house, although Carinthia has not had any since 1933 (see Table 7.1).

Regarding party affiliations, we have seen that in the U.S. House of Representatives the numerical superiority of Democrats among the women can at least partially be explained by the fact that the Democrats have controlled the House for many years, frequently by large majorities. A similar explanation would not make sense in Austria. As a result of 16 elections held in the 60 years between 1919 and 1979, the Socialists have held 1,229 seats and the Christian Socials and their People's party successors 1,262. Yet of the 61 women elected, three have belonged to minor parties, 19 to the ÖVP and their predecessors, and 42 to the Socialists. There is, therefore, a clear indication that the leftist party was at first more inclined to put up female candidates, or at least to place them into positions where they could be elected. This agrees with what we have observed in the previous chapter on Germany. However, the ÖVP seems to be making a determined effort to have more female representatives. Having never had more than three women serving at one time, they brought the figure up to five in 1975 and to an all-time high of seven in 1979. This recent effort is also comparable to what we have found in the German Federal Republic. However, women deputies of both parties have expressed the desirability of having more female colleagues elected, and although none spoke of any resistance by the national leadership, many acknowledged resistance by men and women on the local level.

Although the extreme Right in Germany's First Republic opposed women in politics, some were elected by the more moderate Right. In Austria, as we have seen, the Pan-Germans elected two, and the National Economic Bloc sent one woman to the Nationalrat before 1934. The Freiheitlichen today, who speak of individual

TABLE 7.1

Women in the Nationalrat by Party and Province

Province	First Republic				Second Republic			Grand Total
	Christian Social	Socialist	Others	Total	ÖVP	SPÖ	Total	
Burgenland	0	0	0	0	1	0	1	1
Carinthia	0	1	0	1	0	0	0	1
Lower Austria	0	3	0	3	2	4	6	9
Salzburg	0	0	0	0	1	2	3	3
Styria	1	1	0	2	4	4	8	10
Tyrol	0	0	0	0	0	2	2	2
Upper Austria	0	0	0	0	1	4	5	5
Vienna	3	7	3	13	4	13	17	30
Vorarlberg	0	0	0	0	0	0	0	0
Total	4	12	3	19	13	29	42	61

Source: Compiled by the author.

rights for everybody (and who, in private conversation, stress the concept of equality for all persons), have never yet been represented by a woman in Parliament. Neither have the Communists, who in the first four elections after World War II were able to gain a handful of seats.

The nomination process is all-important. This leaves the possibility of female representation squarely up to the party leadership, who not only determines the names of the candidates but also their numerical order. If one is placed at the lower end of the list, there is no chance for success, and a woman in that position is just so much window dressing. Occasionally, a woman is given a Kampfmandat, a place around which the fight is really centered. Even if she does not win, she may be able to catch the public eye and thus assure herself of a better position the next time, or she may be given a Restmandat, a "remaining seat."*

The only way in which a place on the list may be altered is by writing in someone's name in sufficient numbers to make a change, something that hardly ever happens, especially since write-in votes usually go to well-known party leaders who are elected anyway.[40] However, occasionally there may be further developments. In 1971, the most write-in votes for any ÖVP candidate were received by Schmidt, who was twentieth on the ÖVP list. Her 3,255 votes were certainly not enough to get her elected.[41] But within a few months she was sent to the Bundesrat, and in November 1975 she was indeed elected to the Nationalrat and was reelected in 1979.

There seems, therefore, to be a certain degree of sensitivity to the wishes of the public among the party leaderships, even though this may be more apparent than real due to the complexity of the system. There is also something called a Vorwahl, a kind of primary, which in various forms may now also be found in some parts of Switzerland. These Vorwahlen are quite different from the U.S. primaries where anyone can participate by declaring a party affiliation. In Austria, usually only a proportion of the dues-paying, regular party members participate. Nevertheless, it is an important step away from the closed, intimate party executive meeting,

---

*This is precisely what happened to Wieser in 1971. She was given the fourth position on the list in Salzburg, but this was not quite enough, since the ÖVP was able to get only three seats. However, a few remaining mandates were allocated from a larger pool comprising several provinces, and she received one of them. Four years later, she was well-known enough to be placed in the second spot in Salzburg, and this made her election a certainty.

with its "smoke-filled room" atmosphere. Several of the women now in the Nationalrat have said that they owe their good positions on the list, and therefore their election, to a favorable outcome of such a Vorwahl.

Because of the interruption of parliamentary life during the period from 1933 to 1945, there were not many women who served 20 years or longer. Only two who were present when Austrian democracy was terminated came back in 1945, one adding eight and the other 14 years to her service in the Nationalrat. Serving 20 years or more were Proft (23 years), Jochmann (22), Rehor (21), Solar (21), and Rück (20). Seven women served between 15 and 18 years and another seven between ten and 14. Of the 18 elected to the Nationalrat in 1979, the one with the most seniority has been a member since 1963. If the other 43 women who have terminated their services are included, the length of office for female members in the lower chamber averages little more than nine years.

Looking at age at entrance, we find that the average for women in the First Republic was 45.3 years. After 1945, there were quite a few veterans from the struggle against Austro-fascism and Nazism, and they were a little older; the average age of the women entering the Nationalrat for the first time between 1945 and 1960 is exactly 50 years. In this group, only two were in their thirties, only five in their forties, and two were beyond the age of 60. The average age of the 18 women entering since 1970 is 45.94 years, about the same as that of the very first group after World War I. For all 61 women, the average age on entering Parliament is 47.28 years. It is 48.17 years for those coming in since 1945. Thus, the earlier generation was somewhat younger. Table 7.2 gives a breakdown of the various age groups by party in each of the two Republics.

In the official listings, there is very little mention of the marital state of the women in the Nationalrat. Such detail is now regarded as entirely a private matter. In 1949, Pollak and several of her female Socialist colleagues submitted a proposal, which has since been adopted, giving every woman above the age of 21 the right to be designated as Frau rather than the dimunitive Fräulein. [42] This distinction was explained later as being based on the fact that every woman above a certain age was able to fulfill her biological functions, regardless of whether or not she chose to do so, which, after all, was her own private business. Moreover, an unmarried man is not referred to as Männlein or Herrlein ("little man"), which might reflect on his masculinity. [43]

In Austria, women do not take the place of their husbands in the legislature for the same reasons explained in connection with Germany. The sole exception was Wallisch. She worked closely

TABLE 7.2

Ages of Women Entering Austrian Legislature

Age Group	First Republic				Second Republic			Grand Total
	Christian Social	Socialist	Others	Total	ÖVP	SPÖ	Total	
31–40	1	1	1	3	3	3	6	9
41–50	2	7	2	11	6	12	18	29
51–60	1	4	0	5	3	13	16	21
61–70	0	0	0	0	1	1	2	2
Total	4	12	3	19	13	29	42	61

Source: Compiled by the author.

with her husband, who was executed in 1934 for his Socialist activities. After the war, it was perhaps natural that she was chosen to take her husband's position as member of the Nationalrat. At the same time, Oscar and Marianne Pollak returned to Austria, and the party leadership offered a seat in Parliament to one of them. "Without hesitation," Oscar declined in favor of his wife."[44]

Impressionistically, it must be added that women legislators in Austria expressed a very strong feeling of family togetherness, a feeling not particularly evident in the Anglo-Saxon countries and paralleled only in Switzerland. The Catholic church, of course, frowns upon divorce, although Austria claims to have one of the most liberal abortion laws of any Catholic country. As to marriage, women legislators often said their husbands were in full agreement with their being in Vienna, were very willing to perform the necessary tasks at home (including the raising of the children), and had encouraged them to compete for the legislature in the first place.

In terms of giving government positions to women, Austria is not very far advanced. Only in 1966 did Rehor reach a ministerial position. Since that time, other women have been appointed: Wondrack, Firnberg, Karl, and, because membership in Parliament is not absolutely essential for service in the government, Ingrid Leodolter (a physician and former hospital administrator), whom Kreisky named minister of health. After the 1979 elections, some cabinet reshuffling took place. As already mentioned, Eyepeltauer and Albrecht joined the administration. Leodolter was replaced by a male, but two other women not in the legislature joined the government: Johanna Dohnal, member of Vienna's city council, became state secretary in the Federal Chancellery and Franziska Fast, a union official, was named the first secretary for working women in the Ministry for Social Affairs. This brought the number of women in Kreisky's cabinet to six.[45] It must be noted, however, that these women were given portfolios dealing with subjects supposedly of particular interest to women, that is, social affairs, education, health, and the family. Only the area of science and research does not fit into this category. A number of women have served on committees dealing with legal matters and have been involved in the reform of penal law. Although some of the female legislators have taken an interest in foreign policy and defense, these are matters that, by and large, are regarded as being primarily in the male domain.

Progress has undoubtedly been made. However, much is still to be done, especially since Austria is basically quite a conservative country.

TABLE 7.3

Elected Women Members of the Austrian Parliament

Member	Dates	Party	Province	In Office
Hildegard Burjan	1883–1933	Christian Social	Vienna	1919–20
Therese Schlesinger	1863–1940	Socialist	Vienna	1919–23
Emmy Freundlich	1878–1948	Socialist	Vienna	1919–34
Adelheid Popp	1869–1939	Socialist	Vienna	1919–34
Gabriele Proft	1879–1971	Socialist	Vienna	1919–34, 1945–53
Anna Boschek	1874–1957	Socialist	Vienna	1919–34
Marie Tusch	1868–1938	Socialist	Carinthia	1919–34
Amalie Seidel	1876–1952	Socialist	Vienna	March–May 1919, 1920–34
Irene Sponner	1867–1922	Socialist	Vienna	1919–20
Paula Rauscha	1878–1926	Socialist	Lower Austria	1919–23
Lotte Furreg	1873–1961	Pan-German	Vienna	September–November 1920, April–November 1923
Olga Rudel-Zeynek	1871–1948	Christian Social	Styria	1920–27
Emmy Stradal	1877–1925	Pan-German	Vienna	1920–23
Aloisa Schirmer	1878–1951	Christian Social	Vienna	1921–23
Marie Hautmann	1886–1967	Socialist	Lower Austria	1930–34
Marie Köstler	1879–?	Socialist	Styria	1930–34
Fernanda Flossmann	1888–1964	Socialist	Lower Austria	1930–34, 1945–59
Emma Kapral	1877–?	Christian Social	Vienna	1930–34
Marie Schneider	1898–	National Economic Bloc	Vienna	1930–34

Name		Party	Region	
Hilde Krones	1910–1948	SPÖ	Vienna	1945–48
Paula Wallisch	1893–	SPÖ	Styria	1945–56
Wilhelmine Moik	1894–1970	SPÖ	Vienna	1945–62
Rosa Jochmann	1901–	SPÖ	Lower Austria	1945–67
Marianne Pollak	1891–1963	SPÖ	Vienna	1945–59
Nadine Paunovic	1903–	ÖVP	Vienna	1945–49
Frieda Mikola	1881–1958	ÖVP	Styria	1945–49
Maria Pokorny	1888–1966	SPÖ	Vienna	1949
Maria Kren	1892–1966	SPÖ	Lower Austria	1949–59
Margarethe Rehor	1910–	ÖVP	Vienna	1949–70
Lola Solar	1904–	ÖVP	Lower Austria	1949–70
Rosa Rück	1897–1969	SPÖ	Styria	1952–62
Marie Emhart	1901–	SPÖ	Salzburg	1953–65
Marie Enser	1900–	SPÖ	Upper Austria	1954–56
Johanna Bayer	1915–	ÖVP	Styria	1957–73
Rosa Weber	1919–1967	SPÖ	Vienna	1959–67
Anna Czerny	1902–	SPÖ	Lower Austria	1959–68
Stella Klein–Löw	1904–	SPÖ	Vienna	1959–70
Maria Hagleitner	1907–	SPÖ	Tyrol	1960–61
Herta Winkler	1917–	SPÖ	Styria	1962–73
Hella Hanzlik	1912–	SPÖ	Vienna	1962–66
Hertha Firnberg	1909–	SPÖ	Vienna	1963–
Gertrude Wondrak	1920–1971	SPÖ	Vienna	1966–71
Lona Murowatz	1919–	SPÖ	Lower Austria	1968–
Hanna Hager	1916–	SPÖ	Upper Austria	1970–75

(continued)

Table 7.3, continued

Member	Dates	Party	Province	In Office
Marga Hubinek	1926–	ÖVP	Vienna	1970–
Maria Metzker	1916–	SPÖ	Vienna	1970–
Helga Wieser	1940–	ÖVP	Salzburg	1971–
Anneliese Albrecht	1921–	SPÖ	Vienna	1971–
Erika Seda	1923–	SPÖ	Vienna	1971–
Edith Dobesberger	1925–	SPÖ	Upper Austria	1971–
Jolande Offenbeck	1930–	SPÖ	Styria	1973–
Wilhelmine Moser	1930–	ÖVP	Styria	1973–79
Elfriede Karl	1933–	SPÖ	Salzburg	1974–
Beatrix Eypeltauer	1929–	SPÖ	Upper Austria	1975–
Ottilie Rochus	1928–	ÖVP	Burgenland	1975–
Elisabeth Schmidt	1920–	ÖVP	Lower Austria	1975–
Hilde Hawlicek	1942–	SPÖ	Vienna	1976–
Maria Stangl	1928–	ÖVP	Styria	1979–
Ingrid Tichy-Schreder	1941–	ÖVP	Vienna	1979–
Marilies Möst	1925–	ÖVP	Upper Austria	1979–
Wanda Brunner	1930–	SPÖ	Tyrol	1979–

Source: Compiled by the author.

204

TABLE 7.4

Austrian Elected Legislatures and Female Members

	Number of Women	Names
First Republic		
Constituent Assembly (February 16, 1919)	8	Burjan, Schlesinger, Freundlich, Popp, Proft, Boschek, Tusch, Seidel (to May 1919)
Vacancies		Sponner (June 1919), Rauscha (June 1919), Furreg (September 1920)
First Nationalrat (October 17, 1920)	11	Schlesinger, Freundlich, Popp, Proft, Boschek, Tusch, Seidel, Rauscha, Stradal, Rudel-Zeynek
Vacancies		Schirmer (June 1921), Furreg (April 1923)
Second Nationalrat (October 21, 1923)	7	Freundlich, Popp, Proft, Boschek, Tusch, Seidel, Rudel-Zeynek
Third Nationalrat (April 24, 1927)	6	Freundlich, Popp, Proft, Boschek, Tusch, Seidel
Fourth Nationalrat (November 9, 1930)	11	Freundlich, Popp, Proft, Boschek, Tusch, Seidel, Hautmann, Köstler, Flossmann, Kapral, Schneider
Second Republic		
First Nationalrat (November 25, 1945)	9	Proft, Flossmann, Krones (to December 1948), Wallisch, Moik, Jochmann, Pollak, Paunovic, Mikola
Vacancy	1	Pokorny (January 1949)
Second Nationalrat (October 9, 1949)	9	Proft, Flossmann, Wallisch, Moik, Jochmann, Pollak, Kren, Rehor, Solar
Vacancy	1	Rück (September 1952)
Third Nationalrat (February 22, 1953)	10	Flossmann, Wallisch, Moik, Pollak, Kren, Rehor, Solar, Rück, Jochmann, Emhart
Vacancy	1	Enser (February 1954)

(continued)

205

Table 7.4, continued

	Number of Women	Names
Fourth Nationalrat (May 13, 1956)	9	Flossmann, Moik, Jochmann, Pollak, Kren, Rehor, Solar, Rück, Emhart
Vacancy	1	Bayer (April 1957)
Fifth Nationalrat (May 10, 1959)	10	Moik, Jochmann, Rehor, Solar, Rück, Emhart, Bayer, Weber, Czerny, Klein-Löw
Vacancy	1	Hagleitner (June 1960–November 1961)
Sixth Nationalrat (November 18, 1962)	10	Jochmann, Rehor, Solar, Emhart (to January 1965), Bayer, Weber, Czerny, Klein-Löw, Winkler, Hanzlik
Vacancy	1	Firnberg (October 1963)
Seventh Nationalrat (March 6, 1966)	10	Jochmann (to May 1967), Rehor, Solar, Bayer, Weber (to July 1967), Czerny (to February 1968), Klein-Löw, Winkler, Firnberg, Wondrak
Vacancy	1	Murowatz (February 1968)
Eighth Nationalrat (March 1, 1970)*	8	Bayer, Winkler, Firnberg, Wondrak (to July 1971), Hager, Hubinek, Metzker, Murowatz
Ninth Nationalrat (October 10, 1971)	11	Bayer (to October 1973), Winkler (to November 1973), Firnberg, Murowatz, Hager, Hubinek, Metzker, Wieser, Albrecht, Seda, Dobesberger
Vacancies	3	Moser (October 1973), Karl (November 1974), Offenbeck (November 1973)
Tenth Nationalrat (October 5, 1975)	14	Firnberg, Murowatz, Hubinek, Metzker, Wieser, Albrecht, Seda, Dobesberger, Moser (to February 1979), Karl, Offenbeck, Eypeltauer, Rochus, Schmidt
Vacancies	2	Hawlicek (October 1976), Stangl (February 1979)
Eleventh Nationalrat (May 6, 1979)	18	Firnberg, Murowatz, Hubinek, Metzker, Wieser, Albrecht, Seda, Dobesberger, Karl, Offenbeck, Eypeltauer, Rochus, Schmidt, Hawlicek, Stangl, Tichy-Schreder, Möst, Brunner

*Special elections were also held in Vienna on October 4, 1970.
Note: Unless otherwise indicated, dates in parentheses show when members entered the legislature.
Source: Compiled by the author.

The reasons for the lack of women in public life can be summarized in one sentence: Politics is not regarded as a field of activities for women. This view is more strongly held by men than by women, but the latter also subscribe to it to a high degree. Here the continuation of the traditional view of the position of women becomes very clear. Women overwhelmingly regard themselves as less politically interested than men; they, above all, look at their own political activities as less than significant. At most, they are willing to participate in short-term projects, to work in women's organizations, and to take a hand in events that have to do with "women's questions." Men share this attitude. They, too, stress the participation of women primarily in those activities that deal with matters of interest to women. About half of them are opposed to general political engagements of women. Men as well as women agree that it is much more difficult for a woman than for a man to become a politician or to reach a position of political leadership. In contrast, most would agree that women are politically equally capable. Women in political leadership positions regard the concept of marriage as a partnership as an absolute prerequisite for their activities. The double burden caused by family and profession is regarded as a serious obstacle to political activity. Differences in the political interests of women as well as the attitude toward the politically active woman can be detected among the different generations and different social and educational classes. Such differences also exist among the urban and rural populations. [46]

(For a concise listing of the elected women members of the Austrian legislatures, see Tables 7.3 and 7.4.)

NOTES

1. Oswald Knauer, Das österreichische Parlament von 1848-1966 (Vienna: Begland Verlag, 1969), pp. 14-16.

2. Information about pre-1919 conditions has been obtained largely from Erika Weinzierl, Emanzipation? (Vienna: Jugend & Volk, 1975), pp. 33-42.

3. Ibid., pp. 35-36.

4. Ibid., p. 40.

5. Ibid., p. 41. My translation.

6. David F. Strong, Austria (October 1918-March 1919) (New York: Octagon Books, 1974), p. 275.

7. Austria: Fact and Figures (Vienna: Giestel & Cie., 1973), p. 39.

8. Weinzierl, Emanzipation?, pp. 42-43.

9. Ibid., pp. 168-69.

10. Die Abgeordneten zum österreichischen Nationalrat, 1918-1975, und die Mitglieder des österreichischen Bundesrates, 1920-1975 (Vienna: Österreichische Staatsdruckerei, 1975), p. 285. This claims to be "the only authentic reference of its kind" (p. 3).

11. Weinzierl, Emanzipation?, p. 51. My translation.

12. Ibid., p. 49.

13. Knauer, op. cit., p. 201.

14. Weinzierl, Emanzipation?, p. 49.

15. Abgeordneten zum österreichischen Nationalrat, p. 162.

16. Weinzierl, Emanzipation?, p. 50.

17. Anton Pelinka and Manfried Welan, Demokratie und Verfassung in Österreich (Vienna: Europa Verlag, 1971), p. 40. My translation.

18. Weinzierl, Emanzipation?, p. 13. My translation.

19. Ibid., p. 46.

20. Ernst Trost, Figl von Österreich (Vienna: Verlag Fritz Molden, 1972), p. 234. My translation.

21. Helmut Andics, Die Insel der Seligen (Vienna: Molden-Taschenbuch Verlag, 1976), p. 348.

22. Weinzierl, Emanzipation?, p. 51.

23. Bericht über die Situation der Frau in Österreich (Vienna: Bundeskanzleramt, 1975), 7:14.

24. For a brief but concise account of her activities see Erika Weinzierl, "Marianne Pollak als Parlamentarierin," in Wissenschaft und Weltbild: Festschrift für Hertha Firnberg (Europaverlag, Sonderdruck, 1974), pp. 521-43.

25. Abgeordneten zum österreichischen Nationalrat, p. 237.

26. Die Situation der Frau in Österreich, 7:16.

27. Abgeordneten zum österreichischen Nationalrat, p. 215.

28. Weinzierl, Emanzipation?, p. 52.

29. Ibid., p. 55.

30. Ibid., p. 51.

31. Ibid., p. 53.

32. Ibid., p. 51.

33. Ibid.

34. Ibid., p. 52.

35. Ibid.

36. Information obtained through personal interviews.

37. Information obtained through personal interviews.

38. Information obtained through personal interviews.

39. Information on the women elected in 1979 is based on Western Union Telex, kindly obtained for me by the Austrian consul general in Chicago to whom I am most grateful.

40. For an explanation of the Austrian system, see Walter S. G. Kohn, "The Austrian Parliamentary Elections of 1971," Parliamentary Affairs 25 (Spring 1972): 163-77.

41. Salzburger Nachrichten, October 23, 1971.

42. Weinzierl, "Marianne Pollak als Parlamentarierin," p. 533.

43. Information obtained in private conversation with a prominent member of the Nationalrat.

44. Weinzierl, "Marianne Pollak als Parlamentarierin," p. 522.

45. Austrian Information, Vol. 32, no. 10.

46. Die Situation der Frau in Österreich, Zusammenfassende Darstellung, p. 9. My translation.

8
THE SWISS PARLIAMENT

HISTORY

Switzerland is unique among the countries here under discussion. It alone still has a genuine multiparty system, somewhat comparable to that in Germany's Weimar Republic, but with public support for each party rather stable and four parties participating in the government on a seemingly permanent basis. Switzerland is committed to democracy on the lowest levels, which implies a high degree of local and cantonal autonomy and the necessity of having constitutional changes approved by the people in a referendum. The Swiss still cling to the concept of a Milizparlament, a part-time legislature whose members are expected to pursue their professions and occupations when Parliament is not in session.* This raises questions of time and money for some members.† Of major importance for this study, however, is that Switzerland has lagged behind the rest of Europe in granting the franchise to women. (Only the neighboring, small Liechtenstein has not as yet taken this step.) Not until 1971 did Switzerland's female population receive

---

*Parliament meets four times a year, in March, June, September, and December for about two to three weeks (George Arthur Codding, The Federal Government of Switzerland [Boston: Houghton Mifflin, 1961], p. 79.

†Compensation for legislators attending parliamentary sessions is described as "modest" and insufficient to make up for lost time (Erich Gruner and Beat Junker, Bürger, Staat und Politik in der Schweiz [Basel: Lehrmittelverlag, 1972], p. 75).

the vote, and only then did the first women enter the national legislature.*

Switzerland claims to be the oldest existing democracy. The Federal Constitution of 1848 states in Article 4: "All Swiss are equal before the law. In Switzerland there are no vassals and no privileges on account of place, birth, family or person."† But it was clear from the start that this provision applied to the male citizenry only. Indeed, it was interpreted in such a manner as to be detrimental to women. Since 1833, property-holding and tax-paying women in Bernese communities had had the right to vote in local affairs, even if the actual votes themselves had to be cast by men. But this was restricted to unmarried women and widows in 1852 and discontinued altogether in 1887 because it supposedly violated Article 4 of the Federal Constitution![1]

The struggle to emancipate women in Switzerland took a century. Before the constitution was revised in 1874, there were demands that women be allowed to vote, demands that did not get very far. Other, perhaps more pressing, problems affecting women were the bad working conditions in the factories and the low wages, and on a different level, the difficulties encountered by women who wanted a university education. In order to press for solutions, a number of women's organizations were established, and publications appeared in support of woman's rights. To this day, there exist in Switzerland a large number of women's organizations, divided along cantonal, party, religious, and other lines and brought together under the Bund Schweizerischer Frauenorganisationen ("League of Swiss Women's Organizations"), which claims credit for much of the progress made by women during the past decades and continues to press for further improvements.

It was this league that, after World War I, took the lead in requesting the introduction of woman suffrage in Switzerland and in a special session in January 1919 demanded unanimously that such a step be taken.[2] The military and industrial tasks performed by the Swiss during the war despite their country's neutrality

---

*A compensating factor is that all women who have been members of the Swiss Parliament were alive at the time of this research, and 19 of the 23 women were able to be interviewed, either during the parliamentary session of June 1979 in Bern or in their home communities.

†The author's translation of "Alle Schweizer sind vor dem Gesetze gleich. Es gibt in der Schweiz keine Untertanenverhältnisse, keine Vorrechte des Orts, der Geburt, der Familien oder Personen."

required major efforts from the entire population, male and female alike. In addition, many European countries, such as Britain, Germany, Austria, and the United States, had set examples by enfranchising women. Had the time not come to do likewise in Switzerland?

There was talk of revising the national constitution and using that opportunity to give the vote to all Swiss citizens regardless of sex. However, no such revision took place. The notion spread that woman's suffrage should come from the bottom up, first in the local communities, then in the cantons, and only after that on the federal level.[3] Between 1919 and 1921, attempts were made in six cantons to give women the vote in cantonal and local affairs. Referenda were held in Neuchâtel, Zurich, Basel-Town, and Geneva, and in Glarus, the Landsgemeinde, the old-fashioned town meeting, took up the question. The answer was the same everywhere; each canton replied with a decisive "no." There were allegations that the demand for votes for women was a left-wing plot. In Basel-Town the Social Democrats, the Radicals, and the Evangelical Labor party favored woman suffrage; the Liberals were noncommittal; and the Catholic People's party, the Citizen and Business party (Bürger-und Gewerbepartei), and the Freisinn were in opposition.[4] That the Great Council, the cantonal legislature, had recently debated and rejected the question of a more liberal abortion law did not help either, because this emotional issue had raised the public temperature to a very considerable extent.

As time went by, further efforts were made to bring about universal suffrage but to no avail. Although Hitler never had much of a following in Switzerland, his supporters loudly argued against political equality for women "because the nature of the woman does not fit into the political struggle, because nowhere has the emancipation of women led to an improvement of the political climate and the already existing over-democratization would, through the emancipation of women, only lead to a further increase in mass politics."[5]

After the war, when the Nazis were discredited and when Switzerland's other neighbors, France and Italy, extended voting rights to their women, the matter was raised again. The Nationalrat (the lower house, whose representation is based on population as compared to the Ständerat, where each canton has two members) debated it on December 12, 1945, led by Social Democrat Hans Oprecht. The following arguments of the opposition sound quite ridiculous today. When the Swiss Confederation was established in 1291, no woman was present. Would a woman in the countryside be willing to take the long walk to the voting place? Who would take care of the children in the meantime? Women in town don't like to go out into the streets, which they would have to if they were to vote. What about voting during childbirth? If a woman were to get elected to office, who would do the cooking? For these and other reasons, women themselves would probably oppose the extension of the franchise.[6]

When the Nationalrat finally voted on the issue, the result was overwhelmingly positive, 104 people were in favor and only 32 opposed. But this was merely the first step. For what was passed was postulate, an invitation to the administration to come up with a report.[7] It took five years before such a report was issued, and it was to the effect that the enfranchisement of women was to be achieved through the passage of a new law, rather than through new interpretation of existing legislation. A request to ask the government to work out details for a partial revision of the constitution failed in the upper house. That body, which had a total membership of 44, rejected the suggestion by a vote of 19 to 17.[8]

More referenda on the question were held on the cantonal level, and they all failed. Before asking the men in Geneva and in Basel for their opinions, the women themselves were polled and in overwhelming numbers showed that they indeed wanted the right to vote. Yet both cantons rejected the request. In Zurich, the support of women was solicited and obtained after a referendum had failed.[9]

It was not until February 1957 that the government, in a long and detailed document, recommended the introduction of woman suffrage. More time passed, and more arguments followed, until the crucial vote was taken in Parliament. On June 13, 1958, the Nationalrat accepted the proposal by a vote of 96 to 43, and the Ständerat did likewise, 26 to 12.[10]

Now the cantons themselves, or rather the population in the different cantons, had to be consulted, with a majority of the total vote plus a positive response in a majority of cantons necessary for passage. On February 1, 1959, the male population made its decision. Two-thirds of the eligible electorate participated, and 323,727 voted for the proposal, and 654,939 voted against it.[11] Only in the three French-speaking cantons of Geneva, Vaud, and Neuchâtel were more positive than negative votes cast. Woman suffrage seemed once again to be dead in Switzerland.

However, such an obituary turned out to be slightly premature. For in Vaud, the citizens not only accepted woman suffrage on the federal basis, but decided at the same time that women should be accorded full citizens' rights on the cantonal and communal levels as well. Thus, Vaud became the first canton where women were now able to vote in provincial and local elections. Neuchâtel and Geneva held special referenda, and there, too, the

female population received the right to vote in provincial and local
contests. In the mid-1960s, there were some setbacks when Ticino
and Zurich rejected similar referenda in 1966. But the same year,
Basel-Town voted yes, followed two years later by Basel-Country.
In 1968, Ticino and Valais reacted favorably, followed in 1970 by
Lucerne and Zurich. St. Gallen, however, decided to remain on
the negative side. Meanwhile, in many cantons, individual communities agreed to grant women the right to participate in their affairs
on a local basis.

When, in 1968, Switzerland joined the Human Rights Convention of the United Nations, it could do so only conditionally, because
this document specifically prohibits discrimination on account of
race, religion, or sex. This was obviously embarrassing for the
homeland of the Red Cross and other humanitarian institutions. On
February 7, 1971, another referendum was held on the question of
woman suffrage in federal elections. This time, the figures of 11
years earlier were almost completely reversed, with 621,109
voting in the affirmative and only 323,882 in opposition.[12] By an
almost two-to-one margin, the same ratio with which they had rejected the idea a decade earlier, the men of Switzerland now
accepted women in the body politic as voters and possibly as candidates for office. At the same time, the cantons of Aargau, Zug,
Fribourg, and Schaffhausen enfranchised their women on the state
and local levels as well. In all, 14 cantons and three half-cantons
had voted in the affirmative, leaving only the five cantons of St.
Gallon, Thurgau, Schwyz, Glarus, and Uri and the three half-
cantons of Obwalden, Appenzell Inner Rhodes, and Appenzell Outer
Rhodes in the minority. The constitutional requirements having
thus been met, women now could vote for, and be elected to, federal office. This also applied in those cantons where the vote had
been negative. Where women had not been allowed to vote on the
provincial and local levels, they were given these rights in most
cases shortly afterwards. The exceptions are the tiny half-cantons
of Appenzell. In both of them, women to this day are excluded
from participating in cantonal affairs, although many a community
lets them vote. But in Appenzell there still exists the old-fashioned
Landsgemeinde, and the appearance of women in such gatherings is
apparently viewed as some kind of a threat. By and large, however,
women have indeed achieved the franchise in Switzerland. They
can vote and hold office on the federal level as well as in most
cantons and local communities (see Table 8.1).

TABLE 8.1

Woman Suffrage in Switzerland

Canton	1959 National Referendum (percent yes)	1971 National Referendum (percent yes)	Cantonal Referenda[a]
Aargau	22.7	50.2	1971—yes
Appenzell Inner Rhodes	4.9	28.9	none
Appenzell Outer Rhodes	15.5	39.9	none
Basel-Country	37.3	79.9	1968—yes
Basel-Town	46.8	82.2	1966—yes
Bern	35.5	66.5	1968—yes
Fribourg	29.8	71.1	1971—yes
Geneva	60.0	91.1	1960—yes
Glarus	19.0	41.3	1961—no[b] 1967—yes (partly)[b]
Graubunden	22.4	54.8	none
Lucerne	21.2	62.7	1960—no 1970—yes
Neuchâtel	52.2	82.0	1959—yes
Nidwalden	19.5	55.8	1965—yes[b]
Obwalden	14.0	46.7	1968—yes
St. Gallen	19.3	46.5	1970—no
Schaffhausen	31.9	56.7	1967—yes 1971—yes
Solothurn	30.0	64.1	1968—no
Schwyz	14.1	42.2	none
Thurgau	19.8	44.1	none
Ticino	37.1	75.3	1962—yes[c] 1966—no 1968—yes
Uri	14.6	31.3	none
Valais	30.5	79.9	1968—yes
Vaud	51.3	83.9	1959—yes
Zug	24.3	75.7	1971—yes
Zurich	36.2	66.8	1966—no 1970—yes

[a]Concerning suffrage on the cantonal and local levels.
[b]Decision of the Landsgemeinde.
[c]Decision of the great council.
Source: Susanna Woodtli, Gleichberechtigung (Frauenfeld: Verlag Huber, 1975).

WOMEN MEMBERS OF THE SWISS LEGISLATURE

It has been said that "the long delay in according the vote to women is typical: Switzerland was behind comparable neighbors in many innovations—railways (1846), emancipation of the Jews (1866), motor traffic, television, as well as the political equality of women."[13] Perhaps so. But somehow the Swiss managed to make up for this tardiness. Their railway system today is among the very best in the world. The Holocaust has passed them by (though probably through very little of their own doing). As to women in politics, it is remarkable how quickly the women got used to their new positions. A few months after they were given full citizen rights, elections were held. Competing for the 200 seats in the Nationalrat in October 1971 were 1,696 candidates, of whom 268 (or 15.8 percent) were women. Four years later, 329 women (16.9 percent of the total) were among the 1,947 aspirants for the lower house.[14] Some parties may have been opposed to woman suffrage before. However, this was all forgotten now, and every party that was to elect some of their candidates to Parliament included a few women on their lists.

Eight years later, when personal interviews of party leaders were conducted, there was not one who did not profess to be fully in favor of complete political equality among the sexes. They sometimes expressed concern about their more conservative electorate, especially in the rural areas. They mentioned the less educated women, who themselves would not favor women in leading political positions, and they bemoaned that women might not be interested sufficiently in the political process to vote in large enough numbers. (This was a special complaint of left-wing politicians, who found a lot of apathy among working-class women.) But none left any doubt about the desirability of having women as voters as well as candidates.

Indeed, as the elections of 1971 approached, the various parties were competing with one another for qualified female candidates. Some of these were put into very electable positions. In order to understand this, a few words must be said about the Swiss election system. We have seen that, in the United States, Britain, and Canada, the aim of the candidates is to be the "first past the post." In Austria, proportional representation prevails, and in the German Federal Republic, half the candidates are elected in individual districts and the other half through the land lists (with the precise number of seats allocated to each party determined by the percentage of votes received by the party on the land list). Switzerland has basically a system of proportional representation but with a number of important modifications. Each canton represents an election district and is given a number of seats according to its population. Where only one seat is allocated, an absolute majority is required by the successful candidate. The same holds true of the upper chamber, the Ständerat, where each canton has two seats, except for the six half-cantons, which have one seat apiece.

In Nationalrat elections in cantons with several seats, each party presents a list of names. How the candidates are placed on the list does influence the voters to a considerable extent. Sometimes the incumbents are listed first, sometimes the others are listed in alphabetical order. There is no countrywide system, and the party leadership in each canton has much leeway. The voters themselves have various options. They may cross out names on the list, vote twice for specific individuals, or write in names from other parties' lists. Or they may take an empty list and fill in names appearing on several different lists. The more such individual votes a candidate can obtain, the better his chances for election. Thus, under the Swiss system, on the one hand the parties play a decisive part, because the voters choose lists made up by the political parties. On the other hand, while the position of a candidate on the list may be decisive, the voter is also in a situation where he can clearly express his preference for a certain candidate.

Into this somewhat complicated arrangement, women were now co-opted, not only as voters, but as candidates as well. Almost all political parties, and certainly the more important ones, attempted to recruit women for the October 1971 elections. Some aimed at a specific percentage of female candidates. Others tried to find as many women as possible without any thought of particular quotas. Still others made it clear that female candidates were welcome and left it at that.[15] Several of the women candidates were given preferable positions on the lists, a factor that contributed greatly to their subsequent elections.[16]

How the voters decide the rankings is of crucial importance, not only for the successful candidates but also for the unsuccessful ones, for it does establish the runner-up positions. A number of vacancies occur during every four-year term of the Nationalrat, and the next highest vote-getter of that particular party in the specific canton simply moves up. Several women have reached Parliament in that way. By the end of 1978, for example, women were first runners-up on 11 lists that had elected members to the Nationalrat. Another 11 women were second in line to succeed, 14 were in third place, and 12 in fourth. In no instance, however, were women either first or second in succession to women who had been elected. No such considerations exist in the Ständerat, where a vacancy necessitates a special election.[17]

The Election of 1971

In October 1971, ten women were elected immediately into the 200-member Nationalrat. The three major government parties, the conservative Christian Democrats, the Social Democrats, and the liberal Freisinn, each had three female representatives, and the small Communist Labor party, the Partei der Arbeit, also had elected one. The 44-member Ständerat had one female member, elected on the Freisinn ticket.* Before the four-year term was over, four more women were to take their seats in the Nationalrat.

The little canton of Schwyz had voted against woman suffrage in 1971 and did not as yet allow women to vote in cantonal and local affairs. Nevertheless, it sent a woman to fill one of its three seats in the Nationalrat as soon as this was possible. Elisabeth Blunschy (1972-), a Christian Democrat, was the daughter of a prominent legislator and judge. Herself a practicing lawyer, she married an attorney who died during her first year in Bern. The mother of three adopted children, she was president of the Swiss Catholic Women's League and well-known not only in her own canton but throughout Switzerland, so that she was almost a "natural" candidate of the Christian Democratic party. She was reelected in 1975. Two years later, the president of the Nationalrat (the position is equivalent to that of the Speaker of the House of Representatives except that it comprises only a one-year term and is passed around among the several parties) had to vacate his position because he had been elected to the executive of his home canton, Valais, a post incompatible with membership in the national legislature. Because of a very intricate interparty arrangement that gave the Christian Democrats the presidency of the Nationalrat in 1977, Bluntsch's name was suggested as a substitute, and she thus became not only the Nationalrat's but, in a sense, Switzerland's first lady for a few months. She herself describes her selection largely as accidental,[18] helped along by the mass media, and the suggestion has been made that letting a woman hold the presidency for a short while was a convenient way out for those who could not bring themselves to choose one for a full year. But there is general agreement that her conduct in office enhanced not only her own reputation but that of Swiss female politicians in general.

---

*Literally translated as "free spirit," the Freisinn is often called Radical because of its former reforming attitudes. Today, the party very roughly corresponds to the Liberals in the rest of Europe, shying away from both the Christian emphasis of the Christian Democrats and the Socialist influence of the Social Democrats.

Also elected in 1971 and reelected in 1975 was Josi Meier (1926-), a Christian Democrat from Lucerne. She has been involved in the struggle for woman's rights for quite a while. A lawyer, she is interested in constitutional questions and was the only female member of a commission dealing with possible constitutional revisions several years before she was elected to Parliament.[19] She was elected to the great council of her canton, has occupied leadership positions in her party, is interested in foreign policy, and is serving as president of the Council of Europe from 1978 to 1980.

Hanny Thalmann (1912-) represented St. Gallen, another canton that rejected woman suffrage in 1971. Prominent in educational circles, she headed a vocational school. She is the sister of a clergyman and a member of the Christian Democratic party. Education on all levels, concern for the young, and a fair share for women are among her chief interests. In private conversation, she emphasized not a struggle but a partnership among the sexes, stressing the "natural mission" of women, the upbringing of children, which she described as a herrliche Aufgabe, a "beautiful task." Reelected in 1975, she decided to retire in 1979.

The Christian Democrats have not always favored political equality for women, but today they are fully committed to it. The same is true of the Freisinn, whose liberal tradition was at first confined only to men. This party also elected three women to the Nationalrat in 1971.

Liselotte Spreng (1912-) holds a medical degree, is married to a physician, and is the mother of four children. She was actively involved in the fight for woman suffrage and served on the Fribourg cantonal council. As a doctor, she has been working with men all her life, and whereas in the beginning women in Parliament seem to have been treated with kid gloves, she seems bemused now that things have become "normal," and men no longer hesitate to attack women politically.[20] She rejects the notion that women should confine their interests to questions dealing with home and family, and she is today the only woman on the parliamentary military commission, having previously served on a commission dealing with foreign economic problems. She, too, was reelected in 1975.

Martha Ribi (1915-) comes from Zurich. She is a widow with two sons and takes a special interest in the administration of hospitals and sanatoriums. When she decided to run for political office, she was not as well known as some of her colleagues. She first competed for local office and lost but gained enough recognition to make her election to the Nationalrat possible.[21] She won again in 1975 but in 1978 lost a contest for a seat in the Ständerat to another woman, Emilie Lieberherr. However, she retains her seat in the

Nationalrat. She expressed concern about replacements for the present generation of women in Parliament and advocated female participation on all levels of politics, because women could not expect to start at the top. In this connection, we should mention the frequently voiced complaint that women just do not have as much exposure as men before entering politics. They lack the many connections men can establish through business, sports organizations, the military, shooting societies, and so forth. Ribi feels that "we may not, shall not and can not make policy for women only, but we make policy in general. Within this framework we expound a responsible policy on all matters, including those pertaining to women."[22]

Tilo Frey (1923-) was born in Africa. She is a teacher and educational administrator in Neuchâtel. Since her canton emancipated women earlier than most, she was able to become a member of the municipal and cantonal legislatures before her election to the Nationalrat in 1971. Four years later, she was unsuccessful in her attempt to retain her seat.

The Social Democrats also elected three women in 1971. Hedi Lang (1931-) is from Zurich and of the working class—a class whose female members were not always in favor of woman suffrage. Her husband was an ardent Social Democrat who at one time was himself a member of the Nationalrat. (This remote connection between a husband's seat and his wife's was the only one discoverable. This is, as we have seen, in striking contrast to the situation in the United States, Britain, and, to some extent, Canada). Lang was for many years a homemaker and helped her husband with the publication of a regional daily newspaper. She became a member of a communal council, where she concerned herself with guardianship and welfare questions. In Bern, she soon became quite prominent, and having been reelected in 1975, she was named in June 1979 as one of the vice-presidents of the Social Democrat faction in the Nationalrat.

Lilian Uchtenhagen (1928-) is another very prominent Social Democrat from Zurich. A student of political science, she is married and the mother of three grown children. She has been active in the women's movement and was a member of the town council of Zurich before being elected to the Nationalrat, to which she was reelected in 1975. She is today a member of the executive of her party and lists economic and financial questions among her particular concerns.

From a number of conversations, it was apparent that having young children presents quite a problem for politically active mothers. Gabrielle Nanchen (1943-), one of the two youngest female members of the Nationalrat, had previously been involved in welfare and social services in her native Valais. She was reelected in 1975 but decided to retire at the end of the 1979 legislative period. Her youngest child was born in the spring of 1978, and she found that family matters had reached a point that necessitated withdrawal from politics for the time being, a decision that was very much regretted by everybody who mentioned it.

The last of the ten women who entered the Nationalrat immediately after the 1971 election was Nelly Wicky (1923-) from Geneva. She represented the Partei der Arbeit, which in Switzerland is the Communist party. She is married to a railway worker and both of them have been active in left-wing politics for many years. A very mild-mannered woman, she has served on the city council of Geneva since 1963.* She is a grade school teacher by profession, and during her term of office in Bern, she alternated between the Nationalrat and her classroom. In 1975, she was defeated for reelection.

Four more women entered the Nationalrat during the next four years. Almost immediately after the 1971 election, a vacancy occurred that was filled by Hanna Sahlfeld (1943-), Social Democrat from St. Gallen. Like Nanchen, she was a young mother who gave birth to a child while she was a member of the legislature. Married to a Protestant clergyman, she is herself an ordained minister who had been conducting services in Protestant churches in St. Gallen and in this way gained publicity and popularity before entering public life. In 1975, she sought and obtained reelection. However, her husband was about to assume a pulpit in Germany, and she resigned in late 1975 in order to go with him.

In 1972, Helen Meyer (1920-) from Zurich joined the Christian Democrats in the Nationalrat. She was the editor of a weekly journal and a member of Zurich's town council. The education of girls and women was one of her special concerns. She was also interested in health matters. She expressed the view that specialization in the legislature may not be very spectacular but was necessitated by time pressures and worthwhile in the long run.[23] She won reelection in 1975 but three years later resigned for professional reasons.

---

*In Switzerland, it is possible to serve on the communal or town council, the cantonal legislature, and the Nationalrat at the same time, and several of the women are indeed members of more than one of these bodies, as are many of the men.

It was a particular set of Swiss circumstances* that led to the entry of Gertrude Girard (1913-) into the Nationalrat in 1974. Wife and mother of three children, she had worked with the mass media and had been actively involved in obtaining voting rights for women. She was from Vaud and a member of the <u>Freisinn</u>. A member of Switzerland's Europe delegation, she at one time headed the Nationalrat's contingent to EFTA.[24]

Elisabeth Lardelli (1921-), who represented the People's party from Graubünden, filled a vacancy in 1974 but was unsuccessful in retaining her seat at the next general election. She studied law and was a member of the local board of education and of the cantonal legislature. So far, she has been the only woman in the Nationalrat from her party and from her canton. She expressed "fascination" with being there because it entailed "a state of equality to an extent hardly realized anywhere else in Switzerland."[25]

The Election of 1975

By the time the 1971-75 legislative period drew to a close, the Nationalrat contained 14 women, which was 7 percent of its total membership. All of them ran for reelection. Frey, Wicky, and Lardelli were not successful; the other 11 were returned. In addition, four new ones were chosen. With the almost immediate resignation of Sahlfeld, there were thus again 14 women in the lower house. During the next four years, three more arrived and one departed, bringing the total by the summer of 1979 to 16 or 8 percent of the 200-member body.

In the 1975 elections, there was even a <u>Frauenliste</u> in Zurich, a list of female candidates only. But this list of, by, and for women irrespective of parties received hardly any support at all, the women clearly prefering to remain within the party constellations.

Monique Bauer (1922-) gave the tiny Liberal party its first female representative in the Nationalrat. She is from Geneva and is married to a physician and the mother of grown children. In order to win the election, she had to defeat a member of her own party, a matter that has left party scars. She was elected to the Geneva legislature and served there for four years. Protection of

---

*The canton of Vaud has the provision that only two members of its executive could at the same time be members of the federal legislature. When a third was chosen in 1974, he had to give up his position in Bern, thus making way for Girard.

the environment is one of her chief concerns, and concentration on this topic does not always suit the party leadership too well.

Youngest among the newcomers in 1975 was Cornelia Füeg (1941-). She was born in Zurich but acquired Solothurn citizenship through marriage to an agricultural engineer. They have four children, all quite small. Hers are the problems of a young wife and mother who wants to be politically active, and she is full of praise for her husband and "the grandmothers" who take care of the children.[26] Representing the rural canton of Solothurn and living in the country, she is a member of Parliament's agricultural commission and has acquired expertise in this area.

Doris Morf (1927-) joined Lang and Uchtenhagen and became the third Social Democratic woman from Zurich. She is a journalist who has worked for Swiss newspapers in New York. Also a publisher, she is interested in human rights. She served on Zurich's town council and is very active in party and women's affairs in Zurich. Apparently, her marriage suffered from her political and professional activities; she is divorced and the mother of grown children.

Gertrud Spiess (1914-), a Christian Democrat, gave Basel-Town its first female representative. She taught high school, served on the local and provincial councils, and was president of the great council of her half-canton. In addition to educational questions, she has been involved in such matters as getting better insurance for unmarried women who take care of their sick parents.[27] But she has argued against too much specialization, contending that a Nationalrätin "ought to take some interest in everything."[28]

Three more women joined during the session. First to arrive was Heidi Deneys (1937-), a Social Democrat from Neuchâtel. Interested in politics since her student days, she studied social sciences, taught in Africa for a few years, and since 1965 has been employed as secondary school teacher in La Chaux-de-Fonds, a position she holds to this day. She has served in provincial and cantonal legislatures. Divorced and the mother of two teenagers, she divides her time between Bern and her home community, and the same day may see her in the federal capital in the morning and in her classroom in the afternoon. Her situation exhibits the difficulties involved in a part-time legislature and its less-than-adequate compensation of its members.

Amelia Christinat (1926-) is a Social Democrat who came to the Nationalrat from Geneva, although she was born in Italian-speaking Ticino. She is married and the mother of a grown daughter. She is a dressmaker by profession, and her interests in consumer affairs led her into Social Democratic politics. Even before women could vote in national elections, she was a member of the communal council of Geneva and later of the cantonal parliament, a position she still holds. She was second vice-president of the Great Council in 1975.

Arriving at the beginning of June 1979 was Susi Eppenberger (1931-). She succeeded as Freisinn deputy from St. Gallen when her predecessor was killed in a car accident. She was at the time still a member of the cantonal parliament but was contemplating giving this up, though constitutionally she was not forced to do so. A homemaker and mother of three children, she was not originally enamored by the concept of women in political posts, but as the wife of a veterinarian and familiar with the problems of agricultural regions, she became more and more enthusiastic about playing a part in the political life of her country.[29]

The Ständerat

Thus, there have been 21 women in the Nationalrat by mid-1979. Membership in the Ständerat has been much more elusive. Consisting of 44 members (46 after the establishment of the new canton of Jura in 1978), only one woman was elected to it in 1971. This was Lise Girardin (1921-), representing the Freisinn from Geneva. An educator whose interests include the judiciary and the police, she joined the legislature of the canton of Geneva in 1961 and the executive of the city of Geneva in 1967. In 1975, she did not manage to win reelection but trailed the Social Democratic candidate by 963 votes. Reasons given for her defeat included the unfavorable reaction against the Freisinn in Geneva because of local budgetary measures, her acceptance of an executive position with a bank shortly after arriving in Bern, her lack of support for an initiative advocating the equality of the sexes,[30] and the disciplined support her opponent received from the Communists.[31] These reasons are interesting because they are partly political and partly personal and directed against an individual politician. But there was apparently also sentiment against a female in public life who did not support a measure many women regarded as being in the interest of their sex. Since the incumbent received over 35,000 votes and yet placed third by fewer than 1,000 votes in a fight for two positions, a variety of circumstances not all sex-related was obviously at work.

This left the Ständerat without female membership until 1978, when in a contest over a vacancy in Zurich, the Freisinnig Ribi was barely defeated by another woman, Social Democrat Emilie Lieberherr (1924-). Lieberherr holds a doctorate in the social sciences, has worked in a bank, and taught. Since 1970, she has been a member of the executive of the town of Zurich, where she presently heads the municipal welfare agency. She has been very active in consumer affairs and the Federal Commission on Women's Questions is headed by her. Her complete absorption in politics is made possible by the absence of day-to-day family obligations. She has worked hard for woman suffrage and is now a strong advocate of more and more female participation on all levels. She deplores polarization among women and demands—and personally receives— full equality with men. She has expressed the hope that in time the legislative agenda will deal "not so much with problems about women but with solutions to human problems."[32]

DISCUSSION

Thus, we can observe that just before the elections of October 1979, the Swiss Nationalrat contained 8 percent women, a respectable proportion when compared with the other countries previously discussed and when the brief period during which the Swiss have had experience with women in politics is taken into consideration. Of course, the percentage is still most unsatisfactory when one remembers that half the adult population consists of women. If both houses are taken together, the figure is 6.9 percent (17 out of 246). Some of the women in the national legislature have been in the forefront of the fight for woman suffrage. Some of them have occupied responsible political positions in their hometowns or cantons before they were able to do so on the national level. Others were relative newcomers to politics and arrived almost by accident in Bern. As to their departures, three were defeated in the next election, two resigned during the session, two more announced that they would not run for reelection in 1979, and the remaining 14 were all trying to get back that year.

Regarding political parties, there are three major ones in the Swiss Parliament: the Social Democrats (SP), the Christian Democrats or Christian People's party (CVP), and the Freisinn (FDP), each of which usually elects more than 40 members to the Nationalrat. These three parties each furnish two of the seven men (there have not as yet been any women!) of the executive, the Bundesrat, the seventh coming from the small Swiss People's party (SVP), a party that in the past has had different names indicating its affinity with farmers, businessmen, and Bürger. The three big parties together have thus far accounted for all but three of the women in the Nationalrat, with the People's party, the Liberals, and the Communists (PdA) electing one woman each (see Table 8.2).

TABLE 8.2

Party Affiliation of Female Members
of the Swiss Parliament

Party	Number
Social Democrat	7*
Freisinn	6*
Christian Democrat	5
Liberal	1
Labor	1
People's	1

*Plus one in the Ständerat.
Source: Compiled by the author.

Table 8.3 indicates the ages of the women upon first entry into the Nationalrat. Their average age came to slightly less than 48 years, which compares with 46.26 years for men in a randomly selected year (1974). The average entry age of the seven Social Democratic women came to just under 40 years, while the men who served in 1974 entered at the average age of 45.3. The Christian Democratic women averaged 53 years as compared with 44.1 for the men of 1974. The Freisinn women's average age came to 51 (46.3 for the men). The female representative of the Liberal party was 53 and so was the one from the People's party (whose male colleagues had entered at the average age of 47.8), while Wicky, the Communist, was 48. There is, therefore, the tendency for the Social Democrats to send younger women to the Nationalrat, while the Christian Democratic women are considerably older. However, the third-youngest was a deputy from the Freisinn, and one of the Social Democrats was in her early fifties. Both women in the Ständerat were 50 years or older when elected.

Repeated references have been made to family relationships. This was done because the Swiss women in particular see quite a problem in raising children and being in Bern at the same time. Location is, of course, important, that is, how far away the capital is from home. Although Switzerland is a small country with excellent trains that run very frequently, the mountain ranges make transportation between certain areas quite difficult. For a young mother to be separated from her small children for several days presents a major difficulty and tends to keep at least some women away from politics, perhaps until their children are older. But of the five youngest female representatives (aged 40 or below when first elected), all but one had small children. They all commented on the hardship this created and how they had to work out a solution for their particular situations. Repeatedly, the women praised their spouses and spoke of a commitment to a partnership between husband and wife without which the problem would be impossible to solve.

TABLE 8.3

Ages of Women Entering Swiss Nationalrat

Age Group	Number of Women	Party
21–30	2	SP, SP
31–40	3	FDP, SP, SP
41–50	7	CVP, CVP, FDP, FDP, PdA, SP, SP
51–60	7	CVP, CVP, FDP, FDP, Liberal, SP, SVP
61–70	2	CVP, FDP

Source: Compiled by the author.

Switzerland has a Milizparlament, a part-time legislature that meets for a few weeks four times a year. On the one hand, this supposedly frees the members for much of the year and enables them to pursue their professions, except that they are still expected to sit on commissions, attend meetings, and make speeches even after Parliament has adjourned. On the other hand, the concept of part-time service prevents adequate financial compensation. People from lower income groups, especially unmarried, widowed, or divorced women with family obligations, find this a much rougher situation than, say, professional politicians and union employees whose salary continues, independent professionals, people with means, or women with wealthy husbands.

Table 8.4 deals with regional distribution. Zurich, which has the largest representation in the Nationalrat, has had more women in its delegation than any other canton. Bern, second in

TABLE 8.4

Cantonal Representation of Women

Canton	Total Seats in Nationalrat (1975)	Women in Nationalrat
Aargau	14	0
Appenzell Inner Rhodes	1	0
Appenzell Outer Rhodes	2	0
Basel-Country	7	0
Basel-Town	7	1 (Spiess)
Bern	31	0
Fribourg	6	1 (Spreng)
Geneva	11	3 (Wicky, Bauer, Christinat)
Glarus	1	0
Graubünden	5	1 (Lardelli)
Lucerne	9	1 (Meier)
Neuchâtel	5	2 (Frey, Deneys)
Nidwalden	1	0
Obwalden	1	0
St. Gallen	12	3 (Thalmann, Sahlfeld, Eppenberger)
Schaffhausen	2	0
Solothurn	7	1 (Füeg)
Schwyz	3	1 (Blunschy)
Thurgau	6	0
Ticino	8	0
Uri	1	0
Valais	7	1 (Nanchen)
Vaud	16	1 (Girard)
Zug	2	0
Zurich	35	5 (Ribi, Uchtenhagen, Lang, Meyer, Morf)

Source: Compiled by the author.

population, has not had any. While Zurich, Geneva, St. Gallen, and Neuchâtel have had several women in Parliament, eight other cantons have elected one apiece. This still leaves ten (11, if the new canton of Jura is included) that have never yet been represented by a woman in the national legislature. Among them is obviously Appenzell, which still denies females the vote on the cantonal level.

It would be foolish to suggest that everything possible has been achieved toward the full emancipation of women in Switzerland. On the other hand, it must be admitted that, considering no woman could vote for or be elected to Parliament a decade ago, much has been accomplished. In a relatively short time, men apparently got used to having women among them in the legislature. "At first, we were afraid of the voices of women who sound so very different," a male party leader told me. He and others expected women to act foolishly and were surprised when they did not, at least not more so than their male colleagues. So perhaps this remark is an indication that they are now accepted, a fact that every Swiss female member of the Nationalrat readily admits. An illustration of this acceptance may be found in this statement by a longtime male incumbent: "In the beginning, we were all very quiet and listened closely whenever a woman went to the rostrum and spoke. Now we don't pay any attention and continue with our private conversations, the same way we do with everybody else!" (For a concise listing of the women members of the Swiss legislature, see Tables 8.5 and 8.6.)

ADDENDUM

On October 21, 1979, the Swiss quadrennial parliamentary elections took place. This was the third time that women were able to vote and to compete for national office, and the rapid advances made in 1971 and in 1975 were improved upon.

In the Ständerat, Emilie Lieberherr managed to retain her seat for the Social Democrats, although by a very narrow margin. But she was no longer the only woman in the upper house. Monique Bauer, who had represented the Liberals from Geneva in the Nationalrat since 1975, was elected to the Bundesrat, as was a newcomer to the national legislature, Esther Bürer, Social Democrat from Schaffhausen. Thus, the Ständerat, which four years earlier had lost the only woman member, now had a female contingent of three which amounted to 6.5 percent of the total.

The outgoing Nationalrat had included 16 women. With the retirement of Hanny Thalmann and Gabrielle Nanchen and with Monique Bauer no longer in contention for the lower house, this

TABLE 8.5

Female Members of the Swiss Legislature

Member	Dates	Party	Canton	In Office	Reason for Departure
Elisabeth Blunschy	1922–	Christian Democrat	Schwyz	1971	n.a.
Josi Meier	1926–	Christian Democrat	Lucerne	1971	n.a.
Hanny Thalmann	1912–	Christian Democrat	St. Gallen	1971–79	retired
Liselotte Spreng	1912–	Freisinn	Fribourg	1971	n.a.
Martha Ribi	1915–	Freisinn	Zurich	1971	n.a.
Tilo Frey	1923–	Freisinn	Neuchâtel	1971–75	defeated
Hedi Lang	1931–	Social Democrat	Zurich	1971	n.a.
Lilian Uchtenhagen	1928–	Social Democrat	Zurich	1971	n.a.
Gabrielle Nanchen	1943–	Social Democrat	Valais	1971–79	retired
Nelly Wicky	1923–	Partei der Arbeit	Geneva	1971–75	defeated
Hanna Sahlfeld	1943–	Social Democrat	St. Gallen	1971–75	resigned
Helen Meyer	1920–	Christian Democrat	Zurich	1972–78	resigned
Gertrude Girard	1913–	Freisinn	Vaud	1974	n.a.
Elisabeth Lardelli	1921–	People's party	Graubünden	1974–75	defeated
Monique Bauer	1922–	Liberal	Geneva	1975	n.a.
Cornelia Füeg	1941–	Freisinn	Solothurn	1975	n.a.
Doris Morf	1927–	Social Democrat	Zurich	1975	n.a.
Gertrud Spiess	1914–	Christian Democrat	Basel-Town	1975	n.a.
Heidi Deneys	1937–	Social Democrat	Neuchâtel	1977	n.a.
Amelia Christinat	1926–	Social Democrat	Geneva	1978	n.a.
Susi Eppenberger	1931–	Freisinn	St. Gallen	1979	n.a.
Lise Girardin	1921–	Freisinn	Geneva	1971–75	defeated
Emilie Lieberherr	1924–	Social Democrat	Zurich	1978	n.a.

Note: n.a., not applicable.
Source: Compiled by the author.

230

left 13 incumbents running for reelection. They were all successful and in a number of instances were the leading vote-getters of
their parties in their respective cantons.

TABLE 8.6

The Swiss Nationalrat and Female Members

	Number of Women	Names
October 31, 1971	10	Blunschy, Meier, Thalmann, Spreng, Ribi, Frey, Lang, Uchtenhagen, Nanchen, Wicky
Vacancies	4	Sahlfeld (1971), Meyer (1972), Girard (1974), Lardelli (1974)
October 26, 1975	15	Blunschy, Meier, Thalmann, Spreng, Ribi, Lang, Uchtenhagen, Nanchen, Sahlfeld (to 1975), Meyer (to 1978), Girard, Bauer, Füeg, Morf, Spiess
Vacancies	3	Deneys (1977), Christinat (1978), Eppenberger (1979)

Note: Unless otherwise indicated, dates in parentheses show
when members entered the Nationalrat.
Source: Compiled by the author.

In addition, eight more women were able to enter the National-
rat, bringing the total to 21 or 10.5 percent of the total. Francoise
Vannay (1946-) replaced Nanchen as Social Democrat from Valais
and Thalmann's seat was retained by Eva Segmüller (1932-) for the
Christian Democrats in St. Gallen. Zurich added yet another woman
to its four female incumbents in the person of Freisinn member
Elisabeth Kopp (1936-). The Social Democrats from Vaud elected
Yvette Jaggi (1941-) and the left-wing Progressive Organisation
(POCH) was successful in Basel-Town with Ruth Mascarin (1945-).
In three cantons where no woman had previously been elected to the
national legislature, the situation was now altered: Ursula Mauch
(1935-) won for the Social Democrats in Aargau, Alma Bacciarini

(1921-) for the Freisinn in Ticino and Genevieve Aubry (1928-) for the Freisinn in Bern. Altogether, the women in Switzerland had every reason to be pleased with the outcome of the 1979 parliamentary elections.

NOTES

1. Susanna Woodtli, Gleichberechtigung (Frauenfeld: Verlag Huber, 1975), p. 12.
2. Ibid., pp. 124-25.
3. Ibid., p. 138.
4. Ibid., pp. 148.
5. Ibid., p. 160. My translation of a quotation from a Zurich captain of the Nazi Eidgenössische Front.
6. Ibid., pp. 163-72.
7. Gruner and Junker, Bürger, Staat und Politik in der Schweiz (Basel: Lehrmi Helverlag, 1972), p. 82.
8. Woodtli, op. cit., p. 173.
9. Ibid., pp. 173-74.
10. Ibid., p. 176.
11. Ibid., p. 267.
12. Ibid.
13. Christopher Hughes, Switzerland (New York: Praeger, 1975), p. 144.
14. Thomas Held, Christoph Reichenau, and Verena Ritter, "Frauen in der Bundesversammlung," Frauenfragen, nos. 1 and 2 (1979), p. 75.
15. Erich Gruner, Martin Daetwyler, and Oscar Zosso, Aufstellung und Auswahl der Kandidaten bei den Nationalratswahlen in der Schweiz (Bern: Eidgenössische Drucksachen- und Materialzentrale, 1975), p. 159.
16. Ibid., p. 161.
17. Held, Reichenau, and Ritter, op. cit., p. 77.
18. Private conversation with the author.
19. Barbara Ryser, "Frauen in der Christlichdemokratischen Volkspartei der Schweiz," Seminar paper written under Professor Urs Altermatt, Universitat Bern (Historisches Institut), 1979, p. 57.
20. Theres Giger, "Freisinnige Frauen in den eidgenössischen Räten," Politische Rundschau 58 (1979): 75-76.
21. Private conversation with the author.
22. Giger, op. cit., p. 78. My translation.
23. Ryser, op. cit., p. 48.
24. Giger, op. cit., p. 76.
25. Quoted in a pamphlet issued by the Schweizer Volkspartei.

26. Private conversation with the author.
27. Ryser, op. cit., p. 53.
28. Ibid., p. 49.
29. Private conversation with the author.
30. Neu Züricher Zeitung, October 28, 1975.
31. Neu Züricher Zeitung, October 29, 1975.
32. Berner Tagwacht, June 11, 1979.

9
CONCLUSION

After having studied the national legislatures of six countries in detail, several points can be made. To start with, the number of women serving in the elected parliaments is still pitifully small. Figure 9.1 draws a graphic comparison and shows that nowhere did women exceed 10 percent of the membership of these bodies. Considering that women make up at least one-half of the adult population they are obviously very much underrepresented. One can argue that an elected official serves all constituents, regardless of sex, and that, therefore, a man in the legislature is serving both men and women, just as a woman does in the same position. While this is correct, nevertheless, given the fact that women are, in terms of mental capability and physical stamina, in no way inferior to men, a very strong case can be made for getting more women elected to decision-making bodies.

There are several traditional views of why women should not be in politics. More than 2,000 years ago, Aristotle spoke of the male as "naturally fitter to command" than the female. [1] The Bible is often cited as establishing man's superiority over woman. Political activities, it is argued, would "unsex and degrade women, destroy domestic harmony, and lead to a decline in the birthrate." [2] Then there is the image of the woman as the happy homemaker. Women "do not long for the factory, they do not long for the office, they do not long for parliament. A cosy home, a beloved husband, a number of happy children are far closer to their hearts." [3] Although this quotation expresses the Nazi creed and is therefore now repudiated as such, the sentiment is still prevalent among many people. Childbearing is a definite biological function of the female, and, as a result, the woman was from the beginning charged not only with bearing children but with their upbringing as well. The affairs of business, defense, and politics were left to the male.

FIGURE 9.1

Women in National Legislatures

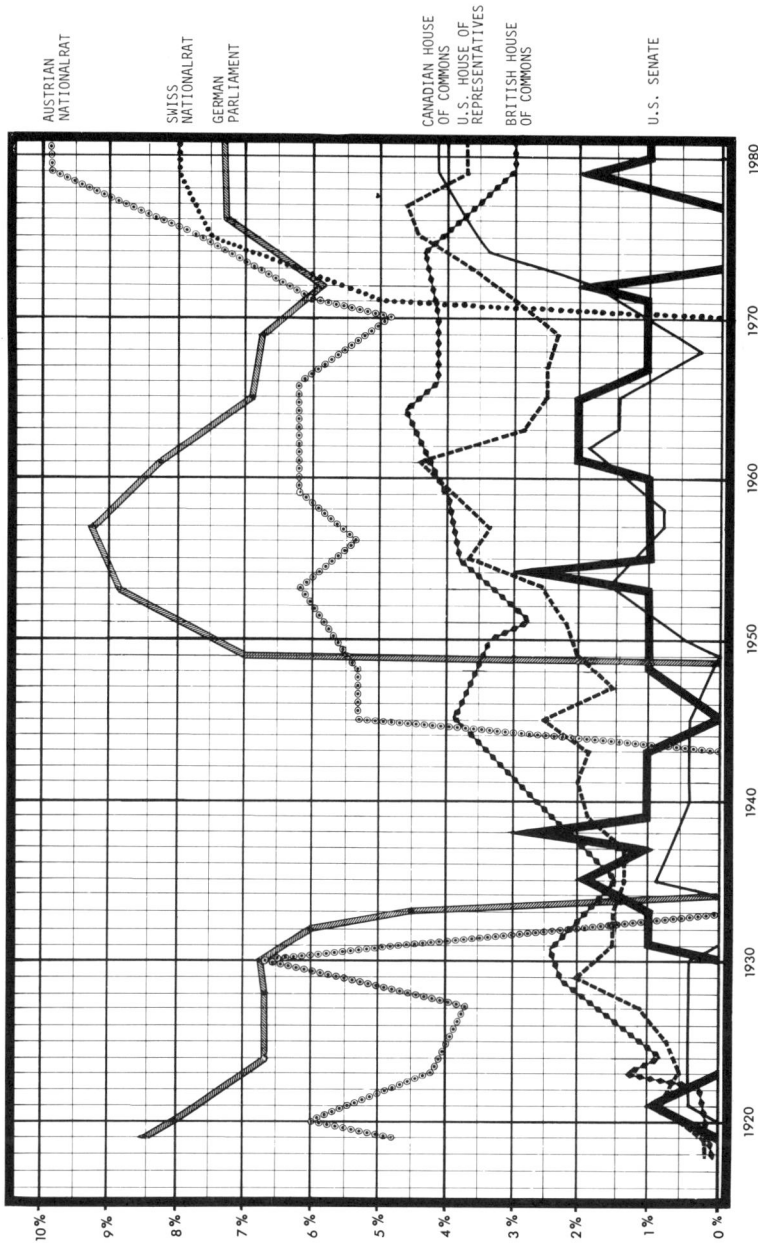

Source: Compiled by the author.

235

Only now are we breaking away from this mind set. We have not yet reached the end of a social and domestic revolution with implications as profound and far-reaching as the Industrial Revolution of an earlier century. Resistance to this change does not only come from men. Many women themselves are not too happy about their new roles and often oppose the idea of having other women playing prominent parts in public life.*

The concept of representative democracy came to Britain, the United States, and Canada much earlier than to most of the European continent. Yet, the Germans and Austrians have a much better record for electing women to the national legislatures. In these five countries, women received the right to vote at approximately the same time, but the English-speaking countries made a much slower start and, in terms of percentages, lagged rather badly behind Germany, Austria, and (since 1971) Switzerland. The reason is probably not so much to be found in degrees of conservatism, tradition, and prejudice, which are fairly widespread in every country. Rather, it is closely connected with particular election systems. In single-member constituencies, the competition is on a one-to-one basis. The candidate needs time, money, and stamina and has to be absent from the family for considerable periods of time. Putting up with abuse and overcoming prejudices are part of the campaign. Contests for the U.S. Senate are good examples of the reluctance of qualified women to subject themselves to such an ordeal. Although larger numbers of women are now competing for office, the picture is still not bright. In the 1978-79 general elections, the two major parties offered 49 female candidates for 435 seats in the U.S. House of Representatives, 83 for 635 seats in the British House of Commons, and 35 for 282 seats in the Canadian House of Commons. The minor parties very frequently have a much larger contingent of female candidates and occasionally get one or two elected. However, the main battle is between the major parties—where women are not very well represented. Even where they are running with major-party endorsement, they often find themselves in situations where they do not even have a fighting chance and are merely <u>Alibifrauen</u>, tokens that give parties an alibi so that the charge of antifeminism cannot be leveled against them.

---

*A woman member of the Swiss Nationalrat, who had received one of those "why don't you go home" letters, pointed out the rather curious fact that such messages are always more numerous right after a national holiday!

Under the list system, on the other hand, the voter is confronted by a number of names selected by the party. The higher one is placed on the list, the better the chance of being elected. When the lists are made up, women often find places on them. The question then is whether they are high enough to be elected almost automatically, occupying positions where they have a fighting chance, or at the lower end where they really have no hope to be elected. We have seen that in Austria the voter has some, and in Switzerland many, possibilities to express preference for certain candidates. But in any event, parties will be very careful to put women on the list, especially if it is a fairly large one. They have to avoid the stigma of being called antifeminist because they want to attract women as voters. On the other hand, they also hope that their more chauvinistic supporters will overlook a few female names tucked away among so many male ones. Under these circumstances, there are greater possibilities for women to be elected under the list system than in situations where one has to be "the first past the post."

The nomination process is of course all-important. The U.S. primary is a general free-for-all, a public contest in which each candidate is for himself. Although a candidate who has enough voter support can overcome reluctance and even hostility on the part of the party leadership, primaries are costly in time and money, and the casualties are high. In Britain, the decision about a person's candidacy is made by a small group of party leaders who interview the contestants and then pick one of them. A basically timid and conservative group may well go with a man because they feel he is "safer" than a female candidate, especially if they feel their party has at least a fighting chance of success. The recent innovation of Vorwahl in Austria and Switzerland broadens the group that makes the decision, and several women in both countries have asserted that their eventual success in winning an election was due to a favorable place on the ballot, won in such a Vorwahl.

Historically, the Social Democrats were in the forefront of the fight for woman's rights. They usually favored female suffrage before other parties and fielded more women candidates than the others as soon as this was possible. In the Weimar Republic, the leftist parties elected many more women than the other parties, especially since the extreme Right opposed women in politics altogether. In Austria, most of the women in Parliament in the First Republic were Socialists, and the same is still true, although recently more People's party legislators have been women. In the Federal Republic, earlier Socialist numerical advantages have completely disappeared. It is interesting that in the case of Denmark, a former Radical Liberal member of Parliament could state that her party "has always had a large percentage of women, whereas Denmark's largest party, the Social Democrats, have been very 'conservative' in this regard. "[4] It might be noted in passing that in 1975 the Danish Parliament included 16 percent women, the Swedish 21 percent, and the Finnish 23 percent.[5] In Britain, the Labour party was a little slow in sending women to Parliament, but made up for this in time. In 1979, despite a Conservative victory, the Labour party elected 11 out of the 19 female members of Parliament. In the less ideologically divided North America, the Democrats have an edge in female representation over the Republicans in the U.S. House of Representatives, just as in Canada, the Liberals have elected more women than the Progressive Conservatives. However, in both countries none of the major parties can claim a monopoly of favoring women in politics, a cause to which they all pay at least lip service.

In the United States, one of the most traveled roads to Congress for a woman is to fill a vacancy. This was true of all but two of the female members of the U.S. Senate. In six cases, women followed their own late husbands. More than one-third of the women in the House of Representatives were first elected as successors to seats left vacant by their spouses. In Britain, eleven women followed their husbands, six after spouses had died, four when the husbands went to the House of Lords, and one when her husband was legally barred to be in Parliament. In Canada, seven of the 33 women followed their husbands into the House of Commons, all of whom were among the first 17 women to be elected to Parliament.

Such a course is practically unknown in Germany, Austria, and Switzerland, although many of the women are indeed Grabspringer, that is, they come in to fill a vacancy during the session when someone elected by their party in that area dies or resigns. However, their predecessors are hardly ever their own husbands. It is different in the English-speaking countries, because special by-elections are scheduled to fill vacancies, and there is the temptation to take advantage of the recognition of the name of the former member, or in case of death, of the sympathy for him. Brookes gives this report on Margaret Wintringham, who competed for a seat in the House of Commons held previously by her deceased husband.

> A tall, well-built woman of forty-two with a high complexion and bright brown eyes she was a good platform speaker and had spoken during many of her husband's campaigns, but throughout the by-election campaign, in deference to her bereavement, she sat silent on the platform in her widow's weeds while eminent Liberals came to speak on her behalf.[6]

Perhaps such demureness was more appropriate in 1921 than it
would be today. Nevertheless, the sympathy vote is often a major
consideration. Under the list system, it is not likely for both
husband and wife to compete and for one to take the place of the
other. Lang might run several years after her husband had re-
linquished his seat in the Swiss Nationalrat, or Pollack might be
suggested by her husband as the one who should be sent to the
Austrian Parliament. But this is as close to the "widow syndrome"
as the European countries here under discussion have come.

There is another good reason for the unlikelihood of a wife's
following her husband to Parliament in the Germanic countries.
Women on the Continent do not seem to get as deeply involved in
their husbands' political careers as they do in the Anglo-Saxon
countries. Lady Astor "worked devotedly among the people of
Plymouth" while her husband was in Parliament.[7] Neuberger had
been a well-known state legislator in her own right in Oregon before her husband became a U.S. Senator, and Sullivan was her
congressman-husband's administrative assistant and campaign
manager. Such a background would, as a rule, be unusual on the
Continent. Although some of the female legislators have related
that they became interested in politics through their husbands, and
others have worked with their spouses on newspapers, more often
than not a wife leaves politics entirely to her husband and does not
even appear at his side when he campaigns or makes a speech.

The list system in West Germany and Austria makes it practically impossible to determine whether candidates have been defeated or resigned of their own accord. In Switzerland, because
of the frequently much smaller cantonal areas and the possibility
of write-ins, victory or defeat is much more personal than in
West Germany or Austria. In the English-speaking nations, the
picture is much clearer. In the House of Representatives, 23 of
the women went down to defeat, and two were later able to return.
The U.S. Senate is a special case. With such a large number of
the women appointed, many retired voluntarily. Defeat came
eventually to the two incumbents with the longest service, Caraway
and Smith, while Allen was unable to win the primary after her
original appointment. In Canada, 15, or more than 50 percent, of
the former female legislators had their service terminated by the
voters, with only Jewett succeeding in a comeback in 1979. In the
British House of Commons, not fewer than 60 female members
were defeated in reelection bids. Of those, 14 were later reelected
(and of those, six met with defeat a second time, two died while in
office, four eventually retired, and two were reelected in 1979.)
Thus, defeats as well as comebacks are more frequent in Britain
than elsewhere. As to the interval between defeat and successful
return, Rankin waited more than two decades and Jewett, 14 years.

In Britain, several female Labour members lost their seats during the 1931 debacle and regained them with the great Labour victory in 1945. Others spent between two and six years outside Parliament before the voters gave them another chance.

In comparing the ages at entrance, it is interesting to note that the average is about 48 for women in the House of Representatives, the German Bundestag, Austria's Nationalrat in the Second Republic, and the Swiss Nationalrat. Britain, based on the available but incomplete data, has a somewhat lower entering age, namely, 42, while the Canadian women elected before 1978 averaged 46.5 years. Only the U.S. female senator is older, 56 years. She serves the least amount of time, an average of 3.5 years, with only one accumulating more than 20 years. In the House of Commons in London, a female member averages more than ten years, with 16 veterans serving more than 20, sometimes interrupted, years. Women in the German Bundestag and the Austrian Nationalrat serve on the average about nine years. Seven German and five Austrian female legislators can look back to 20 years or more in Parliament. None of the Canadian women, whose average length of service is about 5.5 years, has as yet reached the 20-year mark, and obviously none has in Switzerland.

There is not sufficient accumulated information to allow even tentative conclusions about the marital situation of the women under discussion. As we have seen, the existence of young children does present quite a problem for the mother, and there were cases where this has led to the termination of an otherwise very promising legislative career. Certainly, the female legislator without family obligations finds life a lot easier, as several readily admit. In other instances, the key is usually the attitude of the husband, the children themselves, and the availability of grandparents, reliable housekeepers, or close friends. Matters become even more complicated when financial conditions are not too favorable, and a country like Switzerland with its part-time legislature, while providing for more time with one's family and one's job, is nevertheless also creating special difficulties for some of its public servants, who may not find it easy to make ends meet.

A Canadian suffragette remarked earlier in the century that "the demand for women suffrage was merely a 'chapter in the great history of emancipation of the individual, black or white, rich or poor, male or female, from social and political disabilities imposed upon him or her on account of birth alone. '"[8] The chapter she mentioned has been successfully completed. We must now create conditions in our society that will make it possible for all individuals to participate fully in the political life, not merely as voters but as legislators as well. The preceding pages have indicated that a start has been made in the struggle to bring about equality, but much has still to be done in creating a genuine partnership of men and women. Surely the fault is not in our stars but in ourselves.

NOTES

1. Lynne B. Iglitzin, "The Patriarchal Heritage," in <u>Women in the World</u>, ed. Lynne B. Iglitzin and Ruth Ross (Santa Barbara: CLIO Books, 1976), p. 9.

2. Catherine L. Cleverdon, <u>The Woman Suffrage Movement in Canada</u> (Toronto: University of Toronto Press, 1974), p. 6.

3. <u>Bericht über die Situation der Frau in Österreich</u> (Vienna: Bundeskanzleramt, 1975), 1:8. My translation of a quotation from Curt Rosten, "Das ABC des Nationalsozialismus."

4. Lone Dybkjaer, "Now You're Being Unwomanly," <u>Scandinavian Review</u> 65 (1977): 68.

5. Ibid., p. 69.

6. Pamela Brookes, <u>Women at Westminster</u> (London: Peter Davies, 1967), p. 28.

7. Maurice Collis, <u>Nancy Astor</u> (New York: E. P. Dutton, 1960), p. 57.

8. Cleverdon, op. cit., p. xx.

BIBLIOGRAPHY

Die Abgeordneten zum österreichischen Nationalrat, 1918-1975, und die Mitglieder des österreichischen Bundesrates, 1920-1975. Vienna: Österreichische Staatsdruckerei, 1975.

Amundsen, Kirsten. The Silenced Majority. Englewood Cliffs, N.J.: Prentice Hall, 1971.

Andics, Helmut. Die Insel der Seligen. Vienna: Molden-Taschenbuch Verlag, 1976.

_____. Der Staat, den Keiner wollte. Vienna: Molden-Taschenbuch Verlag, 1976.

Aristophanes. The Congresswomen. Translated by Douglass Parker. Ann Arbor: University of Michigan Press, 1967.

Austria: Fact and Figures. Vienna: Giestel & Cie., 1973.

Bamberger, Richart, and Franz Maier Bruck, eds. Österreich Lexikon. Vienna: Österreichischer Bundesverlag and Verlag für Jugend und Volk, 1966.

Beck, J. M. Pendulum of Power. Scarborough, Ont.: Prentice Hall of Canada, 1968.

Behn, Hans Ulrich. Die Bundesrepublik Deutschland. Munich: Gunter Olzog Verlag, 1974.

Berger, Lieselotte, Lenelotte von Bothmer, and Helga Schuchardt. Frauen ins Parlament? Reinbek bei Hamburg: Rowohlt Taschenbuch Verlag, 1976.

Bericht über die Situation der Frau in Österreich. Vienna: Bundeskanzleramt, 1975.

Biographical Directory of the U.S. Congress, 1774-1961. Washington, D.C.: Government Printing Office, 1961.

Bracher, Karl Dietrich. Stufen der Machtergreifung. Cologne: Westdeutscher Verlag, Ullstein Buch, 1974.

Brecht, Arnold. Prelude to Silence. New York: Oxford University Press, 1944.

Breuer, Lore. Frauen in der Politik: Annemarie Renger, Liselotte Funcke. Koblenz: Frauenverlag, 1975.

Brookes, Pamela. Women at Westminster. London: Peter Davies, 1967.

Chamberlin, Hope. A Minority of Members. New York: Praeger, 1973.

Cleverdon, Catherine L. The Woman Suffrage Movement in Canada. Toronto: University of Toronto Press, 1974.

Codding, George Arthur. The Federal Government of Switzerland. Boston: Houghton Mifflin, 1962.

Collis, Maurice. Nancy Astor. New York: E. P. Dutton, 1960.

Craig, F. W. S. British Electoral Facts, 1885-1975. London: The Macmillan Press, 1976.

_____. British Parliamentary Election Statistics, 1918-1970. 2nd ed. Chichester: Political Reference Publications, 1971.

Currell, Melville. Political Woman. London: Croom Helm, 1974.

Devlin, Bernadette. The Price of My Soul. New York: Alfred A. Knopf, 1969.

Dictionary of International Biography. Cambridge: International Biographical Centre.

Dod's Parliamentary Companion. London: Whittaker & Co.

Duverger, Maurice. The Political Role of Women. Paris: UNESCO, 1955.

Elster, Ludwig, Adolf Weber, and Friedrich Wieser. Handwörterbuch der Staatswissenschaften. Jena: Gustav Fischer Verlag, 1927.

Evans, Gwynneth, comp., and Marion C. Wilson, ed. Women in Federal Politics: A Bio-Bibliography. Ottawa: National Library of Canada, 1975.

Eyck, Erich. A History of the Weimar Republic. New York: Athenium, 1970.

Frau und Gesellschaft. Zwischenbericht der Enquete-Kommission, Deutscher Bundestag, 1977.

Frauen im deutschen Bundestag: I. bis. VI. Wahlperiode. Bonn: Deutscher Bundestag Wissenschaftliche Dienste, 1971.

Fulles, Mechthild. Frauen in Partei und Parlament. Cologne: Verlag Wissenschaft und Politik, 1969.

Gast, Gabriele. Die politische Rolle der Frau in der DDR. Düsseldorf: Bertelsmann Universitätsverlag, 1973.

Giger, Theres. "Freisinnige Frauen in den eidgenössischen Räten." Politische Rundschau 58 (1979): 75-79.

Gruberg, Martin. Women in American Politics. Oshkosh, Wis.: Academia, 1968.

Gruner, Erich. Die Parteien in der Schweiz. Bern: Francke Verlag, 1969.

Gruner, Erich, Martin Daetwyler, and Oscar Zosso. Aufstellung und Auswahl der Kandidaten bei den Nationalratswahlen in der Schweiz. Bern: Eidgenössische Drucksachen- und Material-zentrale, 1975.

Gruner, Erich, and Beat Junker. Bürger, Staat und Politik in der Schweiz. Basel: Lehrmittelverlag, 1972.

Halperin, William S. Germany Tried Democracy: A Political History of the Reich from 1918-1933. New York: Thomas Y. Crowell, 1946.

Held, Thomas, Christoph Reichenau, and Verena Ritter. "Frauen in der Bundesversammlung." Frauenfragen, nos. 1 and 2 (1979): 73-101.

Hellwig, Renate. Frauen verändern die Politik. Stuttgart: Aktuell, 1975.

Henkels, Walter. 99 Bonner Köpfe. Frankfurt am Main: Fischer Bücherei, 1965.

Hertzmann, Lewis. DNVP: Right-Wing Opposition in the Weimar Republic, 1918-1924. Lincoln: University of Nebraska Press, 1963.

Hudson, Kenneth. Men and Women: Feminism and Anti-Feminism Today. Newton Abbot: David & Charles, 1968.

Iglitzen, Lynne B., and Ruth Ross, eds. Women in the World. Santa Barbara: CLIO Books, 1976.

Jahrbuch der eidgenössischen Behörden. Bern: Verbandsdruckerei AG. This is an annual and I have used a number of them.

Jaquette, Jane S., ed. Women in Politics. New York: John Wiley & Sons, 1974.

Josephson, Hannah. Jeanette Rankin. Indianapolis: Bobbs-Merrill, 1974.

Kincaid, Diane D. "Over His Dead Body: A New Perspective and Some Feminist Footnotes on Widows in the U.S. Congress." Paper prepared for the 1976 Annual Meeting of the American Political Science Association, Chicago, September 2-5, 1976.

Kirkpatrick, Jeane J. Political Woman. New York: Basic Books, 1974.

Knauer, Oswald. Das österreichische Parlament von 1848-1966. Vienna: Begland Verlag, 1969.

Kohn, Walter S. G. "The Austrian Parliamentary Elections of 1971." Parliamentary Affairs 25 (Spring 1972): 163-77.

Kraditor, Aileen S. The Ideas of the Woman Suffrage Movement, 1890-1920. Garden City, N.Y.: Doubleday, Anchor Books, 1971.

Kuhn, Axel, Eberhard Jäckel, and Detlev Junker. Deutsche Parlamentsdebatten. 3 vols. Frankfurt am Main: Fischer Bücherei, 1970-71.

Kürschners Volkshandbuch: Deutscher Bundestag. Rheinbreitbach: Neue Darmstädter Verlaganstalt, 1978.

Lamson, Peggy. Few Are Chosen: American Women in Political Life Today. Boston: Houghton Mifflin, 1968.

Lee, Jennie. This Great Journey. New York: Farrar and Rinehart, 1942.

Lewis, Russell. Margaret Thatcher. A Personal and Political
Biography. London: Routledge and Kegen Paul, 1975.

Lütkens, Charlotte. "Die Familienverhältnisse der weiblichen
Abgeordneten." Zeitschrift für Politik, vol. 6, no. 1 (1959).

MacPherson, Myra. The Power Lovers. New York: G. P.
Putnams Sons, 1975.

Mann, Jean. Woman in Parliament. London: Odham Press, 1962.

Marriot, Sir J. A. R. Modern England, 1885-1945. London:
Methuen, 1946.

Mikoletzky, Hanns Leo. Österreichische Zeitgeschichte. Vienna:
Austria-Editon, 1969.

Mitchell, B. R., and Klaus Boem. British Parliamentary Election
Results, 1950-1964. London: Cambridge University Press,
1966.

Die Mitglieder des deutschen Bundestages, 1.-8. Wahlperiode
Deutscher Bundestag-Verwaltung-Hauptabteilung Wissenschaftliche
Dienste, 1979.

Mosse, George L. Nazi Culture. New York: Grosset & Dunlap,
Universal Library, 1968.

Nemitz, Rosmarie. "Die Frau in den deutschen Parlamenten."
Gewerkschaftliche Monatshefte, 1958. Köhn, vol. 9, no. 4,
pp. 239-44.

Olzog, Günter, and Arthur Herzig. Die politischen Parteien.
Munich: Günter Olzog Verlag, 1977.

Österreichisches Institut. Österreicher der Gegenwart. Vienna,
1951.

Panorama DDR: Documentation. Auslandspresseagentur, GDR,
1976. Berlin.

Parliamentarierinnen in deutschen Parlamenten, 1919-1976. Bonn: Deutscher Bundestag Wissenschaftliche Dienste, 1976.

Paxton, Annabel. Women in Congress. Richmond, Va.: Dietz Press, 1945.

Pelinka, Anton, and Manfried Welan. Demokratie und Verfassung in Österreich. Vienna: Europa Verlag, 1971.

Puckett, Hugh W. Germany's Women Go Forward. New York: Columbia University Press, 1930.

Ranney, Austin. Pathways to Parliament: Candidate Selection in Britain. Madison: University of Wisconsin Press, 1965.

Reeves, Nancy. Womankind: Beyond the Stereotype. Chicago: Atherton, 1971.

Richards, Peter G. Honorable Members. New York: Frederic A. Praeger, 1959.

Rush, Michael. The Selection of Parliamentary Candidates. London: Thomas Nelson, 1969.

Ryser, Barbara. "Frauen in der Christlichdemokratischen Volkspartei der Schweiz." Seminar paper written under Professor Urs Altermatt, Universitat Bern (Historisches Institut), 1979.

Sänger, Fritz, ed. Handbuch des deutschen Bundestages. Stuttgart: J. G. Cotta'sche Buchhandlung Nachfolger, 1954.

Scandinavian Review, no. 3 (1977).

Schäfer, Friedrich. Der Bundestag. Opladen: Westdeutscher Verlag, 1975.

Schwarz, Max, ed. MdR: Biographisches Handbuch der Reichstage. Hanover: Verlag für Literatur und Zeitgeschehen, 1965.

Schweizer Volkspartei. Frau und Politik (undated pamphlet).

Shirer, William L. Decline and Fall of the Third Reich. New York: Simon and Schuster, 1960.

Sontheimer, Kurt. The Government and Politics of West Germany. New York: Praeger, 1973.

Stadler, Karl R. Austria. New York: Praeger, 1971.

Steiner, Jürg. Das politische System der Schweiz. Munich:
    R. Piper, 1971.

Steiner, Kurt. Politics Austria. Boston: Little, Brown, 1972.

Stern, Carola, ed. Was haben die Parteien für die Frauen getan?
    Reinbek bei Hamburg: Rowohlt Taschenbuch Verlag, 1976.

Stern, Katja, and Brigitte Boeck. Das schöne Geschlecht und die
    Gleichberechtigung in der DDR. Berlin: "Aus erster Hand,"
    1971.

Stewart, Margaret, and Doris French. Ask No Quarter. Toronto:
    Longman, Green, 1959.

Strong, David F. Austria (October 1918-March 1919). New York:
    Octagon Books, 1974.

Stumpfe, Ortrud. "Lebensbilder deutscher Politikerinnen."
    Politische Studien, 1959, pp. 670-84.

Thönnessen, Werner. The Emancipation of Women. Translated by
    Joris de Bres. London: Pluto Press, 1973.

Thorne, J. P., ed. Chamber's Biographical Directory. New York:
    St. Martin's Press, 1969.

The Times Guide to the House of Commons. London: Times Books,
    1964-79.

Tolchin, Susan and Martin. Clout: Women Power and Politics.
    New York: Coward, McCann & Geoghegan, 1974.

Trost, Ernst. Figl von Österreich. Vienna: Verlag Fritz Molden,
    1972.

U.S., Congress. Women in Congress: 1917-1976. 94th Cong.,
    2nd sess., 1976, Rept. 1732.

Weinzierl, Erika. Emanzipation? Vienna: Jugend und Volk, 1975.

Wer ist Wer? Vienna: Selbst Verlag, 1937.

Werner, Emmy E. "Women in Congress, 1917-1964." Western Political Quarterly 19 (March 1966): 16-30.

Who's Who. New York: St. Martin's Press.

Who's Who in Canada. Toronto: International Press.

Who's Who in German Politics. Munich: Verlag Dokumentation Saur KG, 1971.

Who's Who in Switzerland. Geneva: Nagel.

Who Was Who. New York: St. Martin's Press.

Wissenschaft und Welt: Festschrift für Hertha Firnberg. Europaverlag, Sonderdruck, 1974.

Woodtli, Susanna. Gleichberechtigung. Frauenfeld: Verlag Huber, 1975.

ABOUT THE AUTHOR

WALTER S. G. KOHN is professor of political science at Illinois State University, where he has taught since 1956. He has also taught at State University of New York College for Teachers at Buffalo and at Lawrence College, Appleton, Wisconsin.

Kohn has published widely in the area of political science. He is the author of a book on the governments and politics of the German-speaking countries, and his articles have appeared in such journals as Parliamentary Affairs, American Journal of International Law, Military Review, and Policy Studies Journal.

Kohn holds a bachelor degree in Economics from the University of London and an M.A. and Ph.D. in political science from the New School for Social Research in New York City.